AGRICULTURE ISSUES AND POLICIES

AGRICULTURAL TRADE

SANITARY, PHYTOSANITARY AND TECHNICAL BARRIERS

AGRICULTURE ISSUES AND POLICIES

Additional books in this series can be found on Nova's website under the Series tab.

Additional e-books in this series can be found on Nova's website under the e-book tab.

AGRICULTURE ISSUES AND POLICIES

AGRICULTURAL TRADE

SANITARY, PHYTOSANITARY AND TECHNICAL BARRIERS

ROWAN STROUD
EDITOR

nova publishers
New York

For permission to use material from this book please contact us:
Telephone 631-231-7269; Fax 631-231-8175
Web Site: http://www.novapublishers.com

Library of Congress Cataloging-in-Publication Data

ISBN: 978-1-63321-888-8

Published by Nova Science Publishers, Inc. † New York

CONTENTS

PREFACE

Sanitary and phytosanitary (SPS) measures are the laws, rules, standards, and procedures that governments employ to protect humans, animals, and plants from diseases, pests, toxins, and other contaminants. Examples include meat and poultry processing standards to reduce pathogens, residue limits for pesticides in foods, and regulation of agricultural biotechnology. Technical barriers to trade (TBT) cover technical regulations, product standards, environmental regulations, and voluntary procedures relating to human health and animal welfare. Examples include trademarks and patents, labeling and packaging requirements, certification and inspection procedures, product specifications, and marketing of biotechnology. SPS and TBT measures both comprise a group of widely divergent standards and standards-based measures that countries use to regulate markets, protect their consumers, and preserve natural resources. This book describes formal challenges involving SPS/TBT that the United States has brought against some U.S. trading partners, which have resulted in trade disputes that have been, or continue to be, reviewed by the World Trade Organization (WTO). It also discusses the United States and European Union hormone and use of pathogen reduction treatment disputes; and the country-of-origin labeling for foods and the WTO trade dispute on meat labeling.

Chapter 1 - Sanitary and phytosanitary (SPS) measures are the laws, rules, standards, and procedures that governments employ to protect humans, animals, and plants from diseases, pests, toxins, and other contaminants. Examples include meat and poultry processing standards to reduce pathogens, residue limits for pesticides in foods, and regulation of agricultural biotechnology. Technical barriers to trade (TBT) cover technical regulations, product standards, environmental regulations, and voluntary procedures relating to human health and animal welfare. Examples include trademarks and patents, labeling and packaging requirements, certification and inspection procedures, product specifications, and marketing of biotechnology. SPS and TBT measures both comprise a group of widely divergent standards and standards-based measures that countries use to regulate markets, protect their consumers, and preserve natural resources.

According to the World Trade Organization (WTO), SPS and TBT measures have become more prominent concerns for agricultural exporters and policy makers, as tariff-related barriers to trade have been reduced by various multilateral, regional, and bilateral negotiations and trade agreements. The concerns include whether SPS and TBT measures might be used to unfairly discriminate against imported products or create unnecessary obstacles to trade in agricultural, food, and other traded goods. Notable U.S. trade disputes involving SPS and TBT measures have included a European Union (EU) ban on U.S. meats treated with growth-promoting hormones and also certain pathogen reduction treatments, and an EU moratorium on approvals of biotechnology products, among other types of trade concerns with other countries. Foreign countries have also objected to various U.S. trade measures.

Multilateral trade rules allow governments to adopt measures to protect human, animal, or plant life or health, provided such measures do not discriminate or use them as disguised protectionism. This principle was clarified in the mid-1990s by WTO members' approval of the Agreement on the Application of Sanitary and Phytosanitary Measures ("SPS Agreement"). The SPS Agreement sets out the basic rules for ensuring that each country's food safety and animal and plant health laws and regulations are transparent, scientifically defensible, and fair. Similarly, in the late 1970s, the Agreement on Technical Barriers to Trade ("TBT Agreement") addressed the use of technical requirements and voluntary standards for a range of traded goods.

In addition, the United States has entered into, or is currently negotiating, numerous regional and bilateral free trade agreements (FTAs) that contain SPS and TBT language. In an effort to resolve perceived intractable trade problems regarding SPS and TBT matters, many in U.S. agriculture and the food industry are supporting efforts to build on and go beyond rules, rights, and obligations in the SPS Agreement and TBT Agreement, as well as beyond commitments in existing U.S. FTAs. The U.S. meat and poultry industry initially proposed efforts to adopt tougher WTO rules for animal health regulations as part of the ongoing Trans-Pacific Partnership (TPP) negotiations. These concepts were later reinforced by recommendations from U.S. and EU trade officials involved in the ongoing Transatlantic Trade and Investment Partnership (TTIP) negotiations. These efforts are referred to as WTO-Plus rules, SPS-Plus, and TBT-Plus rules.

In Congress, which must approve legislation if a trade agreement is to be implemented, many Members are interested in how a trade agreement might address SPS and TBT matters. Many remain concerned that countries are turning to non-tariff measures, such as SPS and TBT measures, to protect their farmers from import competition. U.S. rights and obligations regarding SPS and TBT measures are also relevant to regulations affecting imported food.

Sanitary and phytosanitary (SPS) measures are laws, regulations, standards, and procedures that governments employ as "necessary to protect human, animal or plant life or health"[1] from the risks associated with the spread of pests, diseases, or disease-carrying and causing organisms, or from additives, toxins, or contaminants in food, beverages, or feedstuffs. SPS measures are designed to protect animals and plants from diseases and pests, and to protect humans from animal- and plant-borne diseases and pests, and foodborne risks. Examples include specific product or processing standards, requirements for products to be produced in disease-free areas, quarantine and inspection procedures, sampling and testing requirements, residue limits for pesticides and drugs in foods, and prohibitions on certain food additives.

Technical barriers to trade (TBTs) cover both food and non-food traded products. TBTs in agriculture include SPS measures, but also include other types of measures related to health and quality standards, testing, registration, and certification requirements, as well as packaging and labeling regulations. TBT measures address technical characteristics of products, such as process and product standards, technical regulations, product environmental regulations, and voluntary procedures relating to health, sanitary, and animal welfare, but also inspection procedures, product specifications, and approval and marketing of biotechnology.

This report broadly refers to SPS and other types of technical requirements, including TBTs in food production, as "SPS/TBT measures." SPS/TBT measures span several broad categories (see text box below), and may vary widely depending on the commodity and importing country. Overall, SPS/TBT measures comprise a group of widely divergent standards and standards-based measures that countries use to regulate markets, protect their consumers, and preserve natural resources, but that can also be used to discriminate against imports in favor of domestic products. Specific examples in agriculture include meat and poultry processing standards to reduce pathogens, residue limits for pesticides in foods, fumigation requirements for grains and wood packaging materials to kill pests, labeling and marketing standards, food safety protocols, and regulation of agricultural biotechnology. This has resulted in a variety of formal trade disputes as well as ongoing trade concerns between the United States and its trading partners.

The United States has initiated several formal trade disputes regarding SPS/TBT measures that have been elevated for review and dispute resolution within the World Trade Organization (WTO). Some high-profile trade disputes include U.S. concerns about the European Union's (EU's) ban on U.S. meats from livestock treated with growth-promoting hormones, the EU's restrictions on chemicals used to treat U.S. poultry, and the EU's moratorium on approvals of biotechnology products. Other disputes have involved U.S. complaints about testing and inspection requirements, among other SPS/TBT measures, applied in other countries. Foreign countries also have objected to various U.S. trade measures. This report describes formal challenges involving SPS/TBT that the United States has brought against some U.S. trading partners, which have resulted in trade disputes that have been, or continue to be, reviewed by the WTO.

Not all U.S. trade concerns regarding SPS/TBT measures rise to the level of a formal WTO trade dispute. A full summary of ongoing SPS/TBT trade concerns based on the most recent annual compilation by the Office of the U.S. Trade Representative (USTR) is provided in **Appendix A** at the end of this report.

Chapter 2 - The United States and the European Union (EU) have engaged in a long-standing and acrimonious trade dispute over the EU's decision to ban hormone-treated meat. Despite an ongoing series of dispute settlement proceedings and decisions by the World Trade Organization (WTO), there is continued disagreement between the United States and the EU on a range of legal and procedural issues, as well as the scientific evidence and consensus concerning the safety of hormone-treated beef. To date, the EU continues to ban imports of hormone-treated meat and restricts most meat exports to the European Union to a limited quantity of beef imports that are certified as produced without the use of hormones.

Starting in 1981, the EU adopted restrictions on livestock production limiting the use of natural hormones to therapeutic purposes, banning the use of synthetic hormones, and prohibiting imports of animals and meat from animals that have been administered the hormones. In 1989, the EU fully implemented its ban on imports of meat and meat products from animals treated with growth promotants. Initially the ban covered six growth promotants that are approved for use and administered in the United States. The EU amended its ban in 2003, permanently banning one hormone—estradiol-17β—while provisionally banning the use of the five other hormones.

The United States has suspended trade concessions with the European Union by imposing higher import tariffs on EU products. The first U.S. action in 1989 imposed retaliatory tariffs of 100% *ad valorem* duty on selected food products, and remained in effect until 1996. The second U.S. action in 1999 again imposed a 100% *ad valorem* duty on selected foods from EU countries.

Over the years, the United States and the EU have attempted to resolve this dispute through a series of WTO dispute consultations, settlement panels, arbitration proceedings, and formal appeals. One of the earlier WTO panel decisions in 1997 ruled against the EU on the grounds that the ban is inconsistent with the EU's WTO obligations under the Sanitary and Phytosanitary (SPS) Agreement because the EU had not conducted a risk assessment. In response, the EU commissioned studies and reviews to address the scientific basis of its ban on hormone-treated meat. Following each of these reviews, the EU reaffirmed its position that there are possible risks to human health associated with hormone-treated meat, given the available scientific data. The EU claims it has complied with its WTO obligations and has challenged the United States for maintaining its prohibitive import tariffs on EU products. The United States disputes whether the EU has conducted an adequate risk assessment to support its position and maintains there is a clear worldwide scientific consensus supporting the safety to consumers of eating hormone-treated meat. In October 2008, the WTO issued a mixed ruling allowing the United States to continue its trade sanctions, but allowing the EU to maintain its ban.

In January 2009, the U.S. Trade Representative (USTR) announced its intent to make changes to the list of EU products subject to increased tariffs under the dispute, including changes to the EU countries and products affected, and higher tariffs on some products. The EU claimed this action constituted an "escalation" of the dispute. In May 2009, following a series of negotiations, the United States and the EU signed a memorandum of understanding (MOU), which phases in certain changes over several years. Currently, the EU has granted market access to U.S. exports of beef raised without the use of growth promotants, and the United States has suspended higher duties for imported EU products listed under the dispute. USTR continues to monitor EU implementation of the MOU and other policies affecting market access for U.S. beef exports.

Chapter 3 - In January 2009, the outgoing Bush Administration escalated a long-running dispute with the European Union (EU) over its refusal to accept imports of U.S. poultry processed with certain pathogen reduction treatments (PRTs). Bush officials requested World Trade Organization (WTO) consultations with the EU on the matter, a prerequisite first step toward the establishment of a formal WTO dispute settlement panel. The U.S. poultry industry supported the WTO filing by the U.S. Trade Representative (USTR) and encouraged the Obama Administration to continue to pursue the case.

PRTs are antimicrobial rinses—including chlorine dioxide, acidified sodium chlorite, trisodium phosphate, and peroxyacids, among others—that have been approved by the U.S. Department of Agriculture (USDA) for use in poultry processing to reduce the amount of microbes on meat. Meat and poultry products processed with PRTs are judged safe by the United States and also by European food safety authorities. Nevertheless, the EU prohibits the use of PRTs and the importation of poultry treated with these substances. The EU generally opposes such chemical interventions and believes that stronger sanitary practices during production and processing are more appropriate for pathogen control than what it views as U.S. overreliance on PRTs.

As PRTs are widely used in U.S. poultry processing, the EU's ban on their use effectively prohibits U.S. poultry meat from entering EU countries. Prior to 1997, when the prohibition took effect, U.S. exports of broiler and turkey meat to the 15 countries that then constituted the EU totaled nearly 38,000 metric tons (MT), valued at $58 million. In 2011, U.S. exports to the same 15 countries were reported to be nearly 9,000 MT, valued at $13 million. USDA analysts believe that almost all of these U.S. exports represent "transshipments," meaning that Europe is not the intended final destination and that virtually no U.S. poultry meat is being purchased for the EU market. Now that the EU consists of 27 countries, it currently imports worldwide about $500 million of fresh, chilled, and frozen poultry meat annually (excluding intra-EU trade), most of which is supplied by Brazil and other Latin American countries. Some estimate the U.S. loss of the EU poultry market at between $200 million and $300 million annually. Still, other foreign buyers continue to make the United States the second-largest exporter of poultry meat in the world, after Brazil.

Despite initial consultations between the United States and the EU, in October 2009, the USTR asked the WTO to establish a dispute settlement panel regarding the EU restrictions on imports of U.S. poultry. The United States has asked the panel to review whether the EU's ban on the import and marketing of poultry meat and poultry meat products processed with PRTs violates the EU's WTO obligations. USTR claims that PRTs are judged safe by U.S. and other public health authorities, citing European scientific opinions indicating that PRTs pose no risk to human health. The latest scientific opinion of the European Food Safety Authority (EFSA) states that "chemical substances in poultry are unlikely to pose an immediate or acute health risk for consumers." In addition, in 2011, the international food safety organization Codex Alimentarius Commission (Codex) issued guidelines for the control of Campylobacter and Salmonella in chicken meat that covers the use of certain hazard-based control measures, including acidified sodium chlorite and trisodium phosphate, among other rinses and oxidants. Some believe the Codex guidelines should effectively resolve concerns about the use of these substances in poultry processing. Nevertheless, USTR and the U.S. poultry industry remain actively engaged in this case, and the United States and EU continue to maintain widely divergent views not only on the poultry issue but on some aspects of their basic approach to food safety regulation.

Chapter 4 - Most retail food stores are now required to inform consumers about the country of origin of fresh fruits and vegetables, fish, shellfish, peanuts, pecans, macadamia nuts, ginseng, and ground and muscle cuts of beef, pork, lamb, chicken, and goat. The rules are required by the 2002 farm bill (P.L. 107-171) as amended by the 2008 farm bill (P.L. 110-246). Other U.S. laws have required such labeling, but only for imported food products already pre-packaged for consumers. The final rule to implement country-of-origin labeling (COOL) took effect on March 16, 2009.

Both the authorization and implementation of COOL by the U.S. Department ofAgriculture (USDA) have been controversial, particularly the labeling rules for meat and meat products.A number of livestock and food industry groups continue to oppose COOL as costly and unnecessary, and they and the main livestock exporters to the United States—Canada and Mexico—view the requirement as trade-distorting. Others, including some cattle and consumer groups, maintain thatAmericans want and deserve to know the origin of their foods.

Less than one year after the COOL rules took effect, Canada and Mexico challenged them in the World Trade Organization (WTO), arguing that COOL has a trade-distorting impact by reducing the value and number of cattle and hogs shipped to the U.S. market, thus violating WTO trade commitments agreed to by the United States. In November 2011, the WTO dispute settlement (DS) panel found that (1) COOL treats imported livestock less favorably than like U.S. livestock (particularly in the labeling of beef and pork muscle cuts), and (2) COOL does not meet its objective to provide complete information to consumers on the origin of meat products.

In March 2012, the United States appealed the WTO ruling. In June 2012 the WTO's Appellate Body (AB) upheld the DS panel's finding that the COOL measure treats imported Canadian cattle and hogs, and imported Mexican cattle, less favorably than like domestic livestock. But the AB reversed the finding that COOL does not fulfill its legitimate objective to provide consumers with information on origin. The Obama Administration welcomed the AB's affirmation of the U.S. right to adopt labeling requirements to inform consumers on the origin of the meat they purchase. Participants in the U.S. livestock sector had mixed reactions, reflecting the ongoing heated debate on COOL.

AWTO arbitrator set May 23, 2013, as the deadline for the United States to comply with the WTO findings. To comply, USDA issued a final rule requiring that labels show where each production step (i.e., born, raised, slaughtered) occurs and prohibiting the commingling of muscle-cut meat from different origins. COOL's supporters applauded the final rule for providing consumers with specific and more useful information on origin.

Opponents of COOL argue that the new rule is more discriminatory than the previous rule and imposes additional recordkeeping burdens on processors and retailers, and in turn, additional costs on consumers. In July 2013, opponents filed suit to stop USDA from implementing the final COOL rule, but in September 2013 they were denied their request for a preliminary injunction against the rule. COOL opponents appealed and await a court ruling.

Opponents of COOL lobbied the farm bill conference committee to either repeal or modify the COOL law to resolve the WTO dispute. However, the conference report to H.R. 2642 did not make such changes.

Canada and Mexico expressed disappointment with USDA's final rule, and argued that it does not bring the United States into compliance with its WTO obligations. In September 2013, Canada and Mexico secured the establishment of a compliance panel to determine if the final COOL rule complies with WTO findings. This panel will hear the COOL case on February 18-19, 2014. Depending on the outcome of the compliance report, any possible appeal, procedural timelines, and whether or not the case progresses to the retaliation phase and arbitration, the WTO COOL case may not be concluded before 2015.

In: Agricultural Trade
Editor: Rowan Stroud

ISBN: 978-1-63321-888-8

Chapter 1

SANITARY AND PHYTOSANITARY (SPS) AND RELATED NON-TARIFF BARRIERS TO AGRICULTURAL TRADE*

Renée Johnson

SUMMARY

Sanitary and phytosanitary (SPS) measures are the laws, rules, standards, and procedures that governments employ to protect humans, animals, and plants from diseases, pests, toxins, and other contaminants. Examples include meat and poultry processing standards to reduce pathogens, residue limits for pesticides in foods, and regulation of agricultural biotechnology. Technical barriers to trade (TBT) cover technical regulations, product standards, environmental regulations, and voluntary procedures relating to human health and animal welfare. Examples include trademarks and patents, labeling and packaging requirements, certification and inspection procedures, product specifications, and marketing of biotechnology. SPS and TBT measures both comprise a group of widely divergent standards and standards-based measures that countries use to regulate markets, protect their consumers, and preserve natural resources.

According to the World Trade Organization (WTO), SPS and TBT measures have become more prominent concerns for agricultural exporters and policy makers, as tariff-related barriers to trade have been reduced by various multilateral, regional, and bilateral negotiations and trade agreements. The concerns include whether SPS and TBT measures might be used to unfairly discriminate against imported products or create unnecessary obstacles to trade in agricultural, food, and other traded goods. Notable U.S. trade disputes involving SPS and TBT measures have included a European Union (EU) ban on U.S. meats treated with growth-promoting hormones and also certain pathogen reduction treatments, and an EU moratorium on approvals of biotechnology products, among other types of trade concerns with other countries. Foreign countries have also objected to various U.S. trade measures.

* This is an edited, reformatted and augmented version of a Congressional Research Service publication R43450, prepared for Members and Committees of Congress dated March 31, 2014.

Multilateral trade rules allow governments to adopt measures to protect human, animal, or plant life or health, provided such measures do not discriminate or use them as disguised protectionism. This principle was clarified in the mid-1990s by WTO members' approval of the Agreement on the Application of Sanitary and Phytosanitary Measures ("SPS Agreement"). The SPS Agreement sets out the basic rules for ensuring that each country's food safety and animal and plant health laws and regulations are transparent, scientifically defensible, and fair. Similarly, in the late 1970s, the Agreement on Technical Barriers to Trade ("TBT Agreement") addressed the use of technical requirements and voluntary standards for a range of traded goods.

In addition, the United States has entered into, or is currently negotiating, numerous regional and bilateral free trade agreements (FTAs) that contain SPS and TBT language. In an effort to resolve perceived intractable trade problems regarding SPS and TBT matters, many in U.S. agriculture and the food industry are supporting efforts to build on and go beyond rules, rights, and obligations in the SPS Agreement and TBT Agreement, as well as beyond commitments in existing U.S. FTAs. The U.S. meat and poultry industry initially proposed efforts to adopt tougher WTO rules for animal health regulations as part of the ongoing Trans-Pacific Partnership (TPP) negotiations. These concepts were later reinforced by recommendations from U.S. and EU trade officials involved in the ongoing Transatlantic Trade and Investment Partnership (TTIP) negotiations. These efforts are referred to as WTO-Plus rules, SPS-Plus, and TBT-Plus rules.

In Congress, which must approve legislation if a trade agreement is to be implemented, many Members are interested in how a trade agreement might address SPS and TBT matters. Many remain concerned that countries are turning to non-tariff measures, such as SPS and TBT measures, to protect their farmers from import competition. U.S. rights and obligations regarding SPS and TBT measures are also relevant to regulations affecting imported food.

Sanitary and phytosanitary (SPS) measures are laws, regulations, standards, and procedures that governments employ as "necessary to protect human, animal or plant life or health"[1] from the risks associated with the spread of pests, diseases, or disease-carrying and causing organisms, or from additives, toxins, or contaminants in food, beverages, or feedstuffs. SPS measures are designed to protect animals and plants from diseases and pests, and to protect humans from animal- and plant-borne diseases and pests, and foodborne risks. Examples include specific product or processing standards, requirements for products to be produced in disease-free areas, quarantine and inspection procedures, sampling and testing requirements, residue limits for pesticides and drugs in foods, and prohibitions on certain food additives.

Technical barriers to trade (TBTs) cover both food and non-food traded products. TBTs in agriculture include SPS measures, but also include other types of measures related to health and quality standards, testing, registration, and certification requirements, as well as packaging and labeling regulations. TBT measures address technical characteristics of products, such as process and product standards, technical regulations, product environmental regulations, and voluntary procedures relating to health, sanitary, and animal welfare, but also inspection procedures, product specifications, and approval and marketing of biotechnology.

This report broadly refers to SPS and other types of technical requirements, including TBTs in food production, as "SPS/TBT measures." SPS/TBT measures span several broad categories (see text box below), and may vary widely depending on the commodity and importing country. Overall, SPS/TBT measures comprise a group of widely divergent standards and standards-based measures that countries use to regulate markets, protect their consumers, and preserve natural resources, but that can also be used to discriminate against imports in favor of domestic products. Specific examples in agriculture include meat and poultry processing standards to reduce pathogens, residue limits for pesticides in foods, fumigation requirements for grains and wood packaging materials to kill pests, labeling and marketing standards, food safety protocols, and regulation of agricultural biotechnology. This has resulted in a variety of formal trade disputes as well as ongoing trade concerns between the United States and its trading partners.

The United States has initiated several formal trade disputes regarding SPS/TBT measures that have been elevated for review and dispute resolution within the World Trade Organization (WTO). Some high-profile trade disputes include U.S. concerns about the European Union's (EU's) ban on U.S. meats from livestock treated with growth-promoting hormones, the EU's restrictions on chemicals used to treat U.S. poultry, and the EU's moratorium on approvals of biotechnology products. Other disputes have involved U.S. complaints about testing and inspection requirements, among other SPS/TBT measures, applied in other countries. Foreign countries also have objected to various U.S. trade measures. This report describes formal challenges involving SPS/TBT that the United States has brought against some U.S. trading partners, which have resulted in trade disputes that have been, or continue to be, reviewed by the WTO.

Not all U.S. trade concerns regarding SPS/TBT measures rise to the level of a formal WTO trade dispute. A full summary of ongoing SPS/TBT trade concerns based on the most recent annual compilation by the Office of the U.S. Trade Representative (USTR) is provided in **Appendix A** at the end of this report.

SPS/TBT Measures and International

Trade Rules Multilateral Trade Agreements

SPS/TBT measures regarding food safety and related public health protection are addressed in various multilateral trade agreements and are regularly notified to and debated within the WTO. International trade rules recognize the rights and obligations of governments to adopt and enforce such requirements.[2] (Present multilateral rules date back to the development and signing of the General Agreement on Tariffs and Trade (GATT) in 1947, which were followed by a number of subsequent negotiating rounds leading up to the establishment of the WTO on January 1, 1995.)[3] These rules are spelled out primarily in two WTO agreements dealing with food safety and animal (sanitary) and plant (phytosanitary) health and safety and with other types of technical product standards in general:

- The Agreement on Sanitary and Phytosanitary Measures (or "SPS Agreement"), which resulted from the Uruguay Round of the General Agreement on Tariffs and Trade (GATT).[4]
- The Agreement on Technical Barriers to Trade ("TBT Agreement"), which also resulted from the Uruguay Round of GATT negotiations as a revision of the agreement of the same name that emerged from negotiations during the Tokyo Round that concluded in 1979.[5]

Both agreements were entered into force on January 1, 1995, as part of the establishment of the WTO, following the Uruguay Round of multilateral negotiations. These agreements establish rules regarding the use of certain human, animal, and plant health protection measures, as well as the technical requirements, standards and procedures intended to ensure such protections are met, for a range of traded goods. These agreements apply only to governmental measures that may directly or indirectly affect international trade.

Although both the SPS and TBT Agreements explicitly recognize the rights of each country to set their own standards, these standards must be science-based and applied only to the extent necessary to protect human, animal or plant health. These standards cannot be arbitrary or used to unjustifiably discriminate domestically or between trading partners. Member countries also are encouraged to observe established and recognized international standards. Improper use of SPS and TBT measures can create substantial, if not complete, barriers to trade when they are disguised protectionist barriers, are not supported by science, or are otherwise unwarranted.

SPS/TBT measures are considered types of non-tariff measures or barriers, and refer to trade policies such as quotas, import licensing systems, sanitary regulations, and other types of prohibitions—other than import tariffs—that may restrict trade.[6] In general, as import tariffs have been reduced to relatively low levels in most countries following multilateral trade negotiations as well as bilateral and regional free trade agreements, non-tariff measures have emerged, in some cases, as significant barriers to international trade.[7]

Other types of recognized non-tariff measures outside of SPS/TBT measures (and therefore not covered in this report) include quantitative restrictions; non-tariff charges and related policies affecting imports; government participation in trade, restrictive practices, and more general government policies; and customs procedures and administrative practices.[8] These types of potential trade barriers are addressed in other WTO agreements and/or processes.

The rules and procedures governing settlement of trade disputes involving SPS/TBT measures within the WTO are spelled out in the WTO's Understanding on Rules and Procedures Governing the Settlement of Disputes. (For more information see "Formal SPS/TBT Trade Disputes Involving the United States.")

WTO Agreement on Sanitary and Phytosanitary (SPS) Measures

The SPS Agreement addresses the rights and obligations of WTO member nations regarding health protection measures related to humans, animals, and plants. SPS measures are defined as any measure that a WTO Member applies to:[9]

Types of SPS/TBT Measures

SPS Measures

- plant and animal pests and diseases, and disease-carrying and causing organisms in foods, beverages, or feedstuffs (e.g., fire blight, brown rot, canker, potato wart, and fungus in plants; bovine spongiform encephalopathy (BSE, or "mad cow disease"), foot-and-mouth disease, chronic wasting disease, and brucellosis in animals);
- post-harvest treatment and mitigation requirements (e.g., chemical and other treatment options, including fumigation and quarantine);
- import bans on products from specific producing areas (e.g., because of specific pest or disease concerns particular to a region), and import bans on production inputs (e.g., nursery stock, seeds);
- food additives, residues, and contaminants (e.g., maximum residue limits (MRLs) for pesticide residues; limits on veterinary drug residues and use of hormones in meat production);
- product and/or processing specifications (e.g., restrictions on the use of antimicrobials, sulfur dioxide, sorbic acid, potassium sorbate, biotech and genetic materials, wax coating, etc.);
- microbiological contaminants;
- chemical contaminants;
- irradiation and other forms of sanitation measures, including use of antimicrobial rinses on meat;
- agricultural biotechnology (e.g., genetically engineered plants) and animal cloning;
- other types of perceived health risks; and
- various overlapping technical requirements, such as labeling and standards, including Good Agricultural Practices (GAP) or land-use practices, use of third party auditors, etc.

TBT Measures

- import quotas and administration (such as licensing and auctions), and other administrative requirements (e.g., protocols, risk assessments, waivers, licenses, import tolerances, packaging requirements);
- export limitations and bans;
- food laws, including quality standards, food safety, and industrial standards;
- certification schemes, including organic certification and eco-labeling marketing and label requirements, such as health-related claims and country-of-origin;
- input, process, and product standards, including domestic content and mixing requirements, rules-of origin requirements;
- packaging standards and labeling requirements;
- laws and import procedures, including media advertising regulations;

- consumer and food safety regulations (e.g., labeling, packaging, pesticide residue testing, nutritional content labeling, and contamination prevention); and
- measures to prevent consumer fraud (e.g., shipping and financial documentation, standards of identity and measurement, etc.).

Source: Compiled by CRS from various sources, including USTR's annual *Report on Sanitary and Phytosanitary Measures* and *Report on Technical Barriers to Trade*, http://www.ustr.gov; various USDA trade reports including USDA, *U.S. Specialty Crops Trade Issues: 2008 Annual Report to Congress*, January 2009; and USDA, *Analyzing Technical Barriers to Trade*, TB-1876, March 1999; F. J. Adcock, "Examining and Reducing Technical Barriers to Trade," CNAS 98-3, October 1998, Texas A&M University

- protect animal or plant life or health from risks arising from the entry, establishment or spread of pests, diseases, disease-carrying organisms, or disease-causing organisms;
- protect human or animal life or health from risks arising from additives, contaminants, toxins, or disease-causing organisms in foods, beverages, or feedstuffs;
- protect human life or health from risks arising from plant- or animal-carried diseases (zoonoses), and from animal or plant life pests, diseases, or disease-causing organisms, or from the entry, establishment, or spread of pests; or
- prevent or limit other damage caused by the entry, establishment, or spread of pests.

In general, *sanitary regulations* apply to animal based products such as meats, poultry, and dairy products to ensure that they meet or exceed specified sanitary standards. *Phytosanitary regulations* apply to fruits, vegetables, bulk commodities, and other plant based products.

The SPS Agreement establishes general requirements and procedures to ensure that governments adopt and apply SPS measures that protect against risks to human, animal, or plant life or health—including food safety regulations and measures to protect domestic crops, livestock, and poultry. The SPS Agreement also explicitly recognizes the rights of governments to adopt regulations and establish the levels of protection from risk they deem appropriate, provided such measures do not unnecessarily restrict trade.[10] Accordingly, the SPS Agreement reaffirms that no WTO member country should be:[11]

> prevented from adopting or enforcing measures necessary to protect human, animal or plant life or health, subject to the requirement that these measures are not applied in a manner which would constitute a means of arbitrary or unjustifiable discrimination between Members where the same conditions prevail or a disguised restriction on international trade... to improve the human health, animal health and phytosanitary situation in all Members... and noting that sanitary and phytosanitary measures are often applied on the basis of bilateral agreements or protocols.

The SPS Agreement encourages harmonization of SPS measures among WTO member nations, where appropriate.

Under the SPS Agreement member nations are obligated to notify and allow for comments on proposed standards affecting trade, among other obligations relevant to regulations affecting imported foods. The SPS Agreement applies only to SPS measures that may directly or indirectly affect international trade, and does not apply to measures that have no trade effect or are imposed by a private company or trade association.

The Office of the U.S. Trade Representative (USTR) identifies most SPS measures to include:[12]

> all relevant laws, decrees, regulations, requirements, and procedures including, among others: end product criteria; processes and production methods; testing, inspection, certification, and approval procedures; quarantine treatments, including relevant requirements associated with the transport of animals or plants, or with the materials necessary for their survival during transport; provisions on relevant statistical methods, sampling procedures, and methods of risk assessment; and packaging and labeling requirements directly related to food safety.

Key principles and provisions of the SPS Agreement are described in **Appendix B**.

The SPS Agreement established a Committee on Sanitary and Phytosanitary Measures ("SPS committee"[13]) that provides for a periodic review of the agreement's operation and implementation. The first review was conducted in 1999, with subsequent reviews in 2005 and 2010.[14] During these reviews, the committee discussed at length the range of SPS issues and proposals, from equivalence, transparency, and harmonization in standards among countries to technical assistance and special and differential treatment for development countries and dispute resolution. The reports include recommendations on each of these topics. Also discussed at the second review were specific trade-related SPS concerns raised by WTO members, cooperation within the three standard-setting bodies (Codex, OIE, and IPPC, see section "International Standard Setting Organizations"), and clarification of terms and SPS provisions, among other topics. Within other articles of the agreement are provisions that permit developing countries to delay compliance with SPS measures affecting imports.

At the time of the second review, the committee reported that some WTO members were "still in the process of adjusting to and implementing the new disciplines." The committee review stated that the SPS Agreement "is serving its purpose to the benefit of both importing and exporting [member countries]" and that no member country "has proposed changes to the basic provisions of the SPS Agreement, or questioned its science-based requirements, the encouragement of harmonization with international standards, or the obligations for transparency."[15] Other information related to the committee's periodic reviews is in section "SPS/TBT Trade Concerns Raised at the WTO."

WTO Agreement on Technical Barriers to Trade

The TBT Agreement addresses the rights and obligations of WTO member nations regarding "standards-related measures" intended to protect against human, animal, or plant life and the environment, and to ensure the quality of traded goods and prevent deceptive practices.[16] At the same time, the TBT Agreement recognizes that:[17]

> no country should be prevented from taking measures necessary to ensure the quality of its exports, or for the protection of human, animal or plant life or health, of the environment, or for the prevention of deceptive practices, at the levels it considers

appropriate, subject to the requirement that they are not applied in a manner which would constitute a means of arbitrary or unjustifiable discrimination between countries where the same conditions prevail or a disguised restriction on international trade.

Under the agreement, "standards-related measures" include standards, technical regulations, and conformity assessment procedures, and apply with respect to products and related processes and production methods. Technical regulations and standards establish a product's specific characteristics—such as its size, shape, design, functions, and performance, or the way it is labelled or packaged before it is available for sale. Standards are approved by a recognized organization and generally are voluntary, whereas technical regulations are mandatory. Conformity assessment procedures refer to certain technical procedures—such as testing, verification, inspection, and certification—which confirm that a product meets the requirements of the regulations and standards.

The TBT Agreement covers "all technical requirements, voluntary standards and the procedures to ensure that these are met ... , except when these are SPS measures as defined by the SPS Agreement."[18] TBTs also include related health and quality standards, testing, registration, and certification requirements; safety and industrial standards and regulations; conformity assessments;[19] and packaging and labeling regulations, including trademarks; quarantines; and advertising and media regulations.[20]

The TBT Agreement establishes rules on "developing, adopting, and applying voluntary product standards and mandatory technical regulations as well as conformity assessment procedures (such as testing or certification) used to determine whether a particular product meets such standards or regulations," thus helping to distinguish "legitimate standards-related measures from protectionist measures, and ensure that testing and other conformity assessment procedures are fair and reasonable."[21]

Under the TBT Agreement member nations are obligated to notify and allow for comments on proposed standards affecting trade, among other obligations relevant to regulations affecting imported foods (such as developing standards-related measures through transparent processes, and to base these measures on relevant international standards where effective and appropriate). The agreement contains a so-called "Code of Good Practice for the Preparation, Adoption, and Application of Standards," which applies to voluntary standards.

TBTs are widely divergent measures that countries use to regulate markets, protect their consumers, and preserve natural resources, but which can also discriminate against imports in favor of domestic products.

The TBT Agreement also established a committee for members to consult on matters regarding the agreement, which has also conducted a series of reviews of the TBTAgreement.[22] Key principles and provisions of the TBT Agreement are described in **Appendix C**.

U.S. Free Trade Agreements

Bilateral and regional free trade agreements (FTAs) between the United States and other countries also address SPS and TBT matters. In general, such provisions in previously enacted FTAs have not been as extensive as those in the WTO SPS and TBT Agreements.

Table 1 lists some of the SPS-specific provisions in U.S. free trade agreements. These FTAs also include provisions that address TBTs as well. More recently, the United States has entered into free trade negotiations that could go beyond provisions in existing FTAs with regard to SPS and TBT matters.

North American Free Trade Agreement (NAFTA)

The North American Free Trade Agreement (NAFTA) between the United States, Canada, and Mexico (NAFTA) entered into force on January 1, 1994, and contains both SPS and TBT provisions that are nearly as extensive as those in the SPS and TBT agreements.[23]

NAFTA text relating to SPS matters is contained within Chapter Seven (Agriculture and Sanitary and Phytosanitary Measures). NAFTA's SPS agreement imposes disciplines on the development, adoption, and enforcement of SPS measures to protect human, animal, or plant life or health from risks arising from animal or plant pests or diseases, food additives, or contaminants. NAFTA affirms the right of each country to establish the level of SPS protections that it considers appropriate and provides that a NAFT A country may achieve that level of protection through SPS measures that are based on scientific principles and a risk assessment; are applied only to the extent necessary to provide a country's chosen level of protections; and do not result in unfair discrimination or disguised restrictions on trade (Article 712).[24] NAFTA also established a Committee on Sanitary and Phytosanitary Measures to facilitate the enhancement of food safety and SPS conditions as well as activities relating to international standards and equivalence, and to provide for technical cooperation and consultation on specific bilateral issues (Article 722).

NAFTA text relating to TBT matters is contained within Chapter Nine (Standards-Related Measures). The agreement's TBT provisions apply to standards-related measures under the TBT Agreement and all other international agreements, including environmental and conservation agreements, other than those covered by SPS provisions. NAFTA affirms the right of each country to "adopt, maintain or apply any standards-related measure, including any such measure relating to safety, the protection of human, animal or plant life or health, the environment or consumers, and any measure to ensure its enforcement or implementation," as long as such measures are non-discriminatory and do not result in unnecessary obstacles to trade (Article 904). NAFTA also established a Committee on Standards-Related Measures (Article 913).

Other Existing FTAs

Since NAFTA entered into force in 1994, the United States has successfully negotiated several FTAs (with Jordon, Singapore, Chile, Australia, Morocco, El Salvador, Honduras, Nicaragua, Guatemala, Dominican Republic, Costa Rica, Bahrain, Oman, Peru, Colombia, Panama, and South Korea; see **Table 1**). Each of these FTAs address SPS and TBT matters in some way. However, compared to NAFTA, subsequent FTAs do not address SPS and TBT matters as extensively and also do not address any specific SPS or TBT disputes or issues. Instead, subsequent FTAs generally reference each party's rights and obligations under the WTO SPS Agreement and TBT Agreement, and some FTAs establish standing committees to consult on and resolve problems on an ongoing basis.[25] These FTAs also do not establish any dispute settlement procedures to address disputes related to SPS and TBT measures. In some cases, U.S. negotiators have taken advantage of the negotiating sessions leading up to an agreement, or the subsequent ratification and implementation period, to raise and attempt to resolve certain outstanding issues.

Table 1. Sanitary and Phytosanitary (SPS) Provisions in FTAs

Agreement	SPS Provisions
North American FTA: NAFTA, between United States, Canada, and Mexico; entered into force 1/1/94.	SPS provisions contained in Section B of Chapter Seven, Agriculture and SPS Measures; much more extensive than in other bilateral and regional FTAs. Generally parallel provisions in UR SPS agreement. Also contains (in Chapter 20) dispute resolution mechanism for challenging SPS barriers. Those bringing dispute can choose either the WTO or NAFTA process; in SPS cases, respondent can steer dispute into NAFTA arena under certain circumstances.
U.S.-Israel FTA: Earliest U.S. FTA; entered into force 9/1/85.	Article 9 (Health) directs two sides to review their veterinary and plant health rules to ensure they are applied in a nondiscriminatory manner and do not obstruct trade. Calls for consultations over any difficulties to "... allow trade in agricultural products insofar as they do not endanger animal and plant health."
U.S.-Jordan FTA: Entered into force 12/17/01.	No SPS section. However, a separate Joint Statement on WTO Issues encourages consultations on SPS equivalence.
U.S.-Singapore FTA: Entered into force 1/1/04.	No SPS section, but declares in preamble both parties' commitment to reduction of technical and SPS barriers to trade.
U.S.-Chile FTA: Entered into force 1/1/04.	Chapter Six reaffirms both parties' rights and obligations under WTO SPS agreement. Establishes bilateral committee to enhance understanding of each other's SPS measures and to consult extensively and regularly on SPS matters.
U.S.-Australia FTA: Entered into force 1/1/05.	Chapter VII reaffirms both parties' rights and obligations under WTO SPS Agreement; establishes committee like that in Chile FTA. Further directs USDA-APHIS and counterpart, Biosecurity Australia, to chair standing technical working group intended to address, on an ongoing basis, all trade-related SPS matters that arise during each country's rulemaking and risk assessment processes. Side letters agree to cooperate on securing science-based international standards on BSE.
U.S.-Morocco FTA: Entered into force 1/1/06	Chapter 3-B reaffirms rights and obligations of both parties under the WTO SPS agreement. No SPS committee. Side letter intended to facilitate exports of U.S. beef and poultry by addressing Morocco's concerns about antibiotics and other substances in beef and poultry.
U.S.-Dominican Republic (DR)-Central American FTA: Between the U.S. and Costa Rica, Guatemala, El Salvador, Nicaragua, DR, and Honduras; entered into force for El	DR-CAFTA reaffirms all parties' rights and obligations under WTO SPS agreement, establishes standing SPS committee like that in the Chile and Australia agreements, but further specifies which agencies in each country to be represented. Side letters with Costa Rica and El Salvador agree to cooperate with the United States on scientific and technical work to achieve market access for poultry. U.S. side letter with DR states that the DR "shall not grant or deny import licenses based on SPS concerns, domestic purchasing

Agreement	SPS Provisions
Salvador 3/1/06; Honduras and Nicaragua, 4/1/06; Guatemala, 7/1/06; DR, 3/1/07; and Costa Rica 1/1/09.	requirements, or discretionary criteria. [DR] shall enforce any SPS measures that it imposes separately from its import-licensing system."
U.S.-Bahrain FTA: Entered into force 8/1/06.	SPS chapter (Six) reaffirms two countries' rights and obligations under the WTO SPS agreement. No SPS committee.
U.S.-Oman FTA: Entered into force 1/1/09.	Reaffirms both parties' rights and obligations under WTO SPS agreement. No SPS committee.
U.S.-Peru Trade Promotion Agreement entered into force 2/1/09. U.S.-Colombia Trade Agreement entered into force 5/15/12.	Chapter Six in both agreements reaffirms parties' rights and obligations under the WTO SPS agreement and creates a standing committee to address SPS matters. Each has a series of SPS side letters attached to agreement.
U.S.-Panama FTA: Entered into force 10/31/12.	Chapter Six reaffirms two countries' rights and obligations under the WTO SPS agreement and creates a standing committee to address SPS matters. In a separate SPS agreement, Panama is to accept equivalency of the U.S. meat and poultry inspection system; to provide access for all U.S. beef and poultry, and related products, on the basis of accepted international standards; to streamline import documentation requirements for U.S. processed foods; and to affirm recognition of the U.S. beef grading system, among other things.
U.S.-South Korea FTA: Entered into force 3/15/12.	Chapter Eight reaffirms two countries' rights and obligations under the WTO SPS agreement and creates a standing committee to address SPS matters. (The FTA does not directly address the reopening of Korea to U.S. beef, which was banned in Dec. 2003 due to BSE concerns.)

Sources: USTR (http://www.ustr.gov/trade-agreements/free-trade-agreements); CRS Report RL31356, *Free Trade Agreements: Impact on U.S. Trade and Implications for U.S. Trade Policy*.

Notes: Although not shown here, most FTAs also include general provisions that address TBT measures.

For example, in the U.S.-Australia FTA, in addition to language reaffirming the parties' commitments to their SPS and TBT obligations, the FTA contains a separate chapter on SPS Measures (Chapter 7 of the FTA) establishing an SPS Committee and also a standing technical working group on animal and plant health (Article 7.4;Annex 7-A). The working group is intended to provide a forum to resolve specific bilateral animal and plant health matters to facilitate trade, and engage in risk assessment and regulatory processes, among other matters.[26] During the U.S.-Australia FTA negotiations, U.S. officials also secured a commitment from Australia that it would work to ease inspection procedures that have impeded U.S. imports of pork, citrus, apples, and stone fruit. The FTA also includes side letters where the United States and Australia agree to cooperate on securing science-based international standards on bovine spongiform encephalopathy (BSE, or "mad cow" disease).[27] Similar side letters have accompanied recent FTAs with Latin American countries.

Ongoing FTA Negotiations

In an effort to resolve perceived obstacles in trade regarding SPS and TBT matters, many in U.S. agriculture and the food industry are supporting efforts by U.S. negotiators to build on and "go beyond" the rules, rights, and obligations in the WTO SPS Agreement and TBT Agreement, as well as beyond commitments in existing U.S. FTAs. These efforts are referred to as "WTO-Plus" rules, or alternatively, as "SPS-Plus" and "TBT-Plus" rules. The U.S. meat and poultry industry initially proposed efforts to adopt tougher WTO rules for animal health regulations as part of the Trans-Pacific Partnership (TPP) negotiations. These concepts were later reinforced by recommendations from U.S. and EU trade officials involved in the Transatlantic Trade and Investment Partnership (TTIP) negotiations.

Trans-Pacific Partnership

The Trans-Pacific Partnership (TPP) is a proposed regional FTA being negotiated among the United States and several countries of the Asia-Pacific region—Australia, Brunei, Canada, Chile, Japan, Malaysia, Mexico, New Zealand, Peru, Singapore, and Vietnam.[28]

A major item in the TPP negotiations on agricultural goods is how to address SPS matters. In a May 2012 white paper, the American Meat Institute and National Chicken Council called for including a "'WTO-Plus' SPS chapter ... , an agreement that strengthens and reinforces the rules and disciplines" of the WTO SPS Agreement "and underscores the importance of science-based regulation."[29] To address concerns such as "unnecessarily trade-restrictive measures that are not science-based" and new measures that "do not conform to science-based international standards" or are based on the use of "questionable testing methods to enforce standards," among other concerns, the May 2012 white paper makes several recommendations. It recommends that the TPP agreement strengthen requirements regarding risk assessment and risk management; reinforce the WTO rule that requires regulators to select the least-trade-restrictive of available risk management options; promote trade-facilitating measures such as equivalence, recognition of inspection systems, and harmonization of export certificates; require parties to provide an adequate grace period before implementing new, nonemergency measures; enhance transparency; and strengthen the role of science-based international standards and promote the harmonization of standards, among other recommendations. "Most importantly, these WTO-plus provisions must be fully enforceable under the agreement."[30] Several Members of Congress have called for the inclusion of "effective and enforceable rules" to strengthen the role of science in resolving trade differences.[31]

Supported by other U.S. agriculture and food groups,[32] U.S. negotiators proposed an SPS chapter that lays out more detailed commitments relating to human health and animal and plant safety issues in ways that go beyond rules in the WTO SPS Agreement.[33] Reports indicate that USTR has tabled legal text (to be resolved by higher-level officials towards the conclusion of the negotiations) that would establish both a "consultative mechanism" to address SPS disputes that arise and a "rapid-response mechanism" designed to quickly resolve SPS barriers that block shipments of perishable products.[34] Other U.S. proposals have included calls for increased transparency, establishing a timeline for carrying out science-based risk assessment, requiring risk assessments be based on relevant scientific data, and consistency with international guidelines, among other proposals.[35] Many in the U.S. agriculture industry have criticized the Administration's efforts to address SPS matters in the TPP negotiations as insufficient.[36]

Some TPP countries that are major agricultural exporters appear to favor a dispute settlement process for SPS obligations.[37] Others have expressed criticism of certain U.S. policies, such as country of origin labeling requirements. Recent reports indicate that the United States may be backing off its earlier position of opposing dispute settlement for SPS rules.[38]

Transatlantic Trade and Investment Partnership (TTIP)

Current negotiations between the United States and EU would establish a free trade area as part of the Transatlantic Trade and Investment Partnership (TTIP).[39] However, given major regulatory differences and non-tariff barriers between the United States and the EU, particularly regarding SPS matters, some have expressed concern about whether the TTIP would be able to address such concerns, or whether the agreement might exclude agriculture products altogether.[40] Some Members of Congress expect the TTIP negotiations to resolve long-standing trade disputes regarding SPS rules between the two trading blocs, as well as enhance disciplines to address SPS issues and other non-tariff barriers.[41] Major concerns revolve around meat and poultry production and processing methods, specifically involving the U.S. use of beef hormones and ractopamine,[42] pathogen reduction and other treatment technologies, BSE-related regulations, and other plant processing regulations. Other SPS concerns between the U.S. and EU involve the use of biotechnology (genetically modified organisms, or GMOs)[43] and pesticide regulations.

At the same time, U.S.-EU negotiators are working to resolve existing SPS disputes, and both parties have made changes to some aspects of their regulatory regimes in an attempt to facilitate some SPS that are viewed as an obstacle to a U.S.-EU trade agreement.[44] Still, some Members of Congress have expressed concern that U.S. companies will become subject to the EU's regulatory requirements on food and agricultural products, in addition to U.S. requirements.[45] USTR has expressed concerns that the EU is openly promoting its own "production values" and is strategizing to "act as a global standard setter to enhance the competitiveness of European industry."[46] Other groups, as well as some Members of Congress, have expressed concern that a U.S.-EU trade deal and harmonization of regulatory standards could result in overall lower health and environmental standards, particularly SPS/TBT measures, by making them enforceable through a dispute settlement process.[47]

As part of the Administration's formal notification to Congress in March 2013 launching the U.S.-EU trade talks, USTR stated that among its specific objectives in negotiating the TTIP is "to eliminate or reduce non-tariff barriers that decrease market opportunities for U.S. exports, provide a competitive advantage to products of the EU, or otherwise distort trade," such as SPS measures "that are not based on science" as well as "unjustified" TBT measures and "other 'behind-the-border' barriers, including restrictive administration of tariff-rate quotas and permit and licensing barriers, that impose unnecessary costs and limit competitive opportunities for U.S. exports."[48] USTR later stated that differences in the U.S. and EU regulatory and standards approaches have resulted in "unnecessary barriers, raising costs, deterring trade and investment, and negatively impacting our competitiveness and our consumers," and also called on EU regulators to adopt a U.S. rulemaking process based on transparency, participation, and accountability.[49]

Similar to the TPP, many in the U.S. agriculture and food industry who are advocating for TTIP agriculture negotiations are hoping to go beyond current WTO rules on SPS and TBT matters as well as address certain perceived concerns regarding science-based decision-making in trade disputes. For example, a final report submitted by U.S. and EU trade officials as part of the so-called U.S.-EU High Level Working Group on Jobs and Growth (HLWG) to advise TTIP negotiations recommended that the United States and EU seek to negotiate both an "ambitious 'SPS-plus' chapter" and an "ambitious 'TBT-plus' chapter" under TTIP.

The HLWG recommendations call for:[50]

1. an "ambitious 'SPS-plus' chapter, including establishing an on-going mechanism for improved dialogue and cooperation" to address bilateral SPS issues by building on key principles of WTO SPS Agreement, including "requirements that each side's SPS measures be based on science and on international standards or scientific risk assessments, applied only to the extent necessary to protect human, animal, or plant life or health, and developed in a transparent manner, without undue delay."
2. an "ambitious 'TBT-plus' chapter, building on horizontal disciplines in the WTO [TBT Agreement], including establishing an ongoing mechanism for improved dialogue and cooperation for addressing bilateral TBT issues," including the goals of "greater openness, transparency, and convergence in regulatory approaches and requirements and related standards-development processes ... , to reduce redundant and burdensome testing and certification requirements, promote confidence in our respective conformity assessment bodies, and enhance cooperation on conformity assessment and standardization issues globally."

The "SPS Plus" and "TBT Plus" concept generally means building on and going beyond the rights and obligations of all WTO members through the WTO's SPS and TBT Agreements. For example, this could mean that the EU and United States would provide for greater transparency and more timely SPS and TBT notifications than required by the WTO, along with—albeit more challenging—some form of "rapid response mechanism" for resolving stoppages of agricultural products at the border and enforcement mechanisms or dispute settlement process.[51]

U.S. agriculture and food groups continue to express concern that ongoing trade negotiations might not adequately address SPS concerns and cover "all significant barriers in a single comprehensive agreement."[52] The U.S. Chamber of Commerce has also expressed the need for "the inclusion of ambitious regulatory provisions" covering "a complete package of all three areas—TBT, SPS, and regulatory cooperation" as part of any agreement.[53] Additionally, several Members of Congress have called for "effective rules and enforceable rules to strengthen the role of science in the marketplace" to resolve international trade differences in the TPP and TTIP.[54]

Geographical Indications

Geographical indications (GIs) are geographical names that act to protect the quality and reputation of a distinctive product originating in a certain region. The term is most often, although not exclusively, applied to wines, spirits, and agricultural products. Examples GIs include Parmesan cheese and Parma ham from the Parma region of Italy, Tuscan olive oil, Champagne from the region of the same name in France, Roquefort cheese, and Irish whiskey.

The WTO's Trade-Related Aspects of Intellectual Property Rights (TRIPS) defines GIs as "indications which identify a good as originating in the territory of a Member, or a region or locality in that territory, where a given quality, reputation or other characteristic of the good is essentially attributable to its geographical origin." (Article 22.1) Under the TRIPS Agreement, member countries have committed to providing a minimum standard of protection for GIs (i.e., protecting GI products to avoid misleading the public and to prevent unfair competition) and an "enhanced level of protection" to wines and spirits that carry a geographical indication, subject to certain exceptions.

In the United States, geographical indications are protected under the U.S. Trademark Act (15 U.S.C. §1051 *et seq.*). Section 4 of the Trademark Act (15 U.S.C. §1054) provides for the registration of "certification marks including indications of regional origin." The U.S. Patent and Trademark Office (PTO) defines GIs as "indications that identify a good as originating in the territory of a Member, or a region or locality in that territory, where a given quality, reputation or other characteristic of the good is essentially attributable to its geographic origin." Examples of GIs from the United States include: "Florida" oranges; "Idaho" potatoes; "Vidalia" onions; and "Washington State" apples. According to the U.S. PTO, "geographical indications serve the same functions as trademarks, because like trademarks they are: source-identifiers, guarantees of quality, and valuable business interests." Establishing a product based on its geography can be complicated, either involving establishing a trademark or a brand name through an extensive advertising campaign.

In the EU, a series of regulations governing GIs was initiated in the early 1990s covering agricultural and food products, as well as wine and spirits. The regulations establish provisions regarding products from a defined geographical area, given linkages between the characteristics of products and their geographical origin. Under the regulations, producers qualify for either a protected geographical indication (PGI) or a protected designation of origin (PDO). For foods, the relevant EU authority overseeing GIs is the Unit on Quality Policy for Agricultural Products and Foodstuffs of the Commission of the European Communities. (Regulation 1151/2012 and Regulation 510/2006 (agricultural products and foodstuffs); Regulation 479/2008 (wine); and Regulation 110/2008 (spirits))

Source: Text of the TRIPS agreement is at WTO's website: http://www.wto.org/english/docs_e/legal_e/27-trips_04b_e.htm. For more information, see *CRS In Focus*, "Geographical Indications in U.S.-EU Trade Negotiations

Working within the framework of the SPS and TBT Agreements, and principles and disciplines of the WTO, among the stated U.S. objectives regarding non-tariff barriers and regulatory issues are:[55]

> greater compatibility of U.S. and EU regulations and related standards development processes, with the objective of reducing costs associated with unnecessary regulatory differences and facilitating trade, inter alia by promoting transparency in the development and implementation of regulations and good regulatory practices, establishing mechanisms for future progress, and pursuing regulatory cooperation initiatives where appropriate

These objectives are alternatively expressed as the need for harmonized standards or convergence in regulatory approaches; regulatory coherence; improved openness; and fewer redundant and/or burdensome testing and certification requirements. Similarly, among the EU's stated objectives of the SPS chapter are to establish regulatory and technical cooperation; improve transparency and discrimination to the adoption and application of SPS measures; and eliminate unnecessary barriers to trade while safeguarding human, animal, and plant health.[56]

Some in the U.S. agriculture and food industry are urging the TTIP agriculture negotiations to address the use and application of the so-called "precautionary principle," which is central to the EU's risk management policy regarding food safety and animal and plant health, as well as the EU's practice of taking a generally more risk adverse approach to risk management. Some contend that the EU's use of the precautionary principle contributes to its practice of taking a generally "more risk-averse approach to risk management"[57] and "allows EU regulators to put in place restrictions on products or processes when they believe that scientific evidence on their potential impact on human health or the environment is inconclusive."[58] Many in thc United States claim that "science-based decision making and not the precautionary principle must be the defining principle in setting up mechanisms and systems" to address SPS concerns.[59] Other TTIP objectives for some U.S. agricultural and food groups include calls for changes to the EU's approach for approving and labeling biotechnology products.

Many in the EU continue to defend the application of the precautionary principle to a range of agricultural issues,[60] and U.S. agriculture and food groups have expressed concern that "a resolution regarding the TTIP passed by the European Parliament on April 24 [2013] strongly expresses the intent of the EU to maintain the precautionary principle, which would undermine sound science and ultimately the agreement itself."[61] Additional background on the use and application of the precautionary principle in international trade is provided in the section of this report titled "Application and Use of "Precautionary Principle"."

In addition, some U.S. groups are calling for changes to EU food and beverage designations that derive from production in a specific geographical location, or so-called geographical indications or GIs. (For more information, see text box). These discussions are not part of the SPS chapter, but are being negotiated as part of the TTIP's intellectual property rights (IPR) chapter.

INTERNATIONAL STANDARD SETTING ORGANIZATIONS

The SPS Agreement and the TBT Agreement both encourage the international harmonization of food standards. Specifically, the SPS Agreement recognizes three international standard setting organizations for "facilitating international trade and protecting public health."[62] These include the Codex Alimentarius Commission (Codex);[63] the World Organisation for Animal Health (OIE);[64] and the International Plant Protection Convention (IPPC).[65] These organizations are often referred to as the "Three Sister" organizations of the WTO. Each of these organizations is directly recognized in the SPS Agreement as the primary "relevant" (or reference) organizations for developing international standards, guidelines, and recommendations on animal health, food safety, and plant health.[66] As stated in the SPS Agreement (Article 3):

> To harmonize sanitary and phytosanitary measures on as wide a basis as possible, Members shall base their sanitary or phytosanitary measures on international standards, guidelines or recommendations, where they exist,.... Members shall play a full part, within the limits of their resources, in the relevant international organizations and their subsidiary bodies, in particular the Codex Alimentarius Commission, the International Office of Epizootics, and the international and regional organizations operating within the framework of the International Plant Protection Convention, to promote within these organizations the development and periodic review of standards, guidelines and recommendations with respect to all aspects of sanitary and phytosanitary measures.

As such, Codex, IPPC, and OIE directly and actively participate in and contribute to discussions of the SPS committee. The TBT Agreement further encourages members to participate in the work of international bodies for the preparation of standards and other procedural guidelines (Articles 2.6 and 5.5).

Prior to the creation of the WTO and negotiation of the SPS and TBT Agreements, the United Nations General Assembly stated as part of a 1985 resolution, *Guidelines for Consumer Protection*:[67] "Governments should take into account the need of all consumers for food security and should support and, as far as possible, adopt standards from the Food and Agriculture Organization of the United Nations and the World Health Organization Codex Alimentarius or, in their absence, other generally accepted international food standards." Arguably, however, there is no single and categorical obligation for WTO member governments to adopt internationally recognized standards, guidelines, or recommendations.

The United States is a member of the WTO and also a member of Codex, OIE, and IPPC.[68] U.S. government scientists participate actively in these organizations, which meet periodically to discuss current and anticipated threats to human and agricultural health, evaluate SPS-related disputes, and develop common, scientifically based SPS standards. Such standards are voluntary and are intended to provide guidance for countries in formulating their own national SPS measures and, ultimately, to help resolve trade disputes.

Codex Alimentarius Commission

Codex Alimentarius Commission (Codex) is the international food safety organization that develops internationally adopted food standards, guidelines, and codes of practice. Codex operates as part of a United Nations program jointly funded by the Food and Agriculture Organization (FAO) and the World Health Organization (WHO), known as the Joint FAO/WHO Food Standards Programme.[69] Codex was created in 1963 to develop food standards, guidelines, and codes of practice intended to ensure food safety and hygiene, as well as facilitate international food trade.[70] Codex provides a forum for countries to formulate and harmonize food standards on a global scale. Nearly all countries are members of Codex.[71]

The SPS Agreement identified Codex as the relevant international standard setting organization for food safety. Regarding food safety, Codex sets Maximum Residue Levels (MRLs) for pesticide residues in plant-based foods and for animal drug residues in meat products, and has standards for a range of veterinary drugs.[72]

Codex standards, guidelines, and recommendations are generally regarded as the benchmarks against which "national food measures and regulations are evaluated within the legal parameters" of the WTO agreements, thus giving Codex a key role in helping to resolve some types of trade disputes.[73] Codex standards, guidelines, and recommendations are advisory, not mandatory. However, measures that conform to Codex are generally recognized, under the SPS Agreement, as necessary to protect public health based on available scientific evidence and risk analysis.

Through international negotiations, Codex has formulated standards for specific food commodities, and has also addressed broader areas of concern including pesticide and drug residues, food contaminants and additives, labeling, and food safety. Overall, Codex has developed more than 200 standards covering processed, semi-processed, or unprocessed foods; developed more than 40 hygienic and technological codes of practice; evaluated more than 1,000 food additives and more than 50 veterinary drugs; set more than 3,000 maximum levels for pesticide residues; and specified over 30 guidelines for contaminants.[74] All Codex standards, guidelines, codes of practice, and advisory texts are publicly available at its website.[75]

World Organization for Animal Health

The World Organization for Animal Health (OIE)[76] is responsible for improving animal health worldwide. OIE is not part of the United Nations, but is a separate intergovernmental organization that was founded in 1924 under an international agreement.[77] The SPS Agreement named OIE as the relevant international standard setting organization for animal health, and states that "to harmonize sanitary and phytosanitary measures on as wide a basis as possible, Members shall base their sanitary or phytosanitary measures on international standards, guidelines or recommendations."[78]

OIE's objectives include developing international standards "to promulgate health standards for the safety of international trade in animals and animal products and animal disease surveillance (within its WTO mandate)" as well as "contribute to food safety and food security and to promote animal welfare, through a science-based approach."[79] Historically its mandate has been to "prevent animal diseases from spreading around the world."[80] Among its major functions, OIE collects and disseminates information on the distribution and control of animal diseases, coordinates research on contagious animal diseases, and develops international standards for the safe movement of animals and animal products in international trade.

OIE's codes and manuals are intended as reference documents to help countries establish health regulations for the import and export of live animals and animal products, and avoid the spread of diseases to other animals and humans. OIE also helps develop general principles relating to risk analysis methodology, including import risk assessments, veterinary services assessments, zoning and regionalization guidelines, and surveillance and monitoring tools, such as animal identification and traceability.[81]

International Plant Protection Convention

The International Plant Protection Convention (IPPC) is an international treaty for international cooperation in plant protection, intended to "protect cultivated and wild plants by preventing the introduction and spread of pests."[82] IPPC was established in 1952 and is administered by FAO. The SPS Agreement named IPPC as the relevant international standard setting organization for plant health. IPPC allows for the application of measures by governments intended to protect their plant resources from harmful pests (referred to as "phytosanitary" measures) that may be introduced through international trade.[83] IPPC's major functions apply mostly to quarantine pests in international trade, and its standards and policies are aimed to prevent the spread and introduction of pests to plants and plant products. Other IPPC work includes establishing standards on pest risk analysis and developing requirements for the establishment of pest-free areas.

Application and Use of "Precautionary Principle"

The "precautionary principle" (or precautionary approach) allows a country to take "protective action"—including restricting trade of products or processes—if they believe that scientific evidence is inconclusive regarding their potential impacts on human health and the environment.

No universally agreed upon definition of the precautionary principle exists, and many differently worded or conflicting definitions can be found in international law. WTO rules state:[84]

> Member countries are encouraged to use international standards, guidelines and recommendations where they exist. When they do, they are unlikely to be challenged legally in a WTO dispute. However, members may use measures which result in higher standards if there is scientific justification. They can also set higher standards based on appropriate assessment of risks so long as the approach is consistent, not arbitrary. And they can to some extent apply the "precautionary principle", a kind of "safety first" approach to deal with scientific uncertainty.

More specifically, the precautionary principle suggests that if scientific evidence is insufficient or inconclusive regarding potential dangers to human, environmental, animal, or plant health of a product or practice, that product or practice should be prohibited if reasonable grounds for concern exist.

The WTO acknowledges that "the need to take precautionary actions in the face of scientific uncertainty has long been widely accepted," particularly in the fields of food safety, and plant and animal health protection. Examples might include a sudden outbreak of an animal disease that is suspected of being linked to imports, which may require a country to impose certain trade restrictions while further information about the source and extent of the outbreak is assessed. The WTO also acknowledges that the SPS Agreement allows countries to use different standards and methods of inspecting products. (For other information see text box below.)

PRECAUTIONARY PRINCIPLE: SPS AGREEMENT AND EU LAWS AND REGULATIONS

The WTO acknowledges that the SPS Agreement allows countries to use different standards and different methods of inspecting products. The WTO regards the "precautionary principle" as being reflected in the SPS Agreement, specifically in paragraph 6 of the Preamble, Article 3.3, and Article 5.7 of the agreement.

- Paragraph 6 of the Preamble encourages harmonization of national SPS measures with international standards without requiring countries to change their sovereignly determined appropriate levels of health protection.
- Article 3.3 explicitly permits Members to adopt SPS measures which are more stringent than measures based on the relevant international standards.
- Article 5.7 allows a country "to take provisional measures when sufficient scientific evidence does not exist to permit a final decision on the safety of a product or process." If a country imposes a provisional (temporary) SPS measure, it must seek "additional information necessary for a more objective assessment of risk, and must review the SPS measure within a reasonable period of time."

Source: WTO, "Current Issues, 8.2 The Precautionary Principle." See also: United Nations, *Trading Precaution: The Precautionary Principle and the WTO*, November 2005.

The precautionary principle remains central to the EU's risk management policy regarding food safety and animal and plant health, among other concerns. It was reportedly referenced as part of the 1992 treaty establishing the EU, and its use was further outlined in a 2000 communication and then formally established in EU food legislation in 2002 (Regulation EC No 178/2002).[85] The EU's regulatory definition (Article 7) states:[86]

> In specific circumstances where, following an assessment of available information, the possibility of harmful effects on health is identified but scientific uncertainty persists, provisional risk management measures necessary to ensure the high level of health

protection chosen in the Community may be adopted, pending further scientific information for a more comprehensive risk assessment.

The EU's 2000 communication outlines guidelines for applying the precautionary principle, including implementation, the basis for triggering a decision to invoke the precautionary principle, and the general principles of application.

In international trade, under EU law, application of the precautionary principle provides for "rapid response" to address "possible danger to human, animal, or plant health, or to protect the environment" and can be used to "stop distribution or order withdrawal from the market of products likely to be hazardous."[87] Although its application may not be used as a pretext for protectionist measures, many countries have challenged as "protectionist" some EU actions that have invoked the precautionary principle.

Several U.S. agricultural and manufacturing groups oppose the EU's application of the principle and argue it allows EU regulations to disregard scientific evidence demonstrating that certain food products and processes are safe, based on evidence from available scientific risk assessments, allowing the EU and other importing countries to engage in disguised protectionism.[88] On the other hand, some advocates believe that the SPS agreement too severely limits use of the principle.[89]

Application of the precautionary principle by some countries remains an ongoing source of contention in international trade, particularly by the United States, and is often cited as a reason why some countries may restrict imports of some food products and processes. A 2013 paper authored by researchers at several U.S. land grant universities and USDA cites the following criticisms of the precautionary principle: (1) the ambiguity and lack of definition of the precautionary principle; (2) the arbitrariness in its use and unprincipled ways in which the precautionary principle has been applied; and (3) application of the precautionary principle is biased against new technologies, such as biotechnology and nanotechnology.[90] The authors conclude that the precautionary principle has become "unworkable and counterproductive."[91] Many U.S. agricultural and food organizations contend the precautionary principle undermines "sound science" and results in "unjustifiable restrictions" on U.S. exports.[92] The stated policy of the U.S. Chamber of Commerce also is to support a "science-based approach to risk management, where risk is assessed based on scientifically sound and technically rigorous standards," and "oppose the domestic and international adoption of the precautionary principle as a basis for regulatory decision making."[93] Its strategy aims to "educate consumers, businesses, and federal policymakers about the implications of the precautionary principle."[94]

A 2005 study by the United Nations University recognizes that despite "fundamental differences in perception as to the appropriate role of science and technology in society, ... there must be a mutually acceptable, rational basis for concern that is based on available information when invoking precaution."[95] The report further states: "While science has an important role to play in assessing risk and in informing decision makers on possible approaches to health and environmental concerns, the management of the risks involved invariably falls into the realm of political choice, where determining an acceptable level of risk must take into account a multitude of different considerations."

The study encourages the need for increased bilateral, regional, and multilateral discussion, and notes that unilateral measures adopted by countries without the support of "international standards, multilateral agreements or rigorous risk assessment" are both "economically damaging" and "create skepticism" for other actions where precaution may be truly warranted.

SPS/TBT Trade Concerns Raised at the WTO

SPS Measures

The WTO reports that member countries submitted 344 complaints about trade concerns associated with SPS requirements between 1995 and 2012 (**Figure 1**). The United States, among other developed countries, raised many of the concerns reviewed by the SPS committee.

About 40% of SPS-specific trade concerns involved animal health and zoonotic diseases[96] (**Figure 2**). Another 30% of trade concerns involved food safety, followed by 24% on plant health and 6% concerning other issues such as certification requirements or translation. Within the animal health and zoonoses category, complaints involved foot-and-mouth disease (24%), transmissible spongiform encephalopathy (33%), and avian influenza (9%), among other animal health concerns (34%).[97] About one-third (101) of all SPS-specific trade concerns were reported by the committee to have been resolved, while the remaining issues often required ongoing attention.

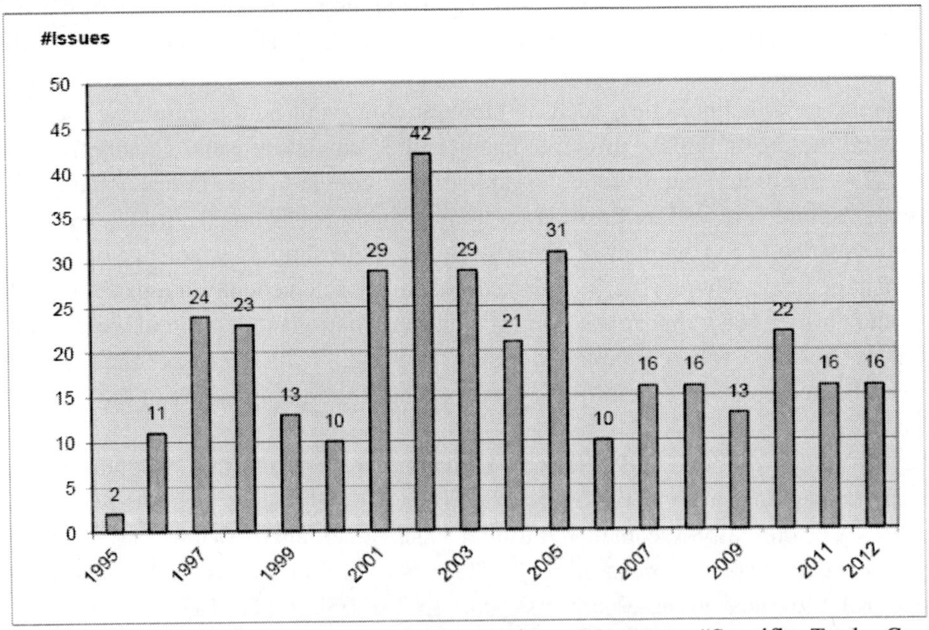

Source: WTO, Committee on Sanitary and Phytosanitary Measures, "Specific Trade Concerns," Overview and Summary Graphs and Tables," G/SPS/GEN/204/Rev.11 (13-1021), February 26, 2013.

Figure 1. SPS-Specific Trade Concerns Raised in the WTO (1995-2012).

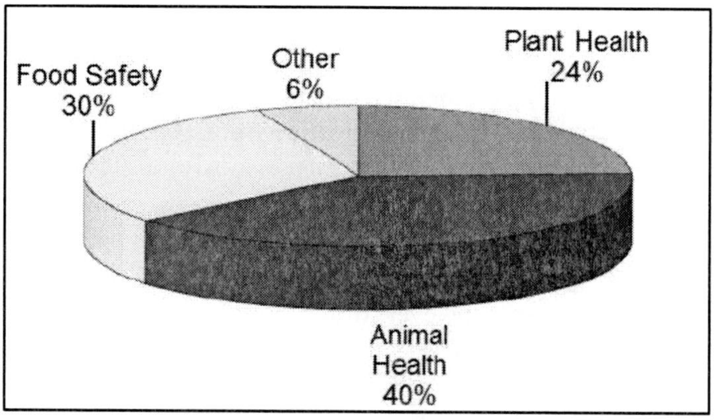

Source: WTO, Committee on Sanitary and Phytosanitary Measures, "Specific Trade Concerns," Overview and Summary Graphs and Tables," G/SPS/GEN/204/Rev.11 (13-1021), February 26, 2013.

Figure 2. SPS-Specific Trade Concerns by Subject (1995-2012).

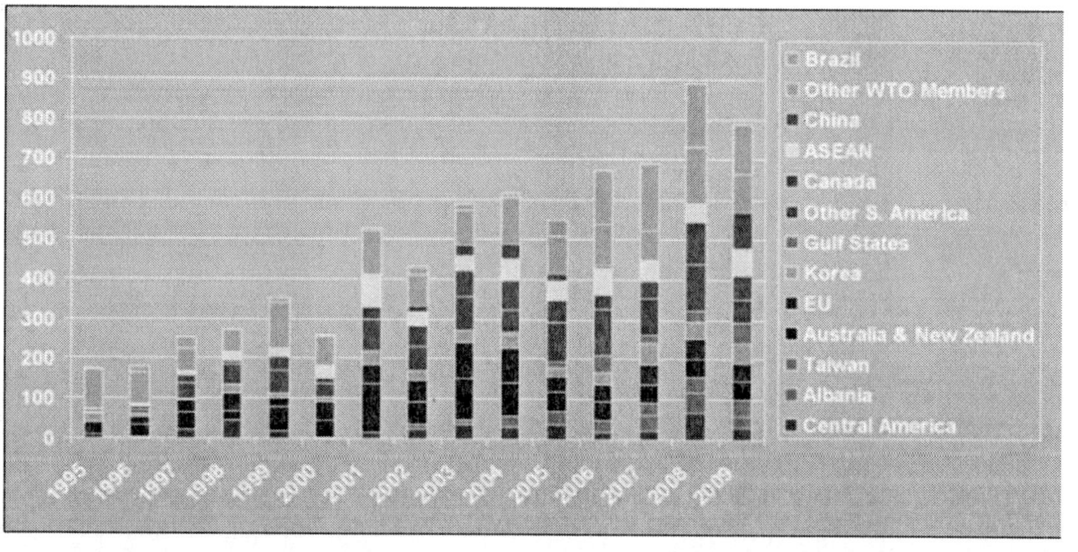

Source: Freese, R., "Monitoring Foreign SPS Measures To Expand U.S. Agricultural Exports," U.S. Department of Agriculture, May 2010. Similar data are not available for TBT measures or for more recent years.

Figure 3. Foreign SPS Measures Reviewed by the United States by Country/Region, 1995-2009.

In the United States, federal agencies continue to review an increasing number of foreign SPS measures notified to the WTO.[98] USDA reports that the number of SPS measures reviewed by U.S. government agencies rose from under 200 notified measures in 1995 to a total of 7,240 notified measures as of 2009, followed by an additional 950 notifications for 2010.[99] More recent data are not available. (Similar information is not available for TBT measures, but would likely also cover other non-food traded goods.) Of these, USDA reports that combined SPS measures by Brazil, China, and other Asian nations account for a large share of total number of SPS notifications (**Figure 3**).

TBT Measures

Trade concerns involving TBT requirements also have been increasing. The WTO reports that member countries submitted 278 new complaints from 1995 to 2012, in addition to the roughly 30-60 complaints per year that had been previously raised to the TBT committee (**Figure 4**). The United States, among other developed countries, raised many of the concerns reviewed by the TBT committee. As the TBT Agreement addresses both food and nonfood traded goods, not all of these trade concerns have involved food products, and data are not available to distinguish foods only. However, of these, "protection of human health and food safety" was the most often single stated objective for the use of TBT measures, accounting for about 30% of all TBT-specific concerns (**Figure 5**).

U.S. Concerns Involving SPS/TBT Measures

The United States has several formal trade disputes regarding SPS/TBT measures with the EU. These include concerns regarding the EU's ban on U.S. meats treated with growth-promoting hormones,[100] the EU's restrictions on chemical treatments ("pathogen reduction treatments" or "PRTs") on U.S. poultry,[101] and the EU's moratorium on approvals of biotechnology products.[102] Other formal complaints have involved U.S. concerns about Korean testing and inspection requirements on U.S. agricultural products,[103] Japan's varietal testing requirement of certain fruits and nuts to control for certain pests,[104] and India's restrictions on poultry products related to concerns about avian influenza.[105] (The United States has also expressed concerns about the expanded use of other types of potential trade barriers, including GIs and intellectual property protections involving agricultural products, as well as wine and spirits.)

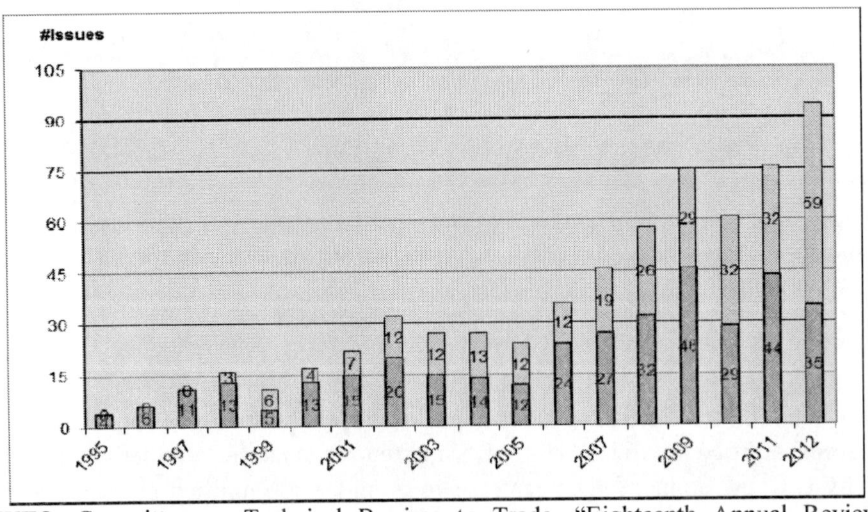

Source: WTO, Committee on Technical Barriers to Trade, "Eighteenth Annual Review of the Implementation and Operation of the TBT Agreement," G/TBT/33/Rev.11 (13-1045), February 27, 2013. Lower part of bar indicates newly raised concerns; upper part of bar indicates previously raised concerns.

Figure 4. Number of TBT-Specific Trade Concerns Raised in (1995-2012).

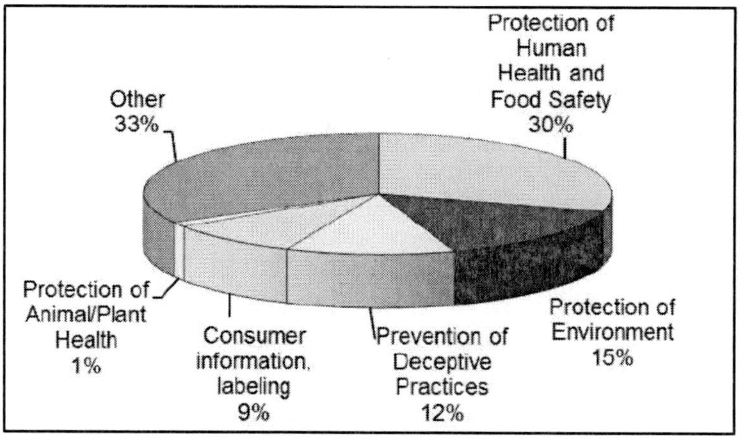

Source: WTO, Committee on Technical Barriers to Trade, "Eighteenth Annual Review of the Implementation and Operation of the TBT Agreement," G/TBT/33/Rev.11 (13-1045), February 27, 2013.

Notes: Shares based on reported "stated objectives for the measures in 1995-2012". For each specific trade concern there can be more than one stated objective.

Figure 5.TBT-Specific Trade Concerns by "Stated Objective" (1995-2012).

Other types of trade concerns with other countries have not risen to the level of a formal WTO dispute. These disputes have involved U.S. concerns over foreign rules and requirements regarding the use and approval of agricultural biotechnology in other WTO member countries,[106] Russia's restrictions on antimicrobial residues and the use of chlorine rinses on U.S. meat and poultry exports,[107] and also ongoing prohibitions against some U.S. livestock products due to concerns about bovine spongiform encephalopathy (BSE, or "mad cow" disease), which was detected in the United States in 2003.

Foreign countries also have objected to various U.S. trade measures as well, including our country of origin labeling (COOL)[108] and "dolphin- safe" labeling standards,[109] as well as U.S. restrictions on poultry product imports from China,[110] among others.[111] Concerns about U.S. standards and procedures involve issues regarding the U.S. plant and animal health approval process, and differences between the United States and EU regarding their respective final approval procedures for products derived using biotechnology as well as labeling requirements for such products, among other types of concerns.[112]

SPS/TBT Trade Concerns Reported by USTR

Annual reports by USTR detail numerous ongoing trade concerns involving U.S. agricultural products and processes under both the SPS and TBTAgreements.[113] Many of these trade concerns have not been formally brought to the WTO, but are addressed on an ongoing basis by U.S. government agencies in an attempt to resolve these issues, perhaps before they become part of a formal complaint or WTO trade dispute.

In 2013, USTR reported about 150 ongoing trade concerns in more than 50 countries or trade regions involving agricultural products under both the SPS and TBT Agreements. A full summary of these ongoing SPS/TBT trade concerns based on the most recent annual report is provided in **Appendix A** at the end of this report. (The information in the tables generally excludes most non-agricultural products, but may include some non-food items such as textiles and fibers, cosmetics and body care products, tobacco products, and reformulated fuels. Cases involving wine are included, but most other alcoholic beverages, such as distilled spirits, are excluded.)

The United States continues to actively pursue the removal of SPS-specific trade barriers on an ongoing and increasing basis. For example, USDA's most recent publicly available report indicates that the U.S. government made the following requests in 2009:[114]

- removal of certain tolerances on food additives, pesticides, and contaminants, tolerances deemed by USDA to be "unscientifically-based" (468 instances);
- submission of risk assessments for actions taken by some U.S. trading partners on certain agricultural products (134 instances);
- adoption of international standards by some U.S. trading partners for certain agricultural products (117 instances);
- adoption of U.S. standards by some U.S. trading partners for certain agricultural products (78 instances); and
- changes to quarantine and inspection requirements by some U.S. trading partners for certain agricultural products (18 instances).

Nearly one-half of the comments pertained to measures regarding processed products; one-third addressed requirements for live animals and fish (and their products, including dairy products); and almost one-quarter were for measures that introduced new standards or entry requirements for plants, bulk commodities (including those made with biotechnology), and horticultural products. The leading countries of U.S. comments were China (82 U.S. comments), South Korea (19 comments), Brazil (18 comments), and Taiwan (15 comments). Moreover, the total number of U.S. comments on foreign SPS measures has been increasing, rising from fewer than 30 comments in 1995 to more than 230 comments in 2009 (**Figure 6**).

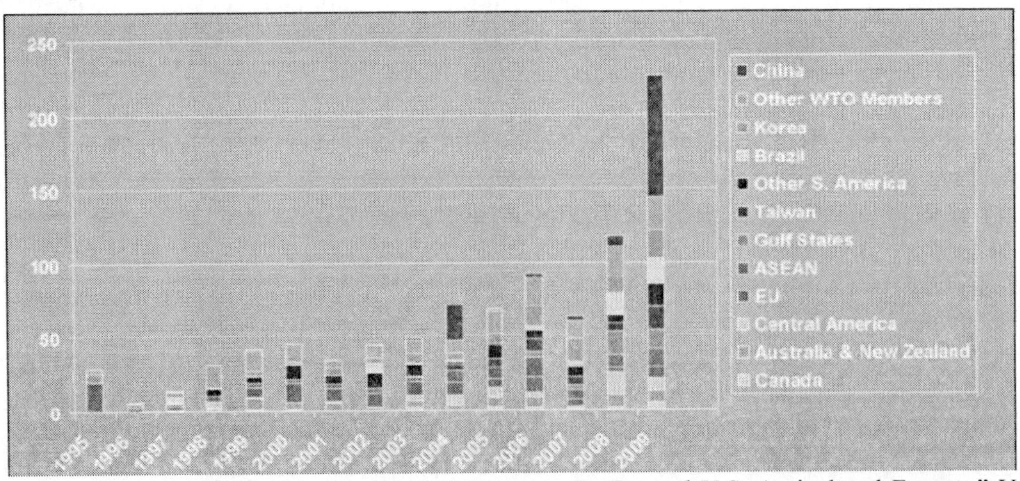

Source: Freese, R., "Monitoring Foreign SPS Measures To Expand U.S. Agricultural Exports," U.S. Department of Agriculture, May 2010.

Notes: Similar data are not available for TBT measures, and would likely also cover non-food traded goods.

Figure 6. Number of U.S. Comments on Foreign SPS Measures by Country/Region, 1995-2009.

Overall, USDA reports that in 2009 the U.S. government commented on about one-third of all foreign SPS notifications submitted to WTO, an increase from previous years when the United States commented on about 10% of all foreign SPS notifications. This rise in U.S. comments on foreign SPS notifications is one indication that SPS measures may increasingly be affecting U.S. agricultural exporters in some international markets. (Similar information is not available for TBT measures, but would likely also cover other non-food traded goods.)

Table 2. WTO Formal Complaints Invoking the SPS and TBT Agreements (Complainant: United States)

WTO Agreement	Complainant: United States	Respondent	Status of Dispute	Dispute Record
SPS, TBT	"Certain Measures Affecting Poultry Meat and Poultry Meat Products from the United States" regarding EC restrictions on the use of chemical treatments ("pathogen reduction treatments" (PRTs)) designed to reduce the level of microbes on the meat.	European Communities	Consultations Requested: January 2009 Current Status: Implementation notified by respondent.	DS389
SPS	"Measures Concerning the Importation of Certain Agricultural Products from the United States" a number of orders issued by India's Department of Animal Husbandry, Dairying, and Fisheries.	India	Consultations Requested: March 2012 Current Status: Panel composed.	DS430
SPS, TBT	"Measures Affecting the Approval and Marketing of Biotech Products" regarding the moratorium applied by the EC since October 1998 on the approval of biotech products.	European Communities	Consultations Requested: May 2003 Current Status: Authorization to retaliate requested (including arbitration).	DS291
SPS	"Measures Affecting the Importation of Apples" regarding Japan's quarantine restrictions on imported apples said to be necessary to protect against introduction of fire blight.	Japan	Consultations Requested: March 2002 Current Status: Mutually acceptable solution on implementation notified.	DS245
SPS, TBT	"Measures Affecting Trade in Live Swine" regarding Mexico's October 1999 definitive anti-dumping measure on live swine for slaughter exported from the United States.	Mexico	Consultations Requested: July 2000 Current Status: In consultations.	DS203
SPS	"Measures Affecting Agricultural Products" regarding Japan's quarantine measures of imports of certain agricultural products.	Japan	Consultations Requested: April 1997 Current Status: Mutually acceptable solution on implementation notified.	DS76

Table 2. (Continued)

WTO Agreement	Complainant: United States	Respondent	Status of Dispute	Dispute Record
SPS, TBT	"Measures Concerning Inspection of Agricultural Products" for the testing, inspection, and other measures required for the importation of agricultural products into Korea.	South Korea	Consultations Requested: May 1996 Current Status: In consultations.	DS41
SPS, TBT	"Measures Concerning Meat and Meat Products (Hormones)" regarding measures taken by the EC to prohibit the use of hormones in livestock production.	European Communities	Consultations Requested: January 1996 Current Status: Mutually acceptable solution on implementation notified.	DS26
SPS	"Measures Affecting the Importation of Salmonids" regarding Australia's prohibition of imports of salmon based on a quarantine regulation.	Australia	Consultations Requested: November 1995 Current Status: Settled or terminated (withdrawn, mutually agreed solution).	DS21
SPS, TBT	"Measures Concerning the Shelf-Life of Products" regarding certain requirements imposed by South Korea on imports.	South Korea	Consultations Requested: May 1995 Current Status: Settled or terminated (withdrawn, mutually agreed solution).	DS5
SPS, TBT	"Measures Concerning the Testing and Inspection of Agricultural Products" with respect to imports of agricultural products into South Korea.	South Korea	Consultations Requested: April 1995 Current Status: In consultations.	DS3
TBT	"Administration of Measures Establishing Customs Duties for Rice" regarding the administration of laws and regulations establishing the customs duties applicable to rice imported from the United States.	Belgium	Consultations Requested: October 2000 Current Status: Settled or terminated (withdrawn, mutually agreed solution).	DS210
TBT	"Measures Affecting Imports of Footwear, Textiles, Apparel and other Items" regarding the imposition of specific duties in excess of the bound rate and other measures by Argentina.	Argentina	Consultations Requested: October 1996 Current Status: Implementation notified by respondent.	DS56

Source: Compiled by CRS from WTO information on trade disputes by agreement: (1) Sanitary and Phytosanitary Measures (SPS) and (2) Technical Barriers to Trade (TBT) from WTO's website (http://www.wto.org/english/tratop_e/dispu_e/dispu_agreements_index_e.htm?id=A19#selected_agreement; http://www.wto.org/english/tratop_e/dispu_e/dispu_agreements_index_e.htm?id=A22#selected_agreement). More detailed information on these disputes is available at the WTO's website by referencing the case numbers shown in the tables. In the WTO, countries of the European Union are referred to as the European Communities.

Notes: Status per WTO's websites, as of March 2014. Excludes disputes where the United States is neither a dispute respondent nor complainant. Generally excludes non-agricultural products.

Table 3. WTO Formal Complaints Invoking the SPS and TBT Agreements (Respondent: United States)

WTO Agreement	Respondent: United States	Complainant	Status of Dispute	Dispute Record
SPS	"Measures Affecting the Importation of Fresh Lemons" regarding certain measures affecting the importation of fresh lemons from the Northwest region of Argentina.	Argentina	**Consultations Requested:** September 2012 **Current Status:** In consultations.	DS448
SPS	"Measures Affecting the Importation of Animals, Meat and Other Animal Products from Argentina."	Argentina	**Consultations Requested:** August 2012 **Current Status:** Panel established but not yet composed.	DS447
SPS	"Measures Affecting the Production and Sale of Clove Cigarettes" regarding the Family Smoking Prevention Tobacco Control Act of 2009 in the United States that restricts clove cigarettes.	Indonesia	**Consultations Requested:** April 2010 **Current Status:** Report(s) adopted, with recommendation to bring measure(s) into conformity.	DS406
SPS	"Certain Measures Affecting Imports of Poultry from China" regarding certain measures taken by the United States in the Omnibus Appropriations Act of 2009, which denied the use of any funding to allow Chinese poultry to be imported to the United States.	China	**Consultations Requested:** April 2009 **Current Status:** Report(s) adopted, no further action required.	DS392
SPS, TBT	"Certain Country of Origin Labeling Requirements" regarding the U.S. implementation of mandatory country of origin labeling (COOL) provisions in 2008.	Mexico and Canada	**Consultations Requested:** December 2008 **Current Status:** Compliance proceedings ongoing	DS386 and DS384

Table 3. (Continued)

WTO Agreement	Respondent: United States	Complainant	Status of Dispute	Dispute Record
SPS, TBT	"Certain Measures Affecting the Import of Cattle, Swine and Grain from Canada" regarding certain measures, imposed by South Dakota and other states, prohibiting entry or transit to Canadian trucks carrying cattle, swine, and grain.	Canada	**Consultations Requested:** September 1998 **Current Status:** In consultations.	DS144
SPS, TBT	"Measures Affecting Imports of Poultry Products" regarding a ban on U.S. imports of poultry and poultry products from the EC under USDA's Food Safety and Inspection Service (FSIS) measures.	European Communities	**Consultations Requested:** August 1997 **Current Status:** In consultations.	DS100
TBT	"Measures Concerning the Importation, Marketing and Sale of Tuna and Tuna Products" regarding dolphin protection measures and "dolphin-safe" labeling requirements for tuna harvested in the Eastern Tropical Pacific ocean by certain large shipping vessels.	Mexico	**Consultations Requested:** October 2008 **Current Status:** Report(s) adopted, with recommendation to bring measure(s) into conformity.	DS381
TBT	"Measures Affecting Textiles and Apparel Products (II)" regarding alleged changes to U.S. rules of origin for textiles and apparel products.	European Communities	**Consultations Requested:** November 1998 **Current Status:** Settled or terminated (withdrawn, mutually agreed solution).	DS151
TBT	"Measures Affecting Textiles and Apparel Products" regarding alleged changes to U.S. rules of origin for textiles and apparel products.	European Communities	**Consultations Requested:** May 1997 **Current Status:** Settled or terminated (withdrawn, mutually agreed solution).	DS85

WTO Agreement	Respondent: United States	Complainant	Status of Dispute	Dispute Record
TBT	"Import Prohibition of Certain Shrimp and Shrimp Products" regarding a ban on the importation of certain shrimp and shrimp products from the Philippines imposed by the United States.	Philippines	**Consultations Requested:** October 1996 **Current Status:** In consultations.	DS61

Source: Compiled by CRS from WTO information on trade disputes by agreement: (1) Sanitary and Phytosanitary Measures (SPS) and (2) Technical Barriers to Trade (TBT) from WTO's website (http://www.wto.org/english/tratop_e/dispu_e/dispu_agreements_index_e.htm?id=A19#selected_agreement; http://www.wto.org/english/tratop_e/dispu_e/dispu_agreements_index_e.htm?id=A22#selected_agreement). More detailed information on these disputes is available at the WTO's website by referencing the case numbers shown in the tables. In the WTO, EU countries are referred to as the European Communities.

Notes: Status per WTO's websites, as of March 2014. Excludes disputes where the United States is neither a dispute respondent nor complainant. Generally excludes non-agricultural products.

Formal SPS/TBT Trade Disputes Involving the United States

Although not all trade concerns about the use of SPS and TBT measures rise to the level of a formal complaint to the WTO, some trade concerns involving SPS/TBT measures have the potential to develop into a formal trade dispute, requiring WTO dispute resolution between the U.S. and its trading partners in some cases.

As of March 2014, in the WTO, 40 cases have cited the SPS Agreement and 49 cases have cited the TBT Agreement (the latter including non-food related disputes). Roughly half of all cases under both agreements have involved the United States as either "complainant" (**Table 2**) or "respondent" (**Table 3**).[115] Many of these cases continue to be debated. These listings include formal cases involving agricultural and fisheries products and processes under the SPS Agreement and TBT Agreement, but exclude nonfood traded goods as well as some other products such as distilled spirits and textiles.

A trade dispute arises when a member government believes another member government is violating a WTO agreement. The complaining member must submit a "request for consultations" identifying the agreements it believes are being violated. Governments can, and often do, resolve SPS and TBT (among other trade) disagreements informally through bilateral and multilateral discussions, usually among technical experts (e.g., scientists, or health professionals) and, if necessary, higher-level trade officials. If such methods are not successful in resolving a particular concern, the countries involved may conclude that a bilaterally agreed approach is not possible. If the trading partner is a WTO Member, and if the United States considers that measure is inconsistent with WTO rules, the United States may decide to assert its rights under the SPS or TBT Agreements through the WTO's dispute settlement system. Disputes that cannot be resolved through bilateral and multilateral discussions may be elevated to formally established dispute procedures. Within the WTO, these procedures are spelled out in the WTO's Understanding on Rules and Procedures Governing the Settlement of Disputes.[116]

If a WTO dispute settlement panel ultimately determines that a country's SPS or TBT measure, for example, is inconsistent with a member's WTO obligations, and WTO members adopt the panel and/or any appellate body report, the defending country is expected to withdraw the measure. Compensation and retaliation are available as temporary remedies. If compensation is not provided to the complaining country by the defending country, and the two still fail to reach a mutually acceptable solution, the WTO panel can authorize trade retaliation if the complaining country so requests. Such retaliation generally takes the form of higher tariffs against a portion of the defending country's exports to the complaining country.[117]

POTENTIAL EFFECTS ON INTERNATIONAL AGRICULTURAL TRADE

The intended purpose of most SPS/TBT measures is to protect the safety and the integrity of the domestic and imported food supply. However, there are concerns that SPS/TBT measures have the potential to restrict international trade. In some cases, this may be an unintentional outcome by an importing country in its efforts to ensure food safety. In other cases, SPS/TBT measures may be used as a form of disguised protectionism by an importing country.[118] The potential of SPS/TBT measures to become non-tariff barriers to trade has increased as monetary tariffs on traded goods have been reduced under multilateral trade agreements and various free trade agreements.[119]

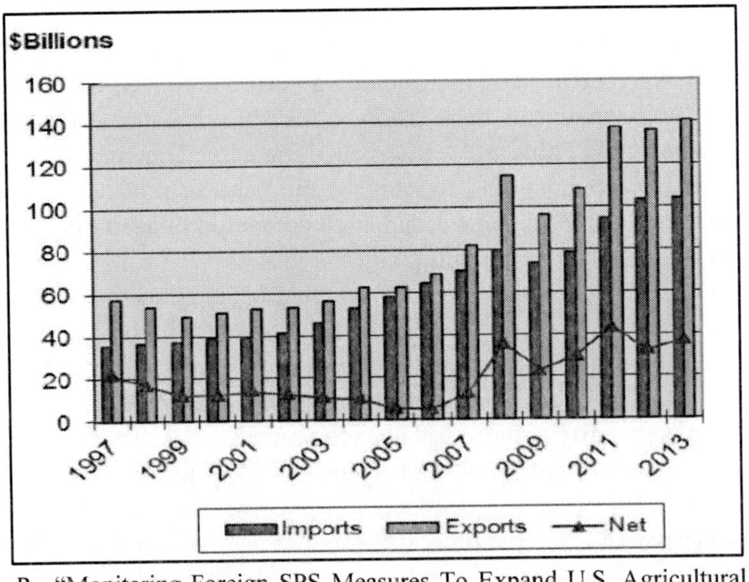

Source: Freese, R., "Monitoring Foreign SPS Measures To Expand U.S. Agricultural Exports," U.S. Department of Agriculture, May 2010.

Notes: Similar data are not available for TBT measures, and would likely also cover non-food traded goods.

Figure 7. U.S. Agricultural Trade, FY1997-FY2013.

In some cases, SPS barriers and agriculture-related TBTs can impose significant economic costs on agricultural and food exporters, by forcing them to make often costly changes in production or marketing in order to comply. A foreign SPS or TBT action can halt all imports of a product, resulting in market or other types of economic losses for the exporting industry. Alternatively, the imposition of technical standards and guidelines may result in certain economic and societal benefits and offset other types of unaccounted for welfare costs that may be associated with trade, such as protection against public health risks from food safety outbreaks or foodborne illness, and also protection against plant and animal pests and disease, and/or degradation of environmental and natural resources. Given the importance of agricultural trade to the U.S. economy, the United States is pursuing ways to reduce and/or remove both tariff and nontariff barriers through multilateral and bilateral negotiations.

Importance of U.S. Agricultural Exports

The United States is a net exporter of agricultural products. Over the past few years, there has been a growing trade surplus in U.S. agricultural trade. Over the 2009-2013 time period, U.S. agricultural exports have averaged $124 billion per year, while imports have averaged about $91 billion per year. This gap between exports and imports has resulted in a U.S. trade surplus of more than $30 billion (**Figure 7**).

USDA's Economic Research Service estimates that each $1 billion in U.S. agricultural exports supports approximately 6,800 jobs throughout the economy, and each $1 of agricultural exports stimulated another $1.29 in business activity (based on 2011 data).[120] Accordingly, ERS reports that U.S. agricultural exports supported nearly 923,000 full-time American jobs both on and off-farm, and also resulted in a total economic output of more than $300 billion in 2011.

Estimated Economic Losses to U.S. Export Markets

Despite the stated policy goals of an importing country for imposing non-tariff measures such as SPS and TBT—namely, to protect public health and the environment—the WTO acknowledges that such measures are often deliberately for protectionist purposes and might impose economic losses on some exporting countries.[121] However, quantifying the potential economic losses from non-tariff measures is not always straightforward.

Previous USDA Analysis (1996 Data)

As a follow-up to the Uruguay Round negotiations in the mid-1990s, USDA published a widely cited report of the aggregate estimated value of lost export revenue to U.S. agricultural exports from foreign technical trade barriers, including barriers due to SPS and TBT measures. The study identified agricultural products and import country regions of concern to U.S. exporters. The study reported the presence of "questionable technical barriers" in more than 60 countries affecting trade in more than 300 agricultural products, valued at an estimated $5.0 billion of U.S. agricultural, forestry, and fishery exports (using 1996 data), accounting for about 7% of total agricultural exports during that year: "Questionable technical barriers were reported for 62 countries. Over 300 market restrictions were identified that threatened, constrained, or blocked an estimated $5.0 billion of U.S. agricultural, forestry, and fishery exports, 7.1% of the $69.7 billion total exported in 1996."[122]

SPS measures accounted for 90% of the estimated revenue losses in USDA's study, with the remainder from revenue losses attributable to TBT measures and other types of trade measures.

The underlying ERS survey data provide more information on these estimated trade effects. Although based on trade data from 1996, the reported underlying relationships may still be useful for understanding how trade may be affected from foreign technical trade barriers.

The ERS study reported that, by regulatory goal, two types of "risk-reducing" measures accounted for most of the total estimated export revenue losses: commercial plant and animal health issues (52% of the estimated export revenue losses) and food safety measures (39% of estimated losses), followed by other goals such as product quality and other concerns (**Figure 8**). By policy instrument, process standards (55%) and product standards (24%) accounted for most estimated trade effects (**Figure 9**), as well as full and partial bans (12%) and other requirements.

The ERS survey data identified a range of agricultural products affected by technical trade barriers (**Figure 10**). By product category, four commodity groups accounted for most of the total estimated export revenue losses: further processed products (26% of estimated losses), grains and oilseeds (24%), animal products (17%), and horticultural products (13%), among other products including cotton, seeds, nuts, fish, and forestry products. Within the meat and produce categories, the bulk of the estimated trade effects was associated with beef products and also fruits. By geographic region, technical barriers affecting U.S. agricultural exports were most prevalent in East Asia, accounting for nearly one-half of all reported trade effects, followed by the Americas with about one-fourth of the estimated loss (**Figure 11**).

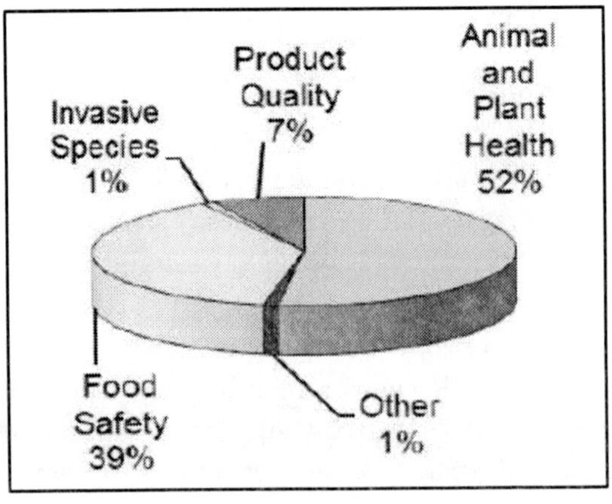

Source: See footnote 122.

Figure 8. Estimated Trade Effects by Regulatory Goal.

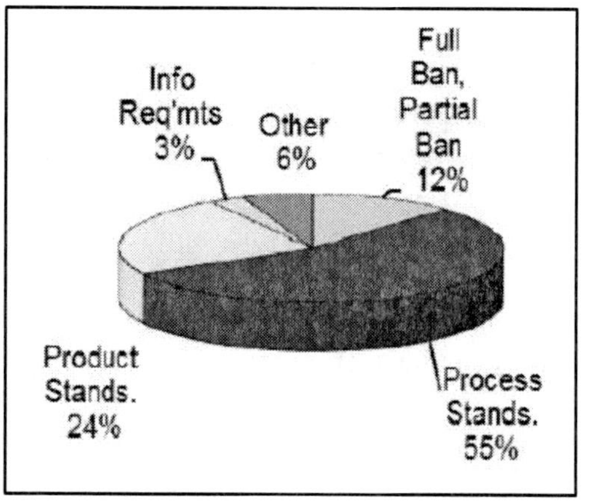

Source: See footnote 122.

Figure 9.EstimatedTrade Effects by Policy Instrument.

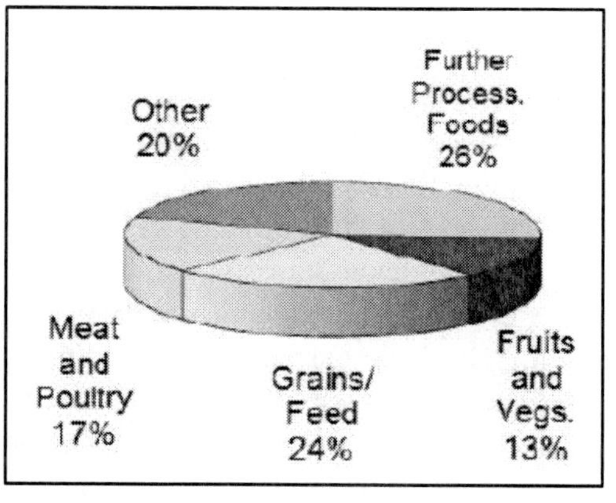

Source: See footnote 122.

Figure 10. Estimated Trade Effects by Product Category.

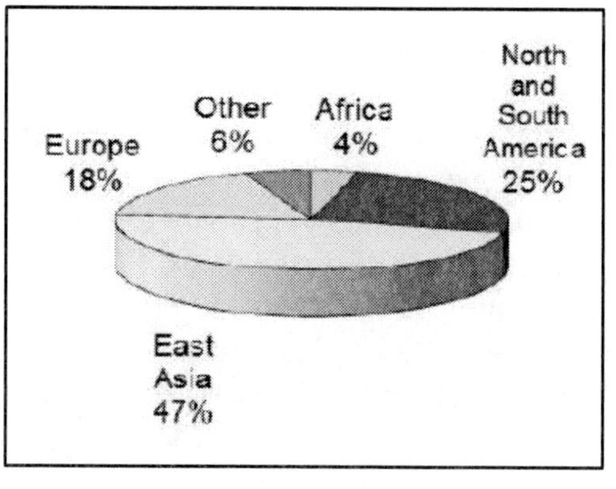

Source: See footnote 122.

Figure 11. Estimated Trade Effects by Geographic Region.

Other Available Estimates

More recent comprehensive analyses of the aggregate costs to U.S. agricultural exports associated with foreign SPS/TBT measures are not available.[123] Efforts to inventory and quantify agricultural non-tariff barriers such as SPS/TBT measures are complicated by the very nature of such measures, given that they often involve complex regulatory schemes and may lack transparency in how these requirements are applied and in the scientific justification supporting their use.[124] It is also difficult to tease out the cost effects of private voluntary standards from government-imposed SPS/TBT measures, and, in some cases, private standards may have more influence on market access into a country than public mandatory standards.[125]

Some studies do provide cost estimates, but often these estimates reflect total costs from all types of nontariff barriers—including prohibitions, and import quotas and licenses, as well as SPS or agricultural TBTs, and may span trade in both food and nonfood merchandise.[126] Other studies instead focus their estimates more narrowly, for example, estimating the economic costs for a specific agricultural product or trade involving regulations between certain countries only, and do not provide aggregate estimates for all product exports globally.

Although more recent formal estimates of U.S. agricultural trade effects are not readily available, USTR continues to assert: "SPS trade barriers prevent U.S. producers from shipping hundreds of millions of dollars worth of goods, hurting farms and small businesses" and states that "elimination of unwarranted SPS foreign trade barriers is a high priority of the U.S. Government."[127] Available estimates indicate that annual trade effects might cost U.S. agricultural exporters well over $1 billion annually. For example, USDA reports that in 2012 the agency's ongoing efforts to "eliminate barriers, open new markets, secure the release of U.S. shipments detained at foreign ports, and ensure the safe movement of agricultural products in a manner consistent with science and international standards" resulted in the agency preserving agricultural exports valued at an estimated $4 billion.[128] Previous estimates by USDA reported that its efforts to resolve SPS barriers in FY2007, for example, allowed U.S. exports with a market value of approximately $1.3 billion to occur.[129] Estimates associated with the ongoing TTIP negotiations indicate that the current regulatory regime and non-tariff trade barriers between the United States and the European Union may have added an estimated $20.2 billion in combined trade costs to U.S.-EU trade in food and beverages in 2011.[130]

In the absence of more precise cost estimates, many U.S. agricultural groups and trade associations continue to actively pursue ways to resolve trade disputes involving SPS and TBT measures, and recognize the increasingly important role that non-tariff measures play in U.S. agricultural export markets.[131]

Other available studies do provide an indication of the potential scale of market and economic implications from non-tariff barriers, including SPS/TBT measures. For example, a 2007 survey showed that among SPS and TBT measures affecting trade in 690 agricultural products exported worldwide, only four products did not face barriers in any importing country.[132] In addition, among the 154 countries reviewed in the study, only 92 notified measures under the SPS and TBT Agreements. Studies also show that SPS and TBT measures may negatively affect exports from other countries, especially developing countries. A 2008 study shows that agricultural exports from Africa and the Caribbean and Pacific nations are often negatively and significantly influenced by SPS and TBT measures in certain import markets for a range of tropical and diversified products such as fruit, nut, and vegetable products and preparation, cereals, oil seed, and also cocoa and cocoa preparations.[133] Researchers at the Organization for Economic Co-operation and Development (OECD) also note that "food regulation compliance costs have a relatively higher overall economic impact in low income countries than in high-income countries."[134]

A 2009 study suggests that nontariff barriers restrict agricultural trade, and may be more restrictive to trade than import tariffs. The study shows that not only are average levels of *ad valorem* equivalents (AVEs)[135] higher for agriculture than for manufacturing goods (27% versus 10%), but overall levels of protection—including calculated AVEs of nontariff barriers and import tariffs—are also much higher. Agricultural goods are estimated to have a higher overall average AVE (44%), compared to manufacturing goods (19%).[136] The overall media nave estimate is also higher: 20% for agriculture and 6% for manufacturing. Similarly, in 2012, the WTO concluded from a literature review of the estimated trade effects of both tariff and non-tariff measures that non-tariff measures may restrict trade far more than tariffs, and that SPS/TBT measures have a negative effect on agricultural trade, especially export market diversification.[137] Another 2009 study looked at the extent to which certain nontariff barriers may result in higher retail prices for some foods, and concluded that nontariff barriers may substantially raise prices for fruits and vegetables, meat products, and also processed foods.[138] The study also concluded that nontariff measures are generally more restrictive in the European Union, United States, and some South East Asian countries, and less restrictive in some African, Eastern European, and Middle Eastern countries.

Finally, other available studies have attempted to estimate the economic impact to specific agricultural products from regulations in certain countries. For example, one study estimated the potential gain in Washington State apple exports to selected countries, including China—where it is believed that if SPS barriers were reduced then U.S. apple exports would be greater. The study concluded that apple exports to China could increase by more than 20% if the tariff equivalent of SPS measures imposed in China were to be reduced, which could translate into possible income gains for Washington State apple exporters.[139]

U.S. Strategy for Addressing SPS/TBT Concerns

Overview of U.S. Process

The United States maintains ongoing interagency processes and mechanisms to identify, review, analyze, and address foreign government standards-related measures that can act as barriers to U.S. exports. These activities are coordinated through the Trade Policy Staff Committee (TPSC), which is chaired by USTR and comprised of representatives from federal agencies with an interest in foreign standards-related measures.[140] Representatives meet formally a few times per year and also maintain ongoing informal consultation and coordination on SPS and TBT issues throughout the year. Representatives of the subcommittee include officials from USDA, the Department of Commerce, and the Department of State, and also officials from the Office of Management and Budget (OMB) and federal regulatory agencies, such as the HHS Department's Food and Drug Administration (FDA) and the Environmental Protection Agency (EPA). More broadly, USTR chairs an interagency group (i.e., both USDA and non-USDA agencies with SPS and TBT responsibilities) that meets regularly on WTO SPS issues. As part of this ongoing interagency process, the United States regularly reviews SPS and TBT measures involving globally traded goods that are notified to the WTO, as required under the SPS and TBT Agreements.

Ongoing Interagency Efforts

Regarding agricultural products, the U.S. process for identifying and dealing with SPS and TBT issues is coordinated, at least in the initial stages, by staff of USDA's Foreign Agricultural Service (FAS), the lead USDA trade agency. An FAS office is the designated WTO "enquiry" point for communicating with other countries on SPS measures, and shares information with and from industry groups and exporters, USTR, FAS's overseas posts, and various regulatory agencies such as USDA's Animal and Plant Health Inspection Service (APHIS) and Food Safety and Inspection Service (FSIS), EPA, and FDA. FAS staff maintain a database on foreign SPS and agriculture-related TBT measures with a potential impact on trade, even those which may comply with WTO or other international trade agreement provisions. FAS chairs regular meetings of USDA technical staff from various USDA agencies to discuss the status of emerging and ongoing SPS/TBT issues, including options for resolving a potential dispute.

As SPS and agriculture-related TBT concerns arise, technical staff and other government officials usually initiate at least informal dialogue with countries concerning the measure in question. They also communicate with affected industries in the private sector. Oftentimes an SPS or TBT issue is most likely to be resolved when USDA or other government experts discuss its scientific aspects with their foreign counterparts. These staff-level discussions often help the importing and exporting parties to clarify their differences, and to determine mutually acceptable conditions for importing the affected product that will not compromise the importing party's safeguards. However, not all problems can be solved in this manner. Eventually, bilateral consultations with the foreign country over an outstanding SPS or TBT issue might be pursued by USTR, with USDA's assistance. USTR also can decide at any point to elevate the issue via a complaint to the WTO or, if a Canadian or Mexican measure, the North American Free Trade Agreement (NAFTA), triggering formal dispute resolution procedures.[141] (Other FTAs generally defer dispute settlement to the WTO procedures.)

Regarding SPS measures, USTR reports that in 2012, the interagency group reviewed 908 SPS notifications by 50 WTO Members and provided comments to these trading partners on 119 proposed or in-force SPS measures.[142]

U.S. Reporting Systems

USTR is required to submit to the President, the Senate Finance Committee, and appropriate committees in the House of Representatives, an annual report on significant foreign trade barriers, the *National Trade Estimate Report on Foreign Trade Barriers* (or NTE report).[143] The NTE report covers significant barriers—including tariffs and various nontariff barriers, including those that are consistent and also inconsistent with international trading rules. The report categorizes, describes, and in some cases quantifies these barriers on a country-by-country basis.

As part of its NTE Report and its other two accompanying reports on SPS and TBT barriers to U.S. trade,[144] USTR reports that SPS and TBT trade barriers continue to threaten, constrain, or block U.S. agricultural exports. These reports address concerns within more than 60 major U.S. trading partners. Recent reports have identified significant SPS-related trade barriers facing U.S. agricultural exporters in several countries. USTR also identified significant standards-related trade barriers to U.S. exports in several countries. A summary of the reported SPS/TBT-related trade concerns is presented in **Appendix A**. Each of these reports is available at USTR's publications website.[145]

Among the types of reported measures that potentially cause concern for U.S. exporters are import policies targeting disease and pest transmission, chemical and pesticide residues, treatment and mitigation requirements, restrictive import and administrative procedures, import bans on products from specific producing areas and bans on certain production inputs, product and/or processing specifications, and perceived health risks. Aside from various standards-related TBT measures, USTR reports that the most significant SPS barriers impeding U.S. exports to multiple foreign markets are "restrictions related to export certifications, biotechnology, bovine spongiform encephalopathy (BSE), avian influenza (AI), and maximum residue limits (MRLs) for pesticides."

Responsibility of U.S. Government Agencies

The United States, like other countries, has in place an extensive, often intersecting, system to protect consumers from unsafe food and agricultural products and to protect its animal and plant resources from foreign pests and diseases. A variety of statutes and implementing regulations, directives, and administrative procedures underpin this system. These essentially constitute the nation's SPS measures. Major authorities are briefly described below.

At the same time, U.S. officials work cooperatively with other governments, frequently within international scientific bodies, to develop commonly recognized guidelines for SPS measures (and TBTs) that will promote balanced but safe trade in plants, animals, agricultural, and food products.

Trade Policy and Negotiations

The Office of the United States Trade Representative (USTR), an agency within the Executive Office of the President, is responsible for developing and coordinating U.S. international trade policy and overseeing negotiations with other countries, including with respect to foreign SPS and TBT measures. USTR meets with governments, business groups, legislators, public interest groups, and other interested parties to gather input on SPS and TBT issues and to discuss trade policy and negotiating positions. USTR coordinates U.S. trade policy through an interagency structure, and also serves as the lead U.S. agency in negotiating bilateral, regional, and multilateral trade agreements and lead U.S. counsel in all WTO disputes.

USTR consults with other government agencies on trade policy matters through the Trade Policy Review Group (TPRG) and the Trade Policy Staff Committee (TPSC), and coordinates processes regarding the specialized subgroups addressing SPS and TBT issues.

Food and Agricultural Products

Within the Department of Health and Human Services, the Food and Drug Administration (FDA) oversees the safety of most human and animal foods and drugs, primarily under the Federal Food, Drug, and Cosmetic Act (21 U.S.C. §301 *et seq.*). The primary exceptions are meat and poultry and their products, which are regulated by USDA's Food Safety and Inspection Service (FSIS) under the Federal Meat Inspection Act (21 U.S.C. §601 *et seq.*) and the Poultry Products Inspection Act (21 U.S.C. §451 *et seq.*).[146] USDA's Animal and Plant Health Inspection Service (APHIS) has lead responsibility for animal and plant health under the Animal Health Protection Act (7 U.S.C. §8301 *et seq.*) and the Federal Plant Protection Act (7 U.S.C. §7701 *et seq.*). Pesticides are regulated by the independent Environmental Protection Agency (EPA) under the Federal Insecticide, Fungicide, and Rodenticide Act (7 U.S.C. §136 *et seq.*).

Each of the responsible agencies has promulgated an extensive body of regulations to implement these laws, all of which apply to imports as well as domestic products. For example, plants, animals, and their products require an APHIS import permit. Whether a product can be imported and the conditions for entry are dependent upon an APHIS risk assessment of a product and where it originated, taking into account internationally recognized scientific guidelines—that is, for animal health, the Office of International Epizootics (OIE), and for plant health, the International Plant Protection Convention (IPPC). The risk assessment usually culminates with formal rules in the *Federal Register*. FSIS evaluates foreign meat and poultry programs to ensure their equivalency with U.S. requirements and reinspects samples at the border. FDA requires imports to comply with the same safety and labeling standards that apply to domestic foods.

Biotechnology

The basic federal guidance for regulating biotechnology products is the Coordinated Framework for Regulation of Biotechnology (51 *Fed. Reg.* 23302), published in 1986 by the White House Office of Science and Technology Policy (OSTP). A key principle is that genetically engineered products should continue to be regulated according to their characteristics and unique features, not their production method—that is, whether or not they were created through biotechnology. The framework relies on existing statutory authority (such as those noted above) and regulations to ensure the safety of biotechnology research and products, including food and agricultural products.[147]

Homeland Security

After the 2001 terrorist attacks, Congress created the Department of Homeland Security, whose agents now play a major role in inspections of imports, including food and agricultural products. Most of APHIS's border inspection functions and personnel were moved into the new department. Congress also passed the Public Health Security and Bioterrorism Preparedness and Response Act of 2002 (the "Bioterrorism Act," P.L. 107-188), which requires all foreign as well as domestic food manufacturing and related companies to register with the FDA, and requires that the FDA receive prior notifications of all food imports into the United States.

Other Relevant Programs

In addition to these major authorities, numerous other laws provide the basis for U.S. SPS measures and TBTs. The Agricultural Marketing Agreement Act of 1937 (7 U.S.C. 601 *et seq.*) is an example of a TBT-related law. This law, among other things, provides the authority for requiring imported commodities to meet the same or similar grade, size, or other quality requirements as domestic products if they are regulated by a federal marketing order. Within the U.S. Department of Commerce, the National Oceanic and Atmospheric Administration enforces provisions of the Marine Mammal Protection Act and the Endangered Species Act that require certain fishing techniques to protect, respectively, dolphins and sea turtles.

CONSIDERATIONS FOR CONGRESS

U.S. government and WTO reports and press releases frequently cite the benefits of the SPS and TBT agreements and progress made, under these agreements, in resolving disputes and facilitating trade between countries. However, some, among them food safety and environmental advocacy organizations, and groups that have more broadly opposed efforts toward globalization and harmonization of world trading rules, have long expressed skepticism. They have argued that implementation of the agreements can result in "downward harmonization" rather than upgraded health and safety standards. This can happen when, for example, a WTO dispute settlement panel questions the scientific underpinnings of a U.S. safeguard, and/or the United States agrees to an effectively lower standard to bring negotiations with another country to a successful conclusion.

Others counter that the current trade agreements explicitly recognize the right of individual nations, as well as states and localities, to enact stronger protections than international guidelines if they believe they are appropriate. The United States is especially well-positioned against challenges, because its health and safety policies are scientifically defensible, U.S. officials have argued. Many believe that the SPS and TBT agreements provide the foundation for developing transparent, science-based trade guidelines, as well as an effective framework for resolving disputes in these areas. Others have argued that ongoing free trade agreements, such as the TPP and TTIP, should revisit aspects of these agreements more closely. The effectiveness and flexibility of the SPS and TBT rules also continues to be tested by rapidly emerging changes in food production technology, such as biotechnology and nanotechnology, which were not imminent concerns when the agreements were finalized in 1994.

Many Members of Congress are following closely a number of ongoing SPS-related trade disputes that, they believe, have negatively affected agricultural producers in their states and districts. The most recent farm bill (Agricultural Act of 2014, P.L. 113-79) reauthorized the Technical Assistance for Specialty Crops (TASC) to address SPS and technical barriers to U.S. exports,[148] and also established an agency position to coordinate SPS matters and address agricultural non-tariff trade barriers across agencies.

The U.S. Congress has held a number of hearings to discuss the ongoing FTA negotiations, and some of these have addressed regulatory matters including SPS and TBT. For example, at a House Ways and Means Trade Subcommittee hearing on TTIP in May 2013, Chairman Devin Nunes stated that any agreement must be "ambitious and comprehensive" and should "identify and eliminate unnecessary regulatory barriers, including sanitary and phytosanitary barriers to U.S. agriculture exports."[149] A July 2013 hearing on TTIP by the House Energy and Commerce Committee's Subcommittee on Commerce, Manufacturing, and Trade discussed in broader terms existing regulatory barriers and the need "greater openness, transparency and convergence in regulatory approaches and standards while reducing unnecessarily redundant requirements."[150]

Previous introduced legislation regarding SPS issues in agricultural trade has included H.R. 2707 (112th Congress) by Representative Devin Nunes. H.R. 2707 sought to establish trade negotiating objectives of the United States with respect to the application of SPS measures to agricultural products to facilitate trade in agriculture.

Some lawmakers also have expressed concern that as additional FTAs further lower agricultural tariffs, countries may turn more and more to SPS and TBT measures to protect their farmers from import competition. These Members have stated that SPS matters will be among the factors they will consider in voting for new FTAs. The President must submit all FTAs to Congress, which in turn must pass implementing legislation if the United States is to participate.

Meanwhile, international SPS and TBT rights and obligations could come into play if the U.S. Congress considers legislation placing new restrictions and requirements on food imports. As noted, such bills are being proposed in the wake of a number of highly publicized adulteration incidents related to food and agricultural imports. Any new measures are likely to be closely scrutinized by U.S. trading partners for their adherence to international trade rules.

APPENDIX A. USTR-REPORTED CONCERNS INVOLVING SPS/TBT MEASURES, 2013

U.S. Trading Partner	SPS/ TBT	Food Product Category	SPS/TBT Category	U.S. Concerns
Argentina	SPS	Live Cattle, Beef, and Beef Products	Food Safety	Prohibits U.S. live cattle, beef, and beef products due to concerns about bovine spongiform encephalopathy (BSE, or "mad cow" disease) following its detection in the U.S. in 2003.
	SPS	Pork	Animal Health	Requires import approval, and U.S. pork products must be shipped frozen or tested for trichinosis.
	SPS	Poultry	Animal Health	Prohibits U.S. fresh, frozen, chilled poultry due to concerns over Avian Influenza (AI) and Exotic Newcastle Disease.
	SPS	Apples, Pears	Plant Health	Restricts U.S. fruit exports due to concerns about the efficacy of post-harvest treatments associated with fire blight.
Australia	SPS	Beef, Beef Products	Food Safety	Prohibits imports of bovine products from countries with reports of one or more indigenous cases of BSE.
	SPS	Pork	Animal Health	Imports of U.S. pork limited to frozen, boneless pork due to concerns about porcine reproductive and respiratory syndrome (PRRS) and post-weaning multi-systemic wasting syndrome (PMWS).
	SPS	Poultry	Animal Health	Limits imports of U.S. fresh, frozen, and cooked turkey meat due to concerns about various risks.
	SPS	Apples	Plant Health	Prohibits U.S. apples due to concerns about fire blight, which can infect apples, pears, and other rosaceous plants.
	SPS	Stone Fruit	Plant Health	Prohibits U.S. stone fruit (peaches, nectarines, plums, and apricots) due to concerns about certain plant pests.
	SPS	Table Grapes	Plant Health	One Australian state, Western Australia, continues to prohibit imports of U.S. table grapes.
China	SPS	Various Products	Biotechnology	Requires biotech-derived products developed in a foreign country to first be approved for use in that country before Chinese authorities will consider approving the product for use in China.

(Continued)

U.S. Trading Partner	SPS/ TBT	Food Product Category	SPS/TBT Category	U.S. Concerns
	SPS SPS	Pork Live Cattle, Beef	Food Safety Food Safety	Bans pork imports containing any residue of ractopamine, a veterinary drug. Prohibits U.S. live cattle, beef, and beef products due to BSE-related concerns.
	SPS	Meat and Poultry	Food Safety	Imposes a zero tolerance limit for Salmonella, Listeria, and other pathogens in imported raw meat and poultry.
	SPS	Processed Meat Products	Food Safety	Imports of U.S. processed meat products (sausages and rendered chicken fat) have been detained without notifying U.S. authorities, citing application of U.S. equivalence agreement regarding (unprocessed) meat products.
	SPS	Animal Feed	Animal Health	Requires foreign regulatory agencies to maintain a list of facilities approved to export feed products, requiring plant-by-plant audits, and requiring manufacturers to provide proprietary information, including photos of facilities.
	SPS	Bovine Products	Animal Health	Prohibits U.S. protein-free tallow because of BSE concerns; also requires compliance with certain requirements.
	SPS	Poultry	Animal Health	Prohibits U.S. products from three states (AR, MN, VA) due to low pathogenic avian influenza (LPAI) concerns.
	SPS	Apples	Plant Health	Allows only two varieties of U.S.-origin apples from three states (ID, OR, WA) due to concerns about fire blight.
	SPS	Potatoes	Plant Health	Prohibits imports of U.S.-origin table stock potatoes based on concerns over various plant pests and diseases.
	SPS	Strawberries	Plant Health	A decision is pending regarding permanent market access to China for California strawberries.
	TBT	Food Additives	Formula Disclosure	Requires foreign food producers to disclose their proprietary food additive formulas on product labels.
Colombia	SPS	Poultry	Food Safety	Imposes a zero tolerance standard for Salmonella on imported raw poultry products.
	SPS	Live Cattle	Animal Health	Prohibits U.S. live cattle, beef, and beef products due to BSE-related concerns.

U.S. Trading Partner	SPS/ TBT	Food Product Category	SPS/TBT Category	U.S. Concerns
	SPS	Pork	Animal Health	U.S. pork products must be shipped frozen or tested for trichinosis.
Croatia	SPS	Food Products	Biotechnology	Prohibits import of all food products that contain even trace amounts of food products derived from biotechnology.
Dominican Rep.	SPS	Beef, Beef Products	Food Safety	Prohibits U.S. beef and beef products from cattle 30 months of age and over due to concerns about BSE.
Ecuador	SPS	Live Cattle, Beef	Food Safety	Prohibits U.S. live cattle, beef, and beef products due to BSE-related concerns.
Egypt	SPS	Animal Products	Food Safety	Imposes European Union (EU) regulations established by regarding Maximum Residue Limits (MRLs) for veterinary products, including growth-promoting hormones.
	SPS	Seed Potatoes	Plant Health	Prohibits most varieties of U.S. seed potatoes due to concerns about Ralstonia (brown rot); registered varieties must undergo mandatory field trials for three seasons and comply with other plant quarantine conditions.
	SPSSPS	Wheat	Plant Health	Imposes a zero tolerance policy for the presence of Ambrosia (ragweed) in wheat imports, although one or more varieties of Ambrosia are present in all major wheat exporting countries, including in Egypt.
		Cotton	Plant Health	Requires inspection by Egyptian authorities prior to shipment.
El Salvador	SPS	Rice	Plant Health	Enforces regulations for rough rice that requires an additional declaration that shipments are free of weeds.
Ethiopia	SPS	Various Products	Biotechnology	Implementing a biosafety law that may require documentation and testing of products derived from biotechnology.
European Union	SPS	Various Products	Biotechnology	Enforces policies restricting imports of products derived from agricultural biotechnology; requires prior approval for a specific use before a product may be imported or used. Several EU countries have biotech-free strategies. -
	SPS	Beef, Beef Products	Food Safety	Prohibits U.S. beef raised with growth promoting hormones.
	SPS	Beef and Poultry	Food Safety	Restricts use of “pathogen reduction treatments” (PRTs), designed to reduce the amount of microbes on the meat.

(Continued)

U.S. Trading Partner	SPS/ TBT	Food Product Category	SPS/TBT Category	U.S. Concerns
	SPS	Cherries	Food Safety	Requires imported cherries be free of Monilinia fructicola (brown rot); requires documentation of field controls.
	SPS	Pork	Food Safety	U.S. pork exporters must verify (and undergo lab testing) that the pork has not been produced using ractopamine.
	SPS	Seafood	Food Safety	Prohibits imports of all U.S.-origin molluscan shellfish other than scallops.
	SPS	Animal By-Products (tallow)	Animal Health	Prohibits U.S. tallow not intended for human consumption, including tallow-containing products, such as pet food and ingredients containing protein-free tallow, and tallow for livestock consumption and other technical uses.
	SPS	Milk	Animal Health	Limits the somatic cell count in milk (below U.S. levels) as part of its public health requirements for dairy imports.
	TBT	Wine	Labeling	Imposes detailed rules regarding designations of origin and geographical indication, traditional terms, and labeling.
	TBT	Honey	Biotech Labeling	Requires honey containing pollen derived from GE crops to be labeled as such according to EU regulations.
	TBT	Food Products	Food Quality	New food quality scheme requires verified certification procedures and labeling systems subject to official controls.
India	SPS	Dairy Products	Food Safety	Requires certification that U.S.-origin milk has been treated to ensure the destruction of paratuberculosis.
	SPS	Pork	Food Safety	Requires certification that imported pork does not contain any residues of pesticides, veterinary drugs, mycotoxins, or other chemicals above the internationally prescribed MRLs. Limits U.S. pork imports to meat derived from animals that were never fed ruminant derived protein, requires animal health attestations, plus extra inspections. Certificates valid for only six months; also separate permits are needed for each lot.
	SPS	Meat Products	Animal Health	Prohibits imports of U.S. poultry, swine, and related products (pet food) due to LPAI outbreaks in the United States.
	SPS	Wheat and Barley	Plant Health	Imposes zero-tolerance standards for certain plant quarantine pests, such as weed seeds and ergot.

U.S. Trading Partner	SPS/ TBT	Food Product Category	SPS/TBT Category	U.S. Concerns
India	TBT	Food Products	Biotech Labeling	Prohibits imports of food and agricultural products containing ingredients derived from biotech crops such as corn and soybeans (except soybean oil).
Indonesia	SPS	Beef and Pork	Food Safety	Does not recognize equivalence of U.S. inspection system; requires questionnaire with proprietary information.
	SPS	Animal Products	Food Safety	Allows imports only from facilities that the Indonesian authorities have individually audited and approved.
	TBT	Horticulture Prods.	Labeling	Regulations impose a range of requirements on imported horticultural products, including labeling requirements.
	TBT	Processed Food	Labeling	Requires imports be labeled exclusively in the Bahasa language; require labels on product containers before shipped.
	TBT	Food (Supplements, Drugs, Cosmetics)	Distribution License Requirements	Requirements for distributors of imported products (e.g., reference letters from the overseas production facility, certifications for health or halal status, certificate that the production process for the product was radiation free).
Israel	SPS	Live Cattle, Beef	Animal Health	Prohibits U.S. live cattle, beef, and beef products due to BSE related concerns.
	SPS	Apples and Pears	Plant Health	Imposes cold treatment requirements to mitigate the risks of two pests, the apple maggot and the plum curculio.
	SPS	Cherries	Plant Health	Prohibits U.S. sweet cherries, citing various plant pests and diseases of concern.
Jamaica	SPS	Pork	Animal Health	Prohibits imports of U.S. pork due to concerns about pseudorabies, a viral disease that can affect swine.
Japan	SPS	Live Cattle, Beef	Food Safety	Prohibits U.S. live cattle, beef, and beef products due to BSE related concerns.
	SPS	Food Additives	Food Safety	Regulates food additives, restricting imports of several U.S. food products, especially processed foods. -
	SPS	Gelatin	Food Safety	Restricts U.S.origin ruminant gelatin and collagen for human consumption, related to BSE concerns. -

(Continued)

U.S. Trading Partner	SPS/ TBT	Food Product Category	SPS/TBT Category	U.S. Concerns
	SPS	Fungicides	Food Safety	Requires separate risk assessments for both pre harvest and post-harvest application of a fungicide.
	SPS	Maximum Residue Limits (MRLs)	Food Safety	Requires industry-wide enhanced surveillance for a given product after a single MRL violation; also, Japan's review process to approve pesticides and fungicides and the lack of established MRLs continue to create trade disruptions.
	SPS	Poultry	Animal Health	Requires U.S. poultry meat and egg products be exported under a protocol aimed at preventing avian influenza (AI).
	SPS	Fresh and Chipping Potatoes	Plant Health	Limits U.S. fresh potato imports from certain states to produce potato chips, and limits shipments to a single chipping facility over a specific shipping period of just five months (February to June), due to phytosanitary concerns.
	SPS	Cherry Varieties	Plant Health	Restricts imports to fresh cherry varieties subject to either fumigation treatment or a systems approach of controls.
	TBT	Certified-Organic Products	Certification, Requirements	Organic labeling requirements impose a zero tolerance policy for pesticide/herbicide residues on organic products, among other requirements. Will not certify products made with alkali extracted humic acid or lignin sulfonate.
Kazakhstan	SPS	Food Products	Systemic Issues	Requires veterinary, phytosanitary, and sanitary-epidemiological control at the customs border under unified epidemiological and hygienic requirements and also a single form of documentation used to confirm product safety.
Kazakhstan	SPS	Various Products	Biotechnology	Considering a draft law to regulate the development and testing of biotechnology products, including labeling.
	SPS	Live Cattle	Food Safety	Bans imports of U.S. cattle due to bluetongue disease, following detection in a shipment of cattle in December 2012.
	SPS	Pork	Food Safety	Requires imported pork to be shipped frozen to mitigate the risk of trichinae.
Kenya	SPS	Various Products	Biotechnology	Under presidential decree, bans imports of food and feed imports derived from biotechnology.

U.S. Trading Partner	SPS/ TBT	Food Product Category	SPS/TBT Category	U.S. Concerns
Kuwait	SPS	Beef, Beef Products	Food Safety	Prohibits all live cattle and beef from Oklahoma due to BSE related concerns.
Kyrgyzstan	SPS	Pork	Food Safety	Prohibits U.S pork exports from several U.S. states due to concerns regarding the H1N1 virus (swine flu).
Macedonia	SPS	Pork	Food Safety	Stopped accepting USDA Food Safety Inspection Service (FSIS) meat inspection system as equivalent.
Malaysia	SPS	Food Products	Food Safety	Stopped issuing import permits for U.S. frozen and chilled pork; issued new requirements with a lengthy application.
	TBT	Meat and Poultry	Halal Standards	Requires all meat (except pork) be certified as halal (produced in accordance with Islamic practices).
Mexico	SPS	Live Cattle, Beef	Food Safety	Bans products from cattle >30 months, but allows imports of U.S. beef from animals <30 months of age.
	SPS	Fresh Potatoes	Plant Health	Prohibits U.S. potatoes shipped beyond a 26-km zone along the U.S.-Mexico border due to nematode concerns.
	SPS	Stone Fruit	Plant Health	U.S. peach, nectarine, and apricot growers are affected by Mexico's controls for oriental fruit moth and other pests.
Morocco	SPS	Live Cattle, Beef and Poultry Products	Food Safety and Animal Health	Restricts imports of U.S. live cattle, beef, and beef products due to concerns over BSE and growth hormones, and restricts imports of U.S. poultry and poultry products due to AI and Salmonella concerns.
New Zealand	SPS	Pork	Animal Health	Restricts imports of fresh U.S. pork in consumer-ready form due to concern about porcine reproductive and respiratory syndrome (PRRS).
Nicaragua	SPS	Poultry	Food Safety	Regulations require a zero tolerance standard for Salmonella on poultry meat.
Norway	SPS SPS	Various Products Beef, Beef Products	Biotechnology Food Safety	With limited exceptions, effectively bans the importation of agricultural biotechnology products. Applies EU regulations that ban imports of meat from animals treated with growth hormones.
Peru	SPS	Biotech products	Biotechnology	Enacted, in 2011, a 10-year moratorium on imports and production of genetically engineered products and animals.

(Continued)

U.S. Trading Partner	SPS/ TBT	Food Product Category	SPS/TBT Category	U.S. Concerns
	SPS	Pork	Food Safety	Requires U.S. pork be shipped to its market either frozen or tested due to concern over trichinae.
	SPS	Live Cattle	Animal Health	Prohibits U.S. live cattle due to BSE-related concerns.
Philippines	SPS	Vegetables	Plant Health	Requires lengthy Pest Risk Assessments (PRAs) for fresh fruits and vegetables.
Russia	SPS	Agricultural Products	Systemic Issues	Requires export certificates for products, including processed agricultural products (e.g., soybean proteins, corn gluten, and distiller's grains) and requests certifications stating the U.S. is free from various livestock diseases.
Russia	SPS	Veterinary Certificates	Systemic Issues	Requires veterinary certificates to include broad statements by U.S. officials that the products satisfy Russia's sanitary and veterinary requirements, including meeting certain chemical, microbiological, and radiological standards.
	SPS	Various Products	Biotechnology	Requires approval of GE foods and feed products, including re-registration of approved products, labeling of GE products; does not provide for an approved system to cultivate GE crops.
	SPS	Tolerances	Food Safety	Maintains a zero tolerance policy (Salmonella, Listeria, and coliforms) in food products, including raw meat/poultry.
	SPS	Veterinary Drugs	Food Safety	Maintains zero tolerances for residues of unapproved veterinary drugs, which are commonly used in United States.
	SPS	Beef, Beef Products	Food Safety	Requires BSE attestations for prepared meat effectively precluding imports of any U.S. cooked beef; prohibits imports of ground beef from cattle of any age.
	SPS	Dairy	Food Safety	Allows shipments only from exporters approved by Russia's veterinary and phytosanitary surveillance agency.
	SPS	Pork, Pork Products	Food Safety	Maintains near-zero tolerance levels for tetracycline-group antibiotics; requires U.S. pork be frozen or tested.
	SPS	Poultry	Food Safety	Prohibits importation/sale of chlorine-treated chicken, and places an upper limit on the amount of water content in chilled and frozen chicken; bans the importation/sale of certain frozen poultry for use in baby food and special diets.

U.S. Trading Partner	SPS/ TBT	Food Product Category	SPS/TBT Category	U.S. Concerns
	SPS	Grains and Oilseeds	Animal Health	Requires U.S. grain and oilseed products for use in animal feed be certified free of animal diseases.
	SPS	Pet Food, Feed	Animal Health	Prohibits use of most ruminant-origin ingredient in pet foods and animal feed due to BSE concerns.
	TBT	Various Products	Food labeling	Imposes labeling requirements, including information regarding nutritional components, allergens, and GE products.
Saudi Arabia	SPS	Beef, Beef Products	Food Safety	Prohibits U.S. live cattle, beef, and beef products due to BSE-related concerns.
Serbia	SPS	Various Products	Biotechnology	Prohibits imports of food products that contain trace amounts of agricultural biotechnology.
Singapore	SPS	Beef, Beef	Food Safety	Prohibits imports of U.S. beef products, except deboned beef from animals under 30 months, due to BSE concerns.
	SPS	Products Pork	Food Safety	Prohibits the use of all PRTs in the production of pork and pork products.
South Africa	SPS	Beef/Beef Products	Food Safety	Prohibits imports of beef cuts and products (except U.S. deboned beef), and other ruminant animals and products.
	SPS	Pork	Animal Health	Enforces various requirements including a 20-day freezing requirement to prevent the transmission of pseudorabies.
	SPS	Table Grapes	Plant Health	Limits imports of California grapes due to pest concerns (European grapevine moth and Light Brown Apple Moth).
South African Devel. Comm.	SPS	Various Products	Biotechnology	South African Development Community (covering 15 member states) bans the importation of agricultural biotechnology products (since 2005).
South Korea	SPS	Various Products	Biotechnology	Regulates trade in agricultural biotech products, including food and seeds for use as feed or for processing.
South Korea	SPS	Beef, Beef Products	Food Safety	Limits U.S. exports to beef and beef products from cattle less than 30 months of age.

(Continued)

U.S. Trading Partner	SPS/ TBT	Food Product Category	SPS/TBT Category	U.S. Concerns
	SPS	Max. Residue Limits	Food Safety	Enforces a national MRL list and a complex deferral approval process.
	SPS	Cherries	Plant Health	Requires U.S. cherries to undergo fumigation with methyl bromide before shipping to control quarantine pests.
	TBT	Certified Organic Foods	Requirements and Conformity Issues	Products claiming to be organic must be certified by Korea's Ministry for Food, Agriculture, Forestry and Fisherie (MIFAFF); imposes certification and accreditation requirements, including zero tolerance for some materials.
Sri Lanka	SPS	Various Products	Biotechnology	Prohibits sale of biotech seeds or products for human consumption unless approved by the Chief Food Authority.
	SPS	Beef, Beef Products	Food Safety	Prohibits U.S. bovine products, including beef, beef products, and beef genetics, due to BSE-related concerns.
Taiwan	SPS	Beef, Beef Products	Food Safety	Prohibits U.S. beef, and beef products due to BSE related concerns.
	SPS	Pork/Beef Products	Food Safety	Delayed implementation of its proposed MRLs for ractopamine for both swine and cattle-derived products.
	SPS	Max. Residue Limits	Food Safety	MRL process for pesticides has resulted in a substantial application backlog and exporter uncertainty.
	SPS	Animal and Pet Feed	Animal Health	Bans imports of all ruminant-origin and many non-ruminant-origin ingredients intended for use in animal feed and pet food, such as tallow (including protein-free tallow), lard, and porcine meal, due to BSE-related concerns.
	SPS	Apples	Plant Health	Imposes a strict "three strikes" penalty structure for codling moth (CM) detections.
	SPS	Potatoes	Plant Health	Limits U.S. fresh potatoes to those grown in selected states (AK, CA, ID, OR, WA).
Thailand	SPS	Animal-derived Products	Food Safety	Prohibits imports of most ruminant-origin products and many non-ruminant origin products for use in pet foods or for livestock feed due to BSE-related concerns.

U.S. Trading Partner	SPS/ TBT	Food Product Category	SPS/TBT Category	U.S. Concerns
	SPS	Beef, Beef Products	Food Safety	Prohibits U.S. live cattle, beef, and beef products due to BSE-related concerns.
	SPS	Pork	Food Safety	Limits imports from countries that allow use of ractopamine, and has not yet established an MRL for ractopamine.
	SPS	Various Products	Food Safety	Imposes food safety inspection fees in the form of import permit fees on all shipments of cooked meat.
Turkey	SPS	Various Products	Biotechnology	Biosafety Law negates approvals of biotech products (e.g., soy and corn products) allowed under previous rules.
	SPS	Meat	Food Safety	Restricts U.S. beef and beef products, plus cattle and sheep for feeding and slaughter.
	TBT	Food/Feed Products	Biotech Labeling	Mandated labeling of ingredients derived from biotechnology in all food and feed if exceeds a certain threshold level.
Ukraine	SPS	Various Products	Biotechnology	Maintains a framework regarding the creation, testing, and use of products of agricultural biotechnology.
	SPS	Pork	Food Safety	Requires U.S. pork to be shipped frozen or tested for trichinosis.
Uruguay	SPS	Live Cattle, Beef	Food Safety	Restricts U.S. live cattle, beef and beef products, due to BSE concerns.
	SPS	Poultry	Animal Health	Bans imports of many U.S. poultry products due to concerns about avian influenza (AI) and Newcastle's disease.
	SPS	Potatoes	Plant Health	Enforces an optional pre-sampling protocol for U.S. exporters of U.S. seed potatoes, due to powdery scab concerns.
Vietnam	SPS	Food Products	General	Imposes a comprehensive food safety law covering regulations for a wide variety of horticultural, seafood, and meat products, which applies to both foreign and domestic producers.
	SPS	Beef, Beef Products	Food Safety	Restricts U.S. beef and beef products, except for products from cattle less than 30 months old.
	SPS	Offal	Food Safety	Bans offal products from all countries.
	SPS	Animal Products	Food Safety	Requires extensive information on individual facilities where food is produced to be eligible to export to Vietnam.

(Continued)

U.S. Trading Partner	SPS/ TBT	Food Product Category	SPS/TBT Category	U.S. Concerns
	SPS	Plant Products	Food Safety	Regulations on imported goods regarding exporter registration requirements, sampling rates, and MRLs.
	TBT	Processed Foods	Food Safety	Requires manufacturers of prepackaged processed foods, food additives, and food packing materials register, certify, and obtain affirmation of a product's conformity to Vietnam's food safety laws and regulations.

Source: USTR, *2013 Report on Sanitary and Phytosanitary Measures* (http://www.ustr.gov/sites/ default/ files/2013%20SPS.pdf) and *2013 Report on Technical Barriers to Trade* (http://www.ustr.gov/sites/default/files/2013%20TBT.pdf).

Notes: Generally excludes non-agricultural products, and does not include cosmetics and body care products, as well as most alcoholic beverages (exclude distilled spirits but includes some wine products).

Appendix B. Key Principles and Provisions of the SPS Agreement[151]

Basic Rights and Obligations: (Articles 1 and 2, Annex A) Members have the right to take SPS measures "necessary for the protection of human, animal, or plant life or health," as long as they are not inconsistent with the language of the SPS Agreement, are "based on scientific principles," "not maintained without sufficient scientific evidence," "do not arbitrarily or unjustifiably discriminate ... ," and are "not applied in a manner which would constitute a disguised restriction on international trade" (excerpts from Article 2). Members could have SPS measures that result in a higher level of protection than relevant international standards, but only if based on scientific justification (Article 3.3) or a risk assessment (Articles 2.3 and 5).

Harmonization: (Article 3) To facilitate trade, countries are encouraged (but not required) to use relevant international standards and work toward harmonization—that is, the adoption of common SPS measures. To promote harmonization, the agreement cites, as sources of scientific expertise and globally recognized standards including Codex Alimentarius Commission for food safety; World Organization for Animal Health (OIE) for animal health and diseases; and International Plant Protection Convention (IPPC) for plant health.

Equivalence: (Article 4) Equivalence means that each importing country must accept the SPS measures of another country as equivalent to its own (even if they are not exactly the same), as long as the exporting country objectively demonstrates to the importing country that its measures achieve the same level of protection.

Risk Assessment: (Articles 2 and 5) SPS measures must be based on a risk assessment taking into account internationally recognized risk assessment techniques, scientific principles and sufficient scientific evidence, while also minimizing trade distortions. SPS measures must be no more trade restrictive than necessary to achieve a country's appropriate level of SPS protection, and "shall avoid arbitrary or unjustifiable distinctions in the levels" considered to be appropriate, if such distinctions result in "discrimination or a disguised restriction on international trade." Countries may adopt a provisional measure to avoid risk, but must seek information and conduct a risk assessment to justify permanent use of a measure that might restrict trade.

Notification and Transparency: (Article 7, Annex B) Requires countries to publish its regulations related to SPS controls and to notify its trading partners in advance about measures that could affect trade. Countries must also provide an "Enquiry Point" to respond to questions about, and provide comments on, new or existing SPS measures. Member governments must report trade measures to the relevant WTO body if the measures might have an effect on other members.

Within the WTO, the SPS Information Management System (SPS IMS, http://spsims.wto.org/) provides access to documents and records relevant under the SPS

Agreement, and allows users to track: information on SPS measures that member governments have notified to the WTO; specific trade concerns raised in the SPS Committee; SPS-related documents circulated at the WTO; member governments' SPS Enquiry Points and Notification Authorities; and the membership of the WTO, Codex, IPPC, and the OIE.

Regionalization: (Article 6) Provides for adaptation to regional conditions, including pest or disease free areas and areas of low pest or disease prevalence. Previously, a country tended to ban an entire country's exports (of a product) from entry, if that product was associated with an unwanted pest or disease in the exporting country.

Dispute Settlement: (Article 11) Provides for formal consultations and the settlement of disputes involving scientific or technical issues, as well as adjudication by a WTO dispute settlement panel, if required. When a dispute arises, a panel seeks advice from experts, an advisory technical experts group, or relevant international organizations, at the request of either party to the dispute or on its own initiative. Decisions by a WTO panel may be appealed to the WTO Appellate Body.

Implementation and Oversight: (Articles 12 and 13, Annex C) Establishes a Committee on Sanitary and Phytosanitary Measures to provide a regular forum for consultations and information exchange, to periodically review implementation of the agreement and governments' compliance with it, to monitor progress in global harmonization of standards, and to work closely with the appropriate technical organizations on SPS matters. The SPS committee meets 3-4 times per year to discuss trade disputes related to SPS measures on an ongoing basis.

APPENDIX C. KEY PRINCIPLES AND PROVISIONS OF THE TBT AGREEMENT[152]

Non-discrimination and Avoiding Unnecessary Obstacles to Trade: (Articles 2, 5.1, and 5.2) Products imported from a Member country shall "be accorded treatment no less favorable than that accorded to like products of national origin and to like products originating in any other country." (Article 2.1) Members must ensure that "conformity assessment procedures are prepared, adopted and applied so as to grant access for suppliers of like products originating in the territories of other Members under conditions no less favorable than those accorded to suppliers of like products of national origin or originating in any other country, in a comparable situation" (Article 5.1.1). Related fees must be equitable (Article 5.2.5) and also respect the confidentiality of information about the results of conformity assessment procedures for imported products in the same way they do for domestic products (Article 5.2.4). Member countries must ensure that the technical regulation is not more trade-restrictive than necessary to fulfill the Member's legitimate objective. (Article 2.2) The obligation to avoid unnecessary obstacles to trade applies also to conformity assessment procedures, which must not be stricter than necessary to provide adequate confidence that products conform to the applicable requirements. (Article 5.1.2)

Alignment and Equivalency: (Articles 2.4, 2.6, and 2.7; also 5.4 and 5.5) Members should use relevant international standards, or the relevant parts of them, as a basis for their technical regulations, as well as relevant international recommendations and guides, or relevant portions of them, as the basis for their conformity assessment procedures (unless they would be ineffective or inappropriate to fulfill the Member's "legitimate objectives") (Articles 2.4 and 5.4). Members should also participate "within the limits of their resources" in the preparation by international standardization bodies, of international standards for products for which they either have adopted, or expect to adopt, technical regulation, and in the elaboration of international guides and recommendations for conformity assessment procedures (Articles 2.6 and 5.5). Members are encouraged to accept technical regulations that other Members adopt as "equivalent" to their own if these regulations adequately fulfill the objectives of their own regulations. (Article 2.7)

Performance-based Requirements: (Article 2.8) Whenever appropriate, product requirements should be set in terms of performance rather than design or descriptive characteristics.

Conformity Assessments: (Articles 9.1, 6.1 and 6.3) Members shall, whenever practicable, formulate and adopt international systems for conformity assessment (Article 9.1). Members must recognize "whenever possible" the results of conformity assessment procedures (e.g., test results or certifications), provided the Member is satisfied that those procedures offer an assurance of conformity that is equivalent as its own, which may require consultation (Article 6.1). Members are encouraged to enter into "mutual recognition agreements" or MRA providing for the mutual recognition of each other's conformity assessment results (Article 6.3).

Transparency: (Articles 2.9 and 2.11; 5.6 and 5.8, 10.1, Annex 3) Members must notify other Members through the WTO Secretariat when it proposes to adopt a technical regulation or conformity assessment procedure and to include in the notification a brief indication of the purpose of the proposed measure (regarding international standard, guide, or recommendation that does not exist or the technical content of a proposed technical regulation or conformity assessment procedure that is not in accordance with the technical content of relevant international standards, guides, or recommendations). Certain requirements apply regarding "reasonable time," codes of practice, and addressing all reasonable questions, among other things.

Technical Assistance: (Article 11) Members should provide technical assistance to other Members with respect to such matters as preparing technical regulations, establishing national standardizing bodies, participating in international standardization bodies, and establishing bodies to assess conformity with technical regulations.

Enforcement and Dispute Settlement: (Article 13 and 14) Establishes the Committee on TBT as the major forum for WTO Members to consult on matters relating to the operation of the Agreement, including specific trade concerns about measures that Members have proposed or adopted (Article 13) and provides for dispute resolution under the WTO and in accordance with the WTO's Dispute Settlement Understanding (Article 14).

End Notes

[1] WTO Agreement on Sanitary and Phytosanitary Measures, Article 2, Basic Rights and Obligations.

[2] With regard to SPS measures, GATT Article XX allows governments to adopt measures necessary to protect human, animal or plant life or health, provided that they do not arbitrarily or unjustifiably discriminate or use this as disguised protectionism.

[3] WTO is responsible for administering multilateral agreements. As of 2013, 159 countries were WTO members. The Uruguay Round of the GATT was intended to establish transparent and fair trade rules and to eliminate policies that distort and reduce trade among countries. Examples of such policies may be domestic and export subsidies, import tariffs, import quotas, restrictions on foreign investment, and arbitrary and unscientific regulations, among others. It also established procedures for global trade cooperation, such as periodically reviewing individual countries' trade commitments, policies and performance, and for the resolution of trade disputes.

[4] Information is at WTO's website: http://www.wto.org/english/tratop_e/sps_e/sps_e.htm.

[5] Information is at WTO's website: http://www.wto.org/english/tratop_e/tbt_e/tbt_e.htm.

[6] Non-tariff measures are often referred to by their abbreviation, NTMs, and also non-tariff barriers, NTBs. See WTO, Glossary, http://www.wto.org/english/thewto_e/glossary_e/glossary_e.htm.

[7] WTO, *World Trade Report 2012*, http://www.wto.org/english/res_e/booksp_e/anrep_e/world_ trade_report12_ e.pdf.

[8] Within these categories of non-tariff measures are: *quantitative restrictions* (import quotas; export limitations; licensing; voluntary export constraints; exchange and other financial controls; prohibitions; domestic content and mixing requirements; discriminatory bilateral agreements; and countertrade); *non-tariff charges and related policies affecting imports* (variable levies; advance deposit requirement; antidumping duties; countervailing duties; and border tax adjustments); *government participation in trade, restrictive practices, and more general government policies* (subsidies and other aids; government procurement policies; state trading, government monopolies, and exclusive franchises; government industrial policy and regional development; government procurement policies; investment restrictions or requirements; national systems of taxation and social insurance; macroeconomic policies; competition policies; foreign investment policies; foreign corruption policies; immigration policies; and various anti-competitive practices); and *customs procedures and administrative practices* (customs valuation procedures; customs classification procedures; and customs clearance procedures). See compilation reported in J. W. Mattson, W. Koo, and R. D. Taylor, "Non-Tariff Trade Barriers in Agriculture." Report No. 531, North Dakota State University, March 2004.

[9] For more information, see the WTO's website, http://www.wto.org/english/tratop_e/sps_e/sps_e.htm.

[10] USTR, *Report on Sanitary and Phytosanitary Measures*; and D. Roberts, and D. Roberts, and K. DeRemer, *Overview of Foreign Technical Barriers to U.S. Agricultural Exports*, ERS Staff Paper. No. 9705, March 1997.

[11] Preamble of the SPS agreement: http://www.wto.org/english/tratop_e/sps_e/spsagr_e.htm

[12] USTR, *Report on Sanitary and Phytosanitary Measures,* http://www.ustr.gov/sites/default/files/2013%20SPS.pdf.

[13] The agreement establishes a Committee on Sanitary and Phytosanitary Measures ("SPS Committee") to provide a forum for information exchange, to periodically review implementation of the agreement and governments' compliance with it, to monitor progress in global harmonization of standards, and to work closely with the appropriate technical organizations on SPS matters.

[14] WTO, Committee on Sanitary and Phytosanitary Measures, *Review of the Operation and Implementation of the Agreement on the Application of Sanitary and Phytosanitary Measures*, March 1999, June 2005, and May 2010.

[15] G/SPS/36, June 2005, p. 2.

[16] USTR, *Report on Technical Barriers to Trade*; and D. Roberts, and D. Roberts, and K. DeRemer, *Overview of Foreign Technical Barriers to U.S. Agricultural Exports*, ERS Staff Paper. No. 9705, March 1997.

[17] Preamble of the TBT agreement: https://www.wto.org/english/docs_e/legal_e/17-tbt_e.htm.

[18] WTO, "SPS and TBT Measures," http://www.wto.org/english/tratop_e/sps_e/sps_agreement_cbt_e/ c1s4p1_ e.htm.

[19] For example, activities such as certification, testing and inspection that may be required by to ensure a company's products and production processes meet minimum health and safety standards. See Annex 1 of the TBT

Agreement for more detailed definitions regarding technical regulations, standards, and conformity assessments. These definitions apply only with respect to products and related processes and production methods, not to services.

[20] See, for example, USTR, *National Trade Estimate Report on Foreign Trade Barriers*, http://www.ustr.gov/; Organization for Economic Co-operation and Development (OECD), "Looking Beyond Tariffs: The Role of Non-Tariff Barriers in World Trade," 2005; and A. V. Deardorff and R. M. Stern, "Measurement of Non-Tariff Barriers," OECD Working Papers, as reported in J. W. Mattson, W. Koo, R. D. Taylor, "Non-Tariff Trade Barriers in Agriculture," Report No. 531, North Dakota State University, March 2004.

[21] USTR, *Report on Technical Barriers to Trade*; and D. Roberts, and D. Roberts, and K. DeRemer, *Overview of Foreign Technical Barriers to U.S. Agricultural Exports*, ERS Staff Paper. No. 9705, March 1997.

[22] The TBT Committee annually reviews implementation and operation of the agreement, including periodic review of provisions relating to transparency and recommendations regarding the rights and obligations under the agreement.

[23] P.L. 103-182. Examples of the reported types of non-tariff barriers to U.S. agricultural products are provided in M. E. Bredahl and E. Holleran, "Technical Regulations and Food Safety in NAFTA," *Proceedings of the 3rd Agricultural and Policy Information Workshop*, 1997. Also see CRS Report R42965, *NAFTA at 20: Overview and Trade Effects*.

[24] USDA, "NAFTA Agricultural Fact Sheet: Sanitary/Phytosanitary," November 18, 2005.

[25] The U.S.-Jordan FTA and U.S.-Singapore FTA do not contain separate SPS sections; however, the FTA with Jordan provides for a separate Joint Statement on WTO Issues encouraging consultations on SPS equivalence, and the preamble in the FTA with Singapore calls for a commitment to reduce technical and SPS barriers to trade.

[26] See, for example, USDA, Animal and Plant Health Inspection Service (APHIS), "Special focus: SPS Issues and Free Trade Agreements," July 2004.

[27] See, for example, report by the Australian Department of Foreign Affairs and Trade, "Australia – United States Free Trade Agreement," Guide to the Agreement, 1st Ed., March 2004, p. 23.

[28] See CRS Report R42694, *The Trans-Pacific Partnership (TPP) Negotiations and Issues for Congress*.

[29] American Meat Institute (AMI), "Trans-Pacific Partnership Negotiations, Dallas Round, Negotiations Regarding Disciplines on Sanitary and Phytosanitary (SPS) Measures," May 2012. Also see "US meat groups back tougher SPS rules in Pacific trade," *Food Chemical News*, May 21, 2012.

[30] Ibid. See also "TPP's Biggest Benefit for Agriculture is Binding SPS Rules, Stallman Says," *Inside U.S. Trade*, November 16, 2012.

[31] Letter to USTR Ron Kirk from Members of the House Agriculture Committee and the House Ways and Means Committees, August 3, 2012.

[32] The white paper is also signed by the American Farm Bureau Federation, American Potato Trade Alliance, American Soybean Association, Corn Refiners Association, Grocery Manufacturers Association, National Corn Growers Association, National Milk Producers Federation, National Oilseed Processors Association, National Pork Producers Council, National Potato Council, Pet Food Institute, USA Poultry & Egg Export Council, USA Rice Federation, US-ASEAN Business Council, U.S. Dairy Export Council, U.S. Grains Council and U.S. Wheat Associates.

[33] "Agriculture, Food Industry Seek WTO-Plus Rules for TPP SPS Chapter," *World Trade Online*, May 16, 2012.

[34] "New U.S. SPS Text Contains "Rapid-Response" Tool for Perishable Goods," *World Trade Online*, May 21, 2013; and J. Murphy, "GMA Explores Rapid Resolution for Food Disputes in TPP," *Food Chemical News*, February 8, 2013.

[35] "TPP Produces Consolidated SPS Text of U.S., Six Other Proposals," *World Trade Online*, September 11, 2011.

[36] Letters from several U.S. agriculture and food groups to Chairman Devin Nunes, Subcommittee on Trade, Committee on Ways and Means (April 15, 2013) and to Michael Froman, Deputy National Security Advisor for International Economic Affairs (April 15, 2013).

[37] "New U.S. SPS Text Includes Consultative Mechanism, RRM Provisions," *Inside U.S. Trade*, May 24, 2013; "Food, Agriculture Groups Blast U.S. Approach to SPS Disputes in TPP," *Inside U.S. Trade*, May 10, 2013.

[38] "U.S. Shows Flexibility On TPP SPS, Now Open To Dispute Settlement," *Inside U.S. Trade*, March 6, 2014.

[39] More information is in CRS Report R43387, *Transatlantic Trade and Investment Partnership (TTIP) Negotiations*.

[40] See, for example, U.S. Senators Worried U.S.-EU Talks Might Not Address Agriculture," *Reuters*, January 24, 2013; letter from several U.S. agriculture and food groups to USTR Ron Kirk, March 4, 2013.

[41] "Baucus, Finance Members Set High Bar for SPS Issues in U.S.-EU Talks," *World Trade Online*, November 6, 2013.

[42] "U.S. Says 'Successful' TTIP Deal Will Eliminate EU Barriers to Meat Exports," *Inside U.S. Trade*, March 11, 2014. Ractopamine is a feed additive that results in more lean meat production in animal raised for meat.

[43] See, for example, letter to USDA Secretary Thomas Vilsack and Acting USTR Demetrios Marantis from 26 farm-state U.S. Senators, May 7, 2013. The letter cites trade barriers to U.S. biotechnology derived crops attributable to regulatory asynchrony, zero tolerance policies, and re-registration requirements. Also see press release by the American Farm Bureau Federation, "U.S.-EU Transatlantic Trade and Investment Partnership Agreement," September 2013.

[44] See, for example, "APHIS Eases Import Restrictions on EU Poultry Products," *Food Chemical News*, April 5, 2013; "APHIS Releases Final BSE Rule, Meeting Longstanding EU Demand To Reopen U.S. Beef Market," *World Trade Online*, November 1, 2013; "EU Lifts Ban on Some U.S. Meat Products in Move Toward Free-Trade Discussions," *Global Insight*, February 2013; and "USDA, "Two Breakthroughs in U.S. Exports to Europe," *GAIN Report* E80004, February 5, 2013.

[45] J. Hatten, "Lawmakers Fear Doubling of Regulations form U.S.-EU Trade Deal," *The Hill*, July 24, 2013. [46] "USTR attacks Europe's bid to "internationalize" its own standards," *Food Chemical News*, April 08 2010.

[47] Institute for Agriculture and Trade Policy (IATP), "Trade Deal to Undermine Health, Environmental Standards," June 26, 2013; and IATP, "Praises and Peril of the TTIP," October 2013. See also: "House Panel Members Offer Conflicting Views of TTIP Regulatory Goals," *Inside U.S. Trade*, July 25, 2013.

[48] Letter to Speaker John Boehner, U.S. House of Representatives, from Demetrios Marantis, Acting USTR, March 20, 2013.

[49] USTR, Remarks by USTR Michael Froman to the German Marshall Fund, September 30, 2013. Also see "Froman Calls on EU Regulators to be More like their U.S. Counterparts," *World Trade Online*, September 30, 2013.

[50] HLWG, "Final Report of the U.S.-EU High Level Working Group on Jobs and Growth," February 11, 2013. These recommendations were submitted to the Presidents of the United States, European Council, and European Commission.

[51] J. Grueff, *Achieving a Successful Outcome for Agriculture in the EU–U.S. Transatlantic Trade and Investment Partnership Agreement*, International Food & Agricultural Trade Policy Council (IFATPC) Discussion Paper, February 2013; and comments and presentation by Ellen Terpstra, IFATPC, February 27, 2013.

[52] Letter to USTR Ron Kirk from several U.S. agriculture and food groups, March 4, 2013.

[53] See U.S. Chamber of Commerce's website, http://www.uschamber.com/issues/regulatory/precautionary-principle.

[54] Letter to USTR Michael Froman from Members of the House Agriculture Committee and House Ways and Means Committee, August 7, 2013. See also: "Ways & Means, Ag Committee Members Demand SPS Enforceability," *Inside U.S. Trade*, September 5, 2013.

[55] USTR, "U.S. Objectives, U.S. Benefits in the Transatlantic Trade and Investment Partnership: A Detailed View," June 2013.

[56] European Commission, "Sanitary and Phytosanitary Issues: Initial EU Position Paper," December 2013.

[57] Testimony by James Grueff of Decision Leaders before the House of Representatives, Committee on Ways and Means, Subcommittee on Trade, May 16, 2013.

[58] "EU Will Not Change 'Precautionary Principle' Through Trade Talks: Official," *Inside U.S. Trade*, May 20, 2013.

[59] G. Marchant et al., "Impact of the Precautionary Principle on Feeding Current and Future Generations," CAST Issue Paper 52-QC June 2013. See also policy statements at the Business Coalition for Transatlantic Trade website.

[60] "European Parliament Back U.S.-EU trade deal talks but Draws "Red Lines," *Food Chemical News*, June 14, 2013; and "EU Will Not Change 'Precautionary Principle' Through Trade Talks: Official," *Inside U.S. Trade*, May 20, 2013.

[61] Letters from several U.S. agriculture and food groups to Michael Froman, Deputy National Security Advisor for International Economic Affairs, May 20, 2013. See also U.S. Food, Ag Groups Want 'Precautionary Principle' On Table in EU Talks," *World Trade Online*, May 22, 2013.

[62] WTO, "The WTO and the FAO/WHO Codex Alimentarius," http://www.wto.org.

[63] See Codex's website (http://www.codexalimentarius.org/). As of year-end 2013, Codex had 186 members.

[64] OIE is based in Paris and still known by its former French abbreviation, OIE (Office International des Épizooties), even though it has been renamed the World Organization for Animal Health. OIE is not part of the United Nations, but is a separate intergovernmental organization that was founded in 1924 under an international agreement. For more information, see OIE's website: http://www.oie.int/index.php. As of September 2013, OIE had 178 members.

[65] See IPPC's website (http://www.ippc.int/). As of September 2013, IPPC had 179 signatories.

[66] See text of the SPS Agreement in the preamble, Articles 3 and 12, and Annex A. Also see WTO, Committee on Sanitary and Phytosanitary Measures, "Relationship with Codex, IPPC and OIE," SPS/GEN/775, May 15, 2007.

[67] United Nations General Assembly, "Guidelines for Consumer Protection," April 16, 1985 A/RES/39/248, http://www.un.org/documents/ga/res/39/a39r248.htm.

[68] The United States is also a member of the North American Plant Protection Organization (NAPPO).

[69] See FAO, http://www.fao.org/about/en/.

[70] See Codex's website (http://www.codexalimentarius.org/about-codex/en/).

[71] Codex currently has 185 members including 184 member countries and EU (considered a member organization). For a country listing, see http://www.codexalimentarius.org/members-observers/en/.

[72] For a current listing, see the Codex Veterinary Drug Residues in Food Online Database (http://www.codexalimentarius.net/vetdrugs/data/index.html).

[73] Joint FAO/WHO Food Standards Programme, *Understanding the Codex Alimentarius*, 3rd Edition, 2006, p. ix. Also see the Commission's website (http://www.codexalimentarius.org/about-codex/en/).

[74] WTO, "The WTO and the FAO/WHO Codex, Alimentarius," http://www.wto.org/.

[75] Listing covers food additives, pesticide and veterinary drug Maximum Residue Levels (MRLs), and other international standards or guidelines (http://www.codexalimentarius.org/standards/en/).

[76] OEI is based in Paris and still known by its former French abbreviation, OIE (Office International des Épizooties), even though it has been renamed the World Organization for Animal Health.

[77] In the 1950s, there was discussion about whether OIE should be dissolved, given that similar work was being done at FAO and WHO. This ultimately did not happen. For more information, see http://www.oie.int/about-us/history/.

[78] See 1998 agreement between WTO and OIE: http://www.wto.org/english/thewto_e/coher_e/wto_oie_e.htm. \[79] OIE, "Presentation of the World Organisation for Animal Health (OIE)," March 2010.

[80] The 4th Strategic Plan 2006/2010 extended the OIE's global mandate to: "The improvement of animal health all around the world." See http://ec.europa.eu/food/animal/diseases/strategy/docs/OIE-pres_en.pdf.

[81] WTO, "The WTO and the World Organization for Animal Health (OIE)."

[82] IPPC's website (http://www.ippc.int/). As of September 2013, IPPC had 178 members.

[83] WTO, "The WTO and the International Plant Protection Convention (IPPC)."

[84] See WTO, "Glossary Term: Precautionary Principle" and WTO, "Understanding the WTO Agreement on Sanitary and Phytosanitary Measures." These are addressed in Article 5.7, Article 3.3, and the preamble of the SPS agreement.

[85] Commission of European Communities, "Communication from the Commission on the precautionary principle," COM(2000) 1, Brussels, February 2, 2000.

[86] Regulation (EC) No 178/2002 of the European Union Parliament and of the Council of 28 January 2002 laying down the general principles and requirements of food law, establishing the European Food Safety Authority and laying down procedures in matters of food safety. Other information is at http://eur-lex.europa.eu.

[87] "Summaries of EU legislation," http://europa.eu/legislation_summaries/consumers/ consumer_safety/ l32042_en.htm.

[88] See, for example, letter from many U.S. agriculture trade associations to Michael Froman, then Deputy National Security Advisor for International Economic Affairs at The White House, May 20, 2013; and statement from U.S. Chamber of Commerce. See also: Council for Agricultural Science and Technology (CAST), "Impact of the Precautionary Principle on Feeding Current and Future Generations" CAST Issue paper number 52, June 2013.

[89] Friends of the Earth International, *Trade and People's Food Sovereignty*, position paper, April 2003. The document also charged that "the Codex is so heavily influenced by food and chemical corporations that the standards it sets may be lower than those already in place in many nations."

[90] G. Marchant et al., "Impact of the Precautionary Principle on Feeding Current and Future Generations," CAST Issue Paper 52-QC June 2013.

[91] Ibid.

[92] See, for example, letters from several U.S. agriculture and food groups to Michael Froman, Deputy National Security Advisor for International Economic Affairs, May 20, 2013.

[93] See U.S. Chamber of Commerce's website, http://www.uschamber.com/issues/regulatory/precautionary-principle.

[94] Ibid.

[95] United Nations University, "Trading Precaution: The Precautionary Principle and the WTO," November 2005.

[96] Zoonotic refers to a disease that may be naturally transmitted from animals to humans under natural conditions (e.g., rabies). Zoonoses may be bacterial, viral, or parasitic, or may involve unconventional agents.

[97] WTO, Committee on Sanitary and Phytosanitary Measures, "Specific Trade Concerns," Overview and Summary Graphs and Tables," G/SPS/GEN/204/Rev.11 (13-1021), February 26, 2013.

[98] WTO members are required to notify the WTO of their SPS/TBT measure whenever there is no international standard or the SPS measure substantially differs from the international standard and the measure may have a significant effect on trade among WTO members (SPS Agreement, Annex B; TBT Agreement, Article 2).

[99] Freese, R., "Monitoring Foreign SPS Measures To Expand U.S. Agricultural Exports," May 2010.

[100] WTO, "Dispute DS26." See also CRS Report R40449, *The U.S.-EU Beef Hormone Dispute*.

[101] WTO, "Dispute DS389." See also CRS Report R40199, *U.S.-EU Poultry Dispute on the Use of Pathogen Reduction Treatments (PRTs)*.

[102] WTO, "Dispute DS291," See also CRS Report RS21556, *Agricultural Biotechnology: The U.S.-EU Dispute*.

[103] SPS disputes DS3, DS5, and DS41. See CRS Report RL34528, *U.S.-South Korea Beef Dispute: Issues and Status*.

[104] See, for example, SPS disputes DS76 and DS245. For a full listing, see WTO, "[SPS] Disputes by Agreement," http://www.wto.org/english/tratop_e/dispu_e/dispu_agreements_index_e.htm?id=A19.

[105] WTO, "Dispute DS430."

[106] As of May 2013, there were currently 159 countries that are members of the WTO.

[107] For more information, see CRS Report RS22948, *U.S.-Russia Meat and Poultry Trade Issues*.

[108] WTO, "Dispute DS384." See also CRS Report RS22955, *Country-of-Origin Labeling for Foods and the WTO Trade Dispute on Meat Labeling*.

[109] WTO, "Dispute DS381."

[110] WTO, "Dispute DS392."

[111] For a full listing, see WTO, "[TBT] Disputes by Agreement," http://www.wto.org/english/tratop_e/dispu_e/dispu_agreements_index_e.htm?id=A22.

[112] CRS communication with staff from the EU Delegation and EC Directorate-General for Trade, December 20, 2013.

[113] USTR, *Report on Sanitary and Phytosanitary Measures* and *Report on Technical Barriers to Trade* (various years).

[114] Freese, R., "Monitoring Foreign SPS Measures To Expand U.S. Agricultural Exports," USDA, May 2010.

[115] Of all cases involving the United States, ten cases cite both the SPS Agreement and the TBT Agreement.

[116] For more information, WTO, "Understanding on rules and procedures governing the settlement of disputes"

[117] See also CRS Report RS20088, *Dispute Settlement in the World Trade Organization (WTO): An Overview*.

[118] WTO, "Standards and Safety," http://www.wto.org/english/thewto_e/whatis_e/tif_e/agrm4_e.htm#TRS.

[119] WTO, *World Trade Report 2012*, http://www.wto.org/english/res_e/booksp_e/anrep_e/world_trade_report12_e.pdf.

[120] USDA, ERS, "Effects of Trade on the U.S. Economy." Based on export-generated employment, income, and purchasing power in both the farm and nonfarm sectors.

[121] See, for example, WTO press release, "Increased use of regulatory measures creates new challenges for the WTO, report says," July 16, 2012; and WTO, *World Trade Report 2012*, July 2012.

[122] D. Roberts, T.E. Josling, and D. Orden, "A Framework for Analyzing Technical Trade Barriers in Agricultural Markets," TB-1876, March 1999. Builds off earlier work: D. Roberts, and K. DeRemer, *Overview of Foreign Technical Barriers to U.S. Agricultural Exports*, ERS Staff Paper. No. 9705, March 1997. Technical trade barriers are defined as "measures that restrict imports of products that fail to meet a country's health, safety, or environmental standards," and include most types of SPS and TBT measures, among other trade-restricting measures.

[123] CRS communications with USDA's ERS and the American Farm Bureau Federation personnel, May-June 2011.

[124] See, for example, Scott Bradford, *The Extent and Impact of Food Non-Tariff Barriers in Rich Countries*, Brigham Young University research paper, January 2006.

[125] OECD, "Non-Tariff Measures in Agri- Food Trade: Improving Policy Coherence for Development," January 2013.

[126] See, for example, a review by Ferrantino, M., "Quantifying the Trade and Economic Effects of Non-Tariff Measures", OECD Trade Policy Papers, No. 28, OECD, 2006.

[127] USTR, *2010 Report on Sanitary and Phytosanitary Measures (SPS Report)*, April 1, 2010, page 5.

[128] USDA, "USDA Preserves $4 Billion in Agricultural Exports in 2012 by Knocking Down Barriers to Trade," February 1, 2013, http://www.aphis.usda.gov/newsroom/2013/02/pdf/trade_results.pdf.

[129] APHIS, *SPS Accomplishments Report, Fiscal 2007*. The SPS issues in the report are limited to those for which APHIS has lead responsibility—that is, animal and plant health but not food safety. Most of this reported value—$1.2 billion—was resolution of trade issues in order to retain existing sales (mostly produce/horticultural shipments to NAFTA partners Mexico and Canada), not to new or expanded markets. The report also notes that APHIS implemented a number of changes to its own import requirements that provided new or expanded market access for 10 countries and a total of 12 commodities. This reverse trade was valued at approximately $5 million in FY2007.

[130] K. Monahan, "U.S.-EU Trade Talks," *Bloomberg Government*, August 6, 2013. 2011 estimates.

[131] See, for example, two coalition letters from more than 50 agricultural trade associations to Chairman Devin Nunes, Subcommittee on Trade Committee on Ways and Means (April 15, 2013) and to Michael Froman, Deputy National Security Advisor for International Economic Affairs (April 15, 2013); also testimony before the U.S.-China Economic and Security Review Commission by Veronica Nigh, American Farm Bureau Federation, April 25, 2013.

[132] A. Disdier, et al.,"The Impact of Regulations on Agricultural Trade: Evidence from SPS and TBT Agreements," Working Paper 2007-04, February 2007. Based on a survey of 92 importing countries notifying measures under the SPS and TBT agreements (of 154 importing countries). Products in the study with no identified SPS or TBT barriers were wool grease, crude ; certain jojoba oils; and raw/whole beaver furskins and musk-rat furskins.

[133] A. Disdier, et al., *Trade Effects of SPS and TBT Measures on Tropical and Diversification Products*, ICTSD Programme on Agricultural Trade and Sustainable Development, May 2008.

[134] OECD, "Non-Tariff Measures in Agri- Food Trade: Improving Policy Coherence for Development," January 2013.

[135] *Ad valorem* equivalent (AVE) refers to import duties or other charges levied on a traded good, expressed as a percentage of the value of the imported item, and not based on the weight, size, or quantity of the item.

[136] H. L. Kee, A. Nicita and M. Olarreaga, "Estimating Trade Restrictiveness Indices," *The Economic Journal*, 19 (172-199), January 2009. Based on estimated AVEs of non-tariff barriers at the tariff line level for each of the 78 countries.

[137] See, for example, WTO press release, "Increased use of regulatory measures creates new challenges for the WTO, report says," July 16, 2012; and WTO, *World Trade Report 2012*, July 2012.

[138] J. M. Dean, et al., "Estimating the Price Effects of Non-Tariff Barriers," *The B.E. Journal of Economic Analysis & Policy*, 2009, vol. 9, issue 1.

[139] L. Nogueira and H. Chouinard, "The Effects of Reducing Sanitary and Phytosanitary (SPS) Barriers to Trade on the Washington State Apple industry," paper presented at the American Agricultural Economic Association meeting, 2006.

[140] For additional information, see USTR's *Report on Technical Barriers to Trade*. This process was established in part to address criticisms highlighted in GAO, *Agricultural Exports: U.S. Needs a More Integrated Approach to Address Sanitary/Phytosanitary Issues*, NSIAD-98-32, December 1997.

[141] Sections 301 et seq. of the Trade Act of 1974 delineate the domestic legal authority and procedures for U.S. officials in investigating and challenging unfair trade practices, and enforcing U.S. rights under international trade agreements. Interested parties, including agricultural groups, can—and do—petition USTR to initiate such procedures under Section 301 if they believe that a challenge is warranted and that the Administration is not addressing the issue. For more information, see House Committee on Ways and Means, *Overview and Compilation of U.S. Trade Statutes*.

[142] USTR's *Report on Sanitary and Phytosanitary Measures*, p. 14.

[143] The NTE report is required in accordance with Trade Act of 1974 (§181), as added by Trade and Tariff Act of 1984 (§303) and amended by the Omnibus Trade and Competitiveness Act of 1988 (§1304), the Uruguay Round Trade Agreements Act (§311), and the Internet Tax Freedom Act (§1202).

[144] USTR, *National Trade Estimate Report on Foreign Trade Barriers* (or NTE Report); also USTR's *Report on Sanitary and Phytosanitary Measures* and *Report on Technical Barriers to Trade*. The annual SPS and TBT reports were first initiated under the Obama Administration starting in 2010 (following a speech by then USTR Ron Kirk in July 2009; see http://www.ustr.gov/trade-topics/enforcement). Previously, SPS and TBT measures were generally described in each country's profile within the NTE Report.

[145] USTR, http://www.ustr.gov/about-us/press-office/reports-and-publications/.

[146] For more information, see CRS Report RS22600, *The Federal Food Safety System: A Primer.*

[147] See CRS Report RL32809, *Agricultural Biotechnology: Background, Regulation, and Policy Issues.*

[148] See CRS Report R42771, *Fruits, Vegetables, and Other Specialty Crops: Selected Federal Programs.*

[149] Opening Statement by Chairman Devin Nunes, House Ways and Means Trade Subcommittee, "Hearing on U.S.-EU Trade and Investment Partnership Negotiations," May 16, 2013.

[150] Opening Statement by Chairman Lee Terry, Subcommittee on Commerce, Manufacturing, and Trade, hearing on "The U.S. – E.U. Free Trade Agreement: Tipping Over the Regulatory Barriers," July 24, 2013.

[151] Compiled by CRS from various sources, including text of the SPS agreement can be accessed through WTO's website. Also see J.C. Buzby, ed., *International Trade and Food Safety*, AER Report 828, USDA, November 2003.

[152] Compiled by CRS from various sources, including USTR, *2013 Report on Technical Barriers to Trade*. Text of the TBT agreement can be accessed through WTO's website.

In: Agricultural Trade
Editor: Rowan Stroud

ISBN: 978-1-63321-888-8

Chapter 2

THE U.S.-EU BEEF HORMONE DISPUTE*

Renée Johnson

SUMMARY

The United States and the European Union (EU) have engaged in a long-standing and acrimonious trade dispute over the EU's decision to ban hormone-treated meat. Despite an ongoing series of dispute settlement proceedings and decisions by the World Trade Organization (WTO), there is continued disagreement between the United States and the EU on a range of legal and procedural issues, as well as the scientific evidence and consensus concerning the safety of hormone-treated beef. To date, the EU continues to ban imports of hormone-treated meat and restricts most meat exports to the European Union to a limited quantity of beef imports that are certified as produced without the use of hormones.

Starting in 1981, the EU adopted restrictions on livestock production limiting the use of natural hormones to therapeutic purposes, banning the use of synthetic hormones, and prohibiting imports of animals and meat from animals that have been administered the hormones. In 1989, the EU fully implemented its ban on imports of meat and meat products from animals treated with growth promotants. Initially the ban covered six growth promotants that are approved for use and administered in the United States. The EU amended its ban in 2003, permanently banning one hormone—estradiol-17β—while provisionally banning the use of the five other hormones.

The United States has suspended trade concessions with the European Union by imposing higher import tariffs on EU products. The first U.S. action in 1989 imposed retaliatory tariffs of 100% *ad valorem* duty on selected food products, and remained in effect until 1996. The second U.S. action in 1999 again imposed a 100% *ad valorem* duty on selected foods from EU countries.

Over the years, the United States and the EU have attempted to resolve this dispute through a series of WTO dispute consultations, settlement panels, arbitration proceedings, and formal appeals. One of the earlier WTO panel decisions in 1997 ruled against the EU on the grounds that the ban is inconsistent with the EU's WTO obligations under the Sanitary and Phytosanitary (SPS) Agreement because the EU had not conducted a risk assessment. In response, the EU commissioned studies and reviews to

---

* This is an edited, reformatted and augmented version of a Congressional Research Service publication R40449, prepared for Members and Committees of Congress dated April 22, 2014.

address the scientific basis of its ban on hormone-treated meat. Following each of these reviews, the EU reaffirmed its position that there are possible risks to human health associated with hormone-treated meat, given the available scientific data. The EU claims it has complied with its WTO obligations and has challenged the United States for maintaining its prohibitive import tariffs on EU products. The United States disputes whether the EU has conducted an adequate risk assessment to support its position and maintains there is a clear worldwide scientific consensus supporting the safety to consumers of eating hormone-treated meat. In October 2008, the WTO issued a mixed ruling allowing the United States to continue its trade sanctions, but allowing the EU to maintain its ban.

In January 2009, the U.S. Trade Representative (USTR) announced its intent to make changes to the list of EU products subject to increased tariffs under the dispute, including changes to the EU countries and products affected, and higher tariffs on some products. The EU claimed this action constituted an "escalation" of the dispute. In May 2009, following a series of negotiations, the United States and the EU signed a memorandum of understanding (MOU), which phases in certain changes over several years. Currently, the EU has granted market access to U.S. exports of beef raised without the use of growth promotants, and the United States has suspended higher duties for imported EU products listed under the dispute. USTR continues to monitor EU implementation of the MOU and other policies affecting market access for U.S. beef exports.

BACKGROUND

The United States and the European Union (EU) have engaged in a long-standing and acrimonious trade dispute over the EU's decision to ban hormone-treated meat, dating back to the early 1980s. Despite an ongoing series of dispute settlement proceedings and decisions by the World Trade Organization (WTO), there is continued disagreement between the United States and the EU on a range of legal and procedural issues, as well as the scientific evidence and consensus concerning the safety of hormone-treated beef. Many in the United States perceive the EU's ban as an example of how sanitary and phytosanitary (SPS) measures and non-tariff barriers are used as disguised protectionism, primarily intended to restrict imports from other countries.

In January 2009, the U.S. Trade Representative (USTR) for the outgoing Bush Administration announced changes to the list of EU products subject to increased tariffs under the dispute. These changes were scheduled to go into effect on March 23, 2009. The EU claimed this action constituted an "escalation" of the dispute and was "more punitive" than current trade sanctions. The EU decided to hold off further action until the Obama Administration reviewed the decision. The Administration delayed implementing the changes, pending further negotiations with the EU.

In May 2009, following a series of negotiations, the United States and the EU signed a memorandum of understanding (MOU), which phases in certain changes over several years. Currently, the EU has granted market access to U.S. exports of beef raised without the use of growth promotants, and the United States has suspended higher duties for imported EU products listed under the dispute. USTR continues to monitor EU implementation of the MOU and other policies affecting market access for U.S. beef.

Use of Hormones in Meat Production

Growth-promoting hormones are used widely in beef production in the United States and in other meat-exporting countries. In the United States, hormones have been approved for use since the 1950s and are now believed to be used on approximately two-thirds of all cattle and about 90% of the cattle on feedlots. In large U.S. commercial feedlots, their use approaches 100%. Cattle producers use hormones because they allow animals to grow larger and more quickly on less feed and fewer other inputs, thus reducing production costs, but also because they produce a leaner carcass more in line with consumer preferences for diets with reduced fat and cholesterol.[1]

Growth-promoting hormones include compounds that either naturally occur in an animal's body or mimic naturally occurring compounds. Estradiol, progesterone, and testosterone (three natural hormones), and zeranol and trenbolone acetate (two synthetic hormones), may be used as an implant on the animal's ear.[2] Melengestrol acetate, which can be used to improve weight gain and feed efficiency, is approved for use as a feed additive. Not all combinations of hormones are approved for use in all classes of cattle. The U.S. Food and Drug Administration (FDA) and the U.S. Department of Agriculture (USDA) cooperate in regulating growth promotants for livestock. Both of these agencies maintain that hormones in beef from an implanted animal have no physiological significance for humans. All animal drug products are approved for safety and effectiveness under the Federal Food, Drug, and Cosmetic Act (21 U.S.C. 301 et seq.).[3] About 30 animal growth-promoting products are marketed in the United States.

In addition to the United States, other countries that have approved the use of growth-promoting hormones in beef production are Canada, Australia, New Zealand, South Africa, Mexico, Chile, and Japan, among other countries. The use of hormones in beef production, however, is not allowed in the European Union, or in other European countries that assume many of the rights and obligations of the EU single market. To date, the EU continues to ban imports of hormone-treated meat and restricts most meat exports to the European Union to a limited quantity of beef imports that are certified as produced without the use of hormones.

The EU Beef Hormone BAN

The European Commission (EC) enacted its ban on both the production and importation of meat derived from animals treated with growth-promoting hormones in the early 1980s.[4] This ban restricts the use of natural hormones to therapeutic purposes, bans the use of synthetic hormones, and prohibits imports of animals and meat from animals that have been administered the hormones. The ban, however, did not go into effect until January 1, 1989. Initially the ban covered meat and meat products from animals treated with six growth promotants that are approved for use and administered in the United States, including estradiol, testosterone, progesterone, zeranol, trenbolone acetate and melengestrol acetate. In 2003, the commission amended its policy to permanently ban one hormone—estradiol-17β—while provisionally banning the use of the five other hormones, as it continued to seek more complete scientific information.[5] The ban reflects the EU's approach to food safety policy, known as the precautionary principle, which supports taking protective action before there is complete scientific proof of a risk.[6] The ban also effectively restricts trade of meat and meat products from countries that regularly treat farm animals with these growth promotants.

The commission has justified its ban as necessary to protect consumer health and safety. This position initially evolved, in part, as a reaction to reports in the 1970s over the illegal use of dethylstilboestrol (DES) in veal production in France, and consumer concerns that this was linked to reports of hormonal irregularities in Italian adolescents.[7] This created concerns over the possible negative health effects of using hormones in livestock production, and contributed to a general climate in Europe that was suspicious of the use of hormones in livestock production and the potentially harmful health effects to consumers.

During the 1990s, EU consumer meat demand was again adversely affected by outbreaks in British cattle herds of bovine spongiform encephalopathy (BSE), a fatal brain disease, commonly known as "mad cow disease."[8] Scientifically established links between BSE and Creutzfeldt-Jakob disease (CJD), the human variant of BSE, added to consumer distrust about the safety of the meat supply. Continued discovery of BSE-infected cattle in a number of European countries has contributed further to an unfavorable political, economic, and social environment for resolving the meat hormone dispute. Although BSE has nothing to do with hormones, many European beef producers are fearful of doing anything, like using hormones, that would give consumers another disincentive to buy meat. Many of these same types of concerns have surfaced in consumer reactions to the introduction of transgenic plants and other forms of biotechnology into the food chain.[9]

Political and economic considerations also have likely contributed to the commission's decision to continue its policy to ban hormone-treated beef. Opposition to hormone-treated meat continues unabated, and both producer and consumer interest groups in the EU continue to exert pressure on EU trade policy officials to hold to their position banning hormone-treated beef. The EU's beef sector benefits from both domestic producer support and trade policies under the EU's Common Agricultural Policy (CAP), which is reported to have resulted in the accumulation of large, costly-to-store beef surpluses.[10] Many European cattle producers support the EU's import ban in part because they are concerned about competition from possibly cheaper imported beef from the United States and other beef exporting countries. Along with responding to consumer concerns, EU agricultural policy makers have been resistant to policies that might accelerate the contraction of the agricultural sector and contribute to increased unemployment.

Hormone Dispute in the WTO

The United States has continued to challenge the EU's beef hormone ban in the World Trade Organization (WTO) and to question whether the ban is consistent with the EU's WTO obligations under the Sanitary and Phytosanitary (SPS) Agreement (see box). After a series of WTO consultations, panel decisions, and appeals in the case, both the United States and the European Union claim these formal proceedings have vindicated their respective positions in the dispute. This case has proven so intractable in part because it involves internal national regulation and domestic policy issues, and rules for dispute settlement and the use of SPS measures to restrict trade, rather than routine commercial disputes over trade or customs regulations.[11]

Although the WTO has issued decisions that have questioned the validity of the ban, the EU has repeatedly voted to maintain it, citing consumer worries, questions of animal welfare, meat quality, and effects of hormones on the EU's beef and milk sectors. The laws governing the EU's ban have been reissued and/or updated numerous times (in 1988, in 1996, and again in 2003).[12]

The EU claims that its position to maintain the ban is supported by studies on the potential human health risks associated with the consumption of hormone-treated beef.

THE SANITARY AND PHYTOSANITARY (SPS) AGREEMENT

The SPS Agreement prescribes rules requiring a scientific basis for measures that restrict imports on the basis of health or safety concerns. It was entered into force on January 1, 1995, as one of the agreements in the Uruguay Round of the General Agreement on Tariffs and Trade (GATT), the multilateral trade negotiations to be administered by the WTO.

The SPS Agreement has a twofold objective. It aims to both (1) recognize the sovereign right of WTO Members to provide the level of health protection they deem appropriate; and (2) ensure that SPS requirements do not represent unnecessary, arbitrary, scientifically unjustifiable, or disguised restrictions on international trade.

Each country may set its own food safety and animal and plant health standards based on risk assessment and its determination of an acceptable level of risk. Countries may use international standards, guidelines, and recommendations where available. The SPS agreement recognizes the right of countries to maintain standards that are stricter than international standards. However, stricter standards should be justified by science or by a nondiscriminatory lower level of acceptable risk that does not selectively target imports. Still, some argue whether countries apply such measures to imports based on considerations of food safety and protection of the health of people, animals, and plants, or whether these actions are driven more by protectionist sentiments.

The SPS Agreement provides that dispute settlement procedures under the WTO apply also to disputes about food safety and health measures. As under the earlier General Agreement on Tariffs and Trade (GATT) system, the WTO dispute settlement process begins with consultations between the affected parties and then proceeds to a panel of experts for adjudication if consultations fail to resolve the dispute.

For more information, see the WTO's website, http://www.wto.org/english/tratop_e/sps_e/sps_e.htm, and CRS Report R43450, *Sanitary and Phytosanitary (SPS) and Related Non-Tariff Barriers to Agricultural Trade.*

The United States continues to question whether the EU has conducted an adequate risk assessment to support its position, and maintains there is a clear worldwide scientific consensus supporting the safety to consumers of eating hormone-treated meat. In retaliation, starting in the late 1980s, the United States imposed trade sanctions—as authorized by the WTO—in the form of high import tariffs on selected EU agricultural products.

To further complicate matters, in October 2008, the WTO issued a mixed ruling that allows the United States to continue its trade sanctions, but also allows the EU to maintain its ban. As a result, the United States has continued to impose its trade sanctions, while the EU has continued to maintain its ban.

A detailed timeline showing a chronology of major events is provided at the end of this report (**Appendix D**).

Overview of WTO Proceedings

In response to the EU's initial ban on hormone-treated meat in the 1980s, the United States first invoked GATT dispute settlement in 1986-1987 under the Tokyo Round's Technical Barriers to Trade Agreement, and also threatened to implement retaliatory tariffs on selected EU imports. This action delayed full implementation of the EU ban until January 1, 1989. Once the ban was implemented, the United States instituted retaliatory tariffs (100% *ad valorem*) on EU imports valued at $93 million, which stayed in effect until May 1996. Earlier in 1996, both the United States and the EU had requested WTO consultations in an attempt to resolve the dispute.

In April 1996, the United States requested a WTO dispute settlement panel case against the EU, claiming that the ban is inconsistent with the EU's WTO obligations under the SPS Agreement.[13] Australia, Canada, and New Zealand joined the United States in the complaint. The EU maintained the ban, and issued updates to its law confirming and extending the prohibitions.

In August 1997, the WTO dispute settlement panel released its report agreeing with the United States that the ban violated several provisions of the SPS Agreement. Specifically, the EU ban was found to violate SPS requirements that such measures:

- be based on international standards, guidelines or recommendations (Article 3.1);
- be based on a risk assessment and take into account risk assessment techniques developed by the relevant international organizations (Article 5.1); and
- avoid arbitrary or unjustifiable distinctions that result in discrimination or a disguised restriction on international trade (Article 5.5).[14]

The EU appealed the ruling, and in February 1998, the WTO Appellate Body found that the EU ban did contravene the EU's obligations under the SPS Agreement, but left open the option for the EU to conduct a risk assessment of hormone-treated meat. AWTO arbitration panel ruled subsequently that 15 months from the date of the decision (i.e., May 13, 1999) would be a reasonable period of time for the EU to conduct its assessment. By the deadline, the EU did not complete its scientific review and decided it would not consider removing the ban before conducting additional review. This led the way for the United States to retaliate by imposing its current trade sanctions against U.S. imports of EU products starting in July 1999.

Following the 1997 WTO decision, the EU commissioned various research studies and conducted scientific reviews of the issue. In 1999, as justification for continuing the ban, the EU offered the first in its series of scientific reviews and opinions that estradiol-17β may be carcinogenic. (Further opinions and studies followed in 2000, 2002, and 2007, as discussed in the section of this report titled "EU Reviews.") In 2003, the EU announced that its scientific review had concluded that estradiol-17β was carcinogenic and that for the five other hormones the current state of knowledge did not make it possible to provide a quantitative assessment of their risks to consumers. An October 2003 EU press release claimed that EU's scientific reviews constitute "a thorough risk assessment based on current scientific knowledge"[15] and thus fulfill the EU's WTO obligations. The United States continues to question whether the EU Commission's studies constitute risk assessments.

Accordingly, in 2003, the EU issued a new directive and revised its ban to permanently ban estradiol-17β and provisionally ban the five other hormones. The EU claims the decision to provisionally ban the five other hormones is necessary, while the commission seeks more complete scientific information. The EU claims that its actions replacing its original ban with a provisional ban comply with its WTO obligations under Article 5.7 of the SPS Agreement.[16]

U.S. trade and veterinary officials have repeatedly rejected the EU studies, claiming that the scientific evidence is not new information nor does it establish a risk to consumers from eating hormone-treated meat.[17] The United States also claims that these findings ignore and contradict numerous scientific studies, including some by European scientists (as discussed in the section titled "U.S. Response to EU Reviews").

Claiming that its ban is justified and in compliance with its WTO obligations, the EU has continued to initiate counteractions against the United States (and Canada), stating that there is no longer a legal basis for the United States to impose trade sanctions against the European Union.[18] In November 2004, the EU requested WTO consultations, claiming that the United States should remove its retaliatory measures since the EU has removed the measures found to be WTO-inconsistent in the original case.[19] In 2005, the EU initiated new WTO dispute settlement proceedings against the United States and Canada. A final panel report was delayed until 2008, owing, the panel said, to the complexity of the dispute and other administrative and procedural matters.

The March 2008 panel report cited fault with all three parties (EU, United States, and Canada) on various substantive and procedural aspects of the dispute. The panel found that the EU had not presented sufficient scientific evidence to justify the import ban, including the EU's 2003 risk assessment report. The panel faulted the United States and Canada for maintaining their imposed trade sanctions. The panels found that both parties had made procedural violations under the WTO Dispute Settlement Understanding (DSU) because of unilateral actions they had taken.[20] Both parties filed appeals citing procedural errors and disagreements with the panel findings.

In October 2008, the WTO Appellate Body issued a mixed ruling that allows for continued imposition of trade sanctions on the EU by the United States and Canada, but also allows the EU to continue its ban on imports of hormone-treated beef. The Appellate Body report reversed the dispute panel decision by stating that the EU's ban is not incompatible with WTO law, thus granting more deference to the EU in deciding the basis for food safety regulations.

The WTO Appellate Body also recommended that the parties initiate a compliance panel proceeding under Article 21.5 of the DSU to determine whether the EU is in compliance with its WTO obligations in the underlying beef hormone dispute. In late December, the EU requested consultations under Article 21.5, and may request a panel at a later date.[21]

The WTO Appellate Body's reversal of the panel on this issue of scientific evidence has led some to argue that this is a potentially precedent-setting decision that might be perceived to instruct dispute settlement panels to be more deferential to national governments when the relevant scientific evidence is not available to make an objective risk assessment. Some claim that this could allow for more flexibility to countries in imposing SPS requirements in future WTO compliance panels, and might also change how panels operate on matters related to the burden of proof and in post-retaliation situations. Typically complainants initiating the compliance panel proceedings bear the burden of proof, because it is in their interest to prove that the respondent has not brought itself into compliance with WTO rules.[22]

In November 2008, following the announcement by USTR that it was seeking comment on possible modification of the list of EU products subject to increased tariffs under the dispute, the EU filed a new WTO challenge against U.S. and Canadian sanctions imposed on imports of EU products in retaliation to the EU's ban on hormone-treated beef.

In January 2009, USTR announced changes to the list of EU products subject to increased tariffs under the dispute, adding countries and raising the tariff on select products. The EU claimed that USTR's action constitutes an "escalation" of the dispute and is "more punitive" than the current trade sanctions. The EU was prepared to challenge the United States in the WTO. In May 2009, following a series of negotiations, the United States and the EU signed a memorandum of understanding (MOU), which phases in certain changes over several years, as discussed later in section "2009 Memorandum of Understanding."

Role of Scientific Reviews in the Dispute

One critical issue in this seemingly intractable debate is an underlying disagreement about the scientific consensus regarding the safety of hormone-treated beef for human consumption.

EU Reviews

The EU continues to maintain that "there is a lack of data on the type and amount of [growth-promoting hormone] residues in meat on which to make a quantitative exposure assessment" that would change the EU's understanding of the "possible risks to human health" associated with hormone-treated meat and meat products. It claims that this position is supported by a series of commissioned research studies and scientific reviews conducted by the EU, although there has been no conclusive testing on the issue.

A 1997 WTO decision found that the EU's ban on imports of hormone-treated meat was inconsistent with the EU's WTO obligations under the Sanitary and Phytosanitary (SPS) Agreement since the EU had not conducted a risk assessment. In response, the EU commissioned 17 studies to address the scientific basis of the import ban on meat and meat products and animals treated with hormones for growth promotion purposes. The studies addressed toxicological and carcinogenicity aspects, residue analysis, potential abuse and control problems, and environmental aspects of six growth promotants (estradiol-17β, progesterone, testosterone, zeranol, trenbolone acetate, and melengestrol acetate) and their metabolites.

Between 1999 and 2002, the EC's Scientific Committee on Veterinary Measures relating to Public Health (SCVPH)[23] issued a series of opinions on the potential risks to human health from hormone residues in bovine meat and meat products. The first review's opinion, issued in April 1999, stated that there is evidence showing that the growth hormone estradiol-17β, used in U.S. cattle production, is carcinogenic, among other potential health risks to consumers.[24] The second review, finalized in May 2000, concluded that new information questioning the findings of the SCVPH's first review did "not provide convincing data and arguments demanding revision of the conclusions drawn in the 1999 SCVPH opinion on the potential risks to human health from hormone residues in bovine meat and meat products."[25] The third opinion, issued in May 2002, concluded that the committee's review of the 17 studies initiated in 1998 again reconfirmed the previous findings of the 1999 and 2000 reviews.[26]

The most recent review was conducted in 2007 by the European Food Safety Authority (EFSA).[27] The review covered new scientific evidence that emerged after the previous risk assessments (1999, 2000, and 2002) relating to the use of certain natural and synthetic growth-promoting hormones in cattle. EFSA's Scientific Panel on Contaminants in the Food Chain (CONTAM) concluded:

> At present, epidemiological data provide convincing evidence for an association between the amount of red meat consumed and certain forms of hormone-dependent cancers. Whether hormone residues in meat contribute to this risk is currently unknown.
>
> The CONTAM Panel concluded that the new data that are publicly available do not provide quantitative information that would be informative for risk characterisation and therefore do not call for a revision of the previous assessments of the Scientific Committee on Veterinary Measures relating to Public Health (SCVPH) (EC, 1999, 2000, 2002).[28]

Among the stated concerns is that excess intake of hormone residues from all six hormones and their metabolites could pose a risk to the consumer. The review cites evidence supporting that estradiol-17β be considered as a carcinogen, and states that all six hormones may pose endocrine, developmental, immunological, neurobiological, immunotoxic, genotoxic, and carcinogenic effects, particularly for susceptible risk groups (such as prepubertal children). The toxicological and epidemiological data reviewed by the commission panels do not allow a quantitative estimate of the risk, leading to the panel's conclusions that no threshold levels can be defined for any of the six hormones.[29]

Based on this series of reviews, the commission maintains that these reviews "reaffirmed public health concerns about the large scale use of hormones administered to cattle for growth promoting purposes," and therefore "provided the scientific basis for community legislation not allowing the use of hormones for growth promoting purposes in the EU."[30] Accordingly, the EU claims that the retaliatory tariffs imposed on EU export to the United States are not in compliance with its WTO obligations and should be discontinued.

U.S. Response to EU Reviews

The United States continues to maintain that U.S. beef from cattle treated with certain approved growth hormones poses no public health risk. Overall, the official U.S. position is that "there is a clear world-wide scientific consensus supporting the safety of these approved and licensed hormones when used according to good veterinary practice."[31] The United States claims that this position is supported by "scientific reviews of the six hormones, international standards pertaining to their use, and a long-standing history of administering the six hormones to cattle for growth promotion purposes."[32] Accordingly, the United States claims that the use of these hormones as growth promoters in beef production is safe, when applied in accordance with good veterinary practices.

The United States claims that numerous U.S. and international scientific studies of the six hormones support its position, including safety assessments by the U.S. FDA and comparable food safety institutions in other countries; the reports of the EC-commissioned 1984 and 1987 Scientific Group on Anabolic Agents in Animal Production (the so-called "Lamming Committee"); the 1983 World Organization for Animal Health Symposium; the Joint Expert Committee on Food Additives (JECFA) reports;[33] the Codex Alimentarius Commission reports;[34] the EC-commissioned 1995 Scientific Conference on Growth Promotion in Meat Production;[35] the EC-commissioned Committee for Veterinary Medicinal Products on the Safety Evaluation of Steroidal Sex Hormones reports;[36] the United Kingdom's 1999 and 2006 Veterinary Products Committee reports;[37] and the 2003 Australian review.[38] In general, these studies report that the three natural hormones—estradiol, progesterone, and testosterone—and their derivatives, when used as growth-promoting agents and according to good veterinary practice, are "safe," are "not hazardous," or "do not pose a risk to consumers." Some reports determined that it was unnecessary to specify maximum residue levels (MRLs) for natural hormones administered according to good veterinary practices, and recommended MRLs or acceptable daily intake levels for two of the three synthetic hormones in dispute.

The United States also points out that the EU's own 1995 Scientific Conference on Growth Promoting Substances in Meat Production concluded that "at present there is no evidence for possible health risks to the consumer due to the use of natural sex hormones for growth promotion."[39] The United States also cites as support the findings of the 1996-1997 WTO panel in the dispute. The panel report states that "[n]one of the scientific evidence referred to by the European Communities which specifically addresses the safety of some or all of the hormones in dispute when used for growth promotion, indicates that an identifiable risk arises for human health from use of these hormones if good practice is followed." The panel noted "that this conclusion has also been confirmed by the scientific experts advising the Panel."[40]

The United States has criticized the EU's scientific opinions for focusing on only one growth promotant—estradiol-17β—and on its potential genotoxicity, while directing relatively little attention toward the other natural and synthetic hormones. The United States also claims that the "EU failed to use solid evaluative methods in their studies and completely disregarded the large body of evidence from epidemiological studies that indicate that estradiol does not contribute to any increased cancer risk and that meat from animals tested with estradiol is safe for consumers."[41]

Regarding the EU's more recent reviews, the United States claims they fail to provide any new evidence that would call into question the findings and conclusions of other authoritative reviews. More broadly, the United States also disputes whether the EU's scientific reviews serve as a risk assessment. The United States claims: "There has been no new risk assessment based on scientific information and reasoning presented by the EU," further claiming that the "17 studies" funded by the commission beginning in 1998 were "not intended as a to serve as a risk assessment, but instead were to fill in the gaps."[42] Accordingly, the United States claims, the EU's 2003 update to its hormone ban is not in compliance with its WTO obligations and should be discontinued.

Industry groups in the United States voice these same criticisms. The National Cattlemen's Beef Association (NCBA), the largest national group of cattle producers, has long opposed the EU's ban on imports of U.S. hormone-treated beef, claiming that the ban is scientifically unjustified and fails to satisfy the EU's WTO requirements under the SPS.[43]

Similar concerns have been expressed by other U.S. farm groups, including American Farm Bureau Federation (AFBF), the Animal Health Institute (AHI), and the American Meat Institute (AMI).[44] Many trade analysts believe that the United States has a strong case against the hormone ban under WTO rules that require SPS restrictions to be based on risk assessment and to have a scientific justification. These various interest groups have continued to exert pressure on U.S. trade policy officials to hold to their position regarding the EU's meat hormone ban.

U.S. Trade Sanctions and Retaliation

Initial 1999 Retaliatory Action

Insisting that the scientific evidence demonstrates that hormone-treated beef is safe to consumers, the United States began to consider retaliatory tariffs on EU imports starting in the 1980s. In 1987, the United States announced but then suspended retaliatory tariffs (100% *ad valorem*) on about $100 million worth of EU imports. On January 1, 1989, the United States instituted 100% tariffs on EU imports valued at about $93 million per year. These higher tariffs remained in effect until May 1996, when the EU sought a WTO panel against the U.S action.[45]

Again, in 1999, following the EU's failure to implement the WTO's recommendations related to its obligations under the SPS Agreement, the United States and Canada formally sought and obtained WTO authorization to suspend tariff concessions and retaliate against trade from the European Union. Initially, the United States requested authorization to impose import duties in excess of bound rates on a list of products equivalent, on an annual basis, to $202 million. The WTO arbitrators set the level at $116.8 million for the United States (and C$11.3 million for Canada).[46]

On July 27, 1999, USTR announced its decision to impose a 100% *ad valorem* rate of duty on a specified list of products from certain EU member states.[47] The list of products includes beef and pork products, goose pâté, Roquefort cheese, truffles, onions, carrots, preserved tomatoes, soups, yarn, Dijon mustard, juices, chicory, toasted breads, French chocolate, and jams, as well as agricultural-based byproducts, such as glue and wool grease. The list targeted France, Germany, Italy, and Denmark, as well as Austria, Belgium, Finland, Greece, Ireland, Luxembourg, the Netherlands, Portugal, Spain, and Sweden. The list did not include products of the United Kingdom because it has indicated support for lifting the ban. **Appendix A** provides a listing of the product imports initially affected by the U.S. trade sanctions imposed in 1999.

According to USTR, the imposition of these higher duties is "intended to restore the balance of trade concessions under the WTO and to induce compliance by the EU with the WTO's rulings and recommendations in the original EC-Hormones dispute."[48] However, some point out that these retaliatory duties have been mostly ineffective since they do not provide any direct benefit to the U.S. beef industry, and claim that it is U.S. and EU consumers who lose by paying higher prices for a wide variety of imported foods.[49] The U.S. beef industry has long maintained that the EU ban is merely a disguised trade barrier, intended to protect EU domestic beef producers.[50] Some in Congress have questioned whether the EU's ban is motivated more by politics than by sound science.[51] Yet the EU continues to claim that the United States is not justified in maintaining its trade sanctions, given its belief that there is a scientific basis for banning hormone-treated beef and given updates to their laws governing the ban in 2003.[52]

Revised 2009 Retaliatory Action

In October 2008, USTR initiated action to modify the retaliation list of EU products subject to 100% tariffs in connection with the U.S.-EU beef hormones dispute. Such an action is consistent with legislation enacted by Congress in 2000, under the Trade and Development Act (P.L. 106-200), which amended the 1974 Trade Act. The law included a so-called "carousel retaliation" provision requiring the Administration periodically to rotate, or change, the types of products targeted for trade retaliation.[53] Prior to this, the provision had not been implemented per the legislation. USTR did consider modifying the retaliation list in 2006, but ultimately decided not to do so, as was recommended by the U.S. beef industry.[54] Public comments sent to USTR in late 2008 reflected support by agricultural industry groups for maintaining higher tariffs on a range of current and expanded products, while some importers recommend removing some products.[55]

In January 2009, the USTR under the outgoing Bush Administration announced changes to the list of EU products subject to increased tariffs under the dispute (**Appendix B**).[56] The modified list added products from many of the newly acceded countries under EU expansion (such as Bulgaria, Cyprus, Czech Republic, Estonia, Hungary, Latvia, Lithuania, Poland, Romania, Slovakia, Slovenia, and Malta). The modified list added additional products (such as pork products, cut flowers and plants, processed fruits, nuts, fruit juices, drinking waters, confectionary and chewing gum, and oats), but deleted some products currently on the list (such as onions, carrots, processed tomatoes, toasted breads, coffee, mustard, fish products, soups, yarns, and glue). The modified list did not include some of the initially proposed products, such as yarns, hair clippers, and motorcycles.[57] The modified list also raised the tariff on Roquefort cheese to 300% from 100% under the current retaliation. These changes were scheduled to go into effect on March 23, 2009. The EU claimed that this action constituted an "escalation" of the dispute, and was "more punitive" than the current trade sanctions.[58]

In February 2009, further consultations between the United States and the EU on the dispute were not successful, and the EU was expected to seek a dispute settlement panel on whether its ban was consistent with the SPS Agreement. In March, USTR announced that it would delay the imposition of additional duties on a modified list of EU products by one month; in April, USTR announced it would further extend this delay until May 2009 in order to provide "more time to negotiate a settlement with the EU."[59] Press reports indicated that among the issues to be resolved were the U.S. demand for increased market access of U.S. non-hormone-treated beef for export to the EU, and the U.S. demand that the EU refrain from seeking a new WTO ruling that its revised ban in 2003 now complies with the SPS Agreement.[60] In March 2009, the United States drafted a "reduced list" of EU import products subject to 100% *ad valorem* duties (**Appendix C**).[61]

2009 Memorandum of Understanding

On May 13, 2009, following a series of negotiations, the United States and the EU signed a memorandum of understanding (MOU) implementing an agreement that could resolve this long-standing dispute. The MOU sets up three phases, as follows.[62]

1. **Phase 1:** (a) Expanded market access for beef to the EU under an annual tariff-rate quota (TRQ) of 20,000 metric tons at zero duty for beef produced without growth-promoting hormones ("High Quality Beef");[63] and (b) agreement by the United States that it will delay implementation of the January 2009 modifications ("increased duties," **Appendix B**) for certain EU imports. The new quota is in addition to the existing 11,500 metric tons of hormone-free beef. The United States will continue to impose U.S. import duties on the "reduced list" of products (**Appendix C**). Phase 1 of the MOU was scheduled to conclude August 3, 2012.
2. **Phase 2:** (a) Further expansion of EU market access for High Quality Beef to 45,000 metric tons; and (b) agreement by the United States to reduce "increased duties" to zero (**Appendix B**).A decision on whether to move to Phase 2 would depend on conditions at the end of Phase 1 and the U.S. beef industry's ability to make full use of the additional quota. Phase 2 would last one year.
3. **Phase 3:** (a) EU maintains the TRQ for High Quality Beef at 45,000 metric tons; and (b) the United States removes import duties on selected EU products under the dispute, leading to the possible longer-term resolution of the dispute. Before the end of the fourth year, a decision on whether to move to Phase 3 would be made following negotiations between the United States and the EU on selected issues (such as duration, withdrawal, and status of WTO litigation, etc.).

Some U.S. farm organizations were unhappy with the MOU because it did not lift the EU's ban on beef from hormone-treated cattle and because the EU did not concede to the terms of the science regarding the safety of hormone-treated beef.[64]

As part of Phase 1, the EC adopted regulations opening a tariff quota for 20,000 metric tons imports of high-quality beef (HQB), effective August 2009.[65] U.S. beef products under this quota must originate from animals that have never been treated with growth hormones; eligibility requirements may be met by participating in USDA's Non-Hormone Treated Cattle (NHTC) Program. In 2010, the United States was reported to have shipped about 16,500 metric tons to the EU under the quota, which was about three times that shipped in 2008 under previous quota levels. (For more information, see the section of this report titled "USDA's Non-Hormone Treated Cattle (NHTC) Program.")

The United States, in Phase 1, agreed not to implement its January 2009 revised ("carousel") sanctions, which would have resulted in higher retaliatory duties on selected EU exports to the United States (see **Appendix B**). In September 2009, USTR announced it was officially terminating its plan to rotate the list of products.[66] Trade sanctions were to remain in effect on certain EU exports (listed in **Appendix C**) until the final phase of the agreement. During the first 18 months of the agreement, the United States or the EU would refrain from further WTO litigation regarding the dispute. In May 2011, USTR announced it was terminating higher duties for imported products listed under the dispute.[67] The removal of retaliatory tariffs under the dispute was ahead of the scheduled date under the MOU, and was reported to have been intended to encourage a successful transition to Phase 2 of the MOU.[68]

DEFINITION OF "HIGH QUALITY BEEF"

The 2009 memorandum of understanding (MOU) between United States and the EU s defines "High Quality Beef" as follows:

> Beef cuts obtained from carcasses of heifers and steers less than 30 months of age which have only been fed a diet, for at least the last 100 days before slaughter, containing not less than 62 percent of concentrates and/or feed grain co-products on a dietary dry matter basis that meet or exceed a metabolisable energy (ME) content greater than 12.26 megajoules (MJ) per one kilogram of dry matter. The heifers and steers fed this diet shall be fed, on average, not less than 1.4 percent of live body weight per day on a dry matter basis.
>
> The carcass from which beef cuts are derived shall be evaluated by an evaluator employed by the national government who bases the evaluation, and a resulting classification of the carcass, on a method approved by the national government. The national government evaluation method, and its classifications, must evaluate expected carcass quality using a combination of carcass maturity and palatability traits of the beef cuts. Such an evaluation method of the carcass shall include, but not be limited to, an evaluation of the maturity characteristics of color and texture of the longissimus dorsi muscle and bone and cartilage ossification, as well as an evaluation of expected palatability traits including a combination of the discrete specifications of intramuscular fat and firmness of the longissimus dorsi muscle.
>
> The cuts shall be labeled in accordance with Article 13 of Regulation (EC) No. 1760/2000. The indication 'High Quality Beef' may be added to the information on the label.

See WTO, European Communities—Measures Concerning Meat And Meat Products (Hormones), Joint Communication from the European Communities and the United States, WT/DS26/28, September 30, 2009.

As part of Phase 2, in June 2012, the EU issued regulations increasing the HQB quota and changing the quota management system to a "first come, first served" basis.[69] The HQB quota was raised to 48,200 MT and is consistent with Phase 2 in the MOU on the beef hormone dispute, fully effective byAugust 2012. Changes to the HQB quota management are intended to "provide easier quota access to new and smaller importers of U.S. beef, as well as to terminate the trade in quota import licenses that occurred as demand for import licenses exceeded the quota volume."[70]

In October 2013, the EU approved a two-year extension of the deal, allowing for access of U.S. beef raised without the use of growth promotants in exchange for continued U.S. suspension of retaliatory import duties on some EU food products.[71] The extension will remain in place until August 2015. By extending Phase 2, the EU and U.S. are opting not to proceed to Phase 3, which would require the EU to maintain its annual TRQ of 45,000 metric tons and require that the United States end its retaliatory import duties and give up its ability to reimpose higher duties.[72]

USTR continues to monitor EU implementation of the MOU and other policies affecting market access for U.S. beef products.

The U.S-EU beef hormone dispute has been raised as an issue as part of the current negotiations between the United States and the EU seeking to establish a free trade area as part of the Transatlantic Trade and Investment Partnership (TTIP).[73] Specifically, some Members of Congress expect the TTIP negotiations to resolve long-standing trade disputes regarding SPS rules between the two trading blocs, as well as enhance disciplines to address SPS issues and other non-tariff barriers.[74] Major concerns revolve around meat and poultry production and processing methods, specifically involving the U.S. use of beef hormones and ractopamine,[75] pathogen reduction and other treatment technologies, BSE-related regulations, and other plant processing regulations. In February 2014, European Commissioner Karl De Gucht indicated that the EU would not change its regulations prohibiting imports of meat raised with growth promotants.[76]

Other issues also need to be resolved. According to press reports, the U.S. government will consider implementation of Phase 2 following resolution of an outstanding issue regarding the EU's disapproval of the common U.S. practice in the beef industry of using antimicrobial treatments to ensure that meat is not contaminated with pathogens.[77] The EU has claimed that the use of such washes is cover for unsanitary production methods.[78] EU representatives have stated that they would be unwilling to accept U.S. beef products treated with antimicrobial washes. In 2013, EU lifted its previous ban to allow the use of lactic acid as a pathogen reduction treatment (PRT) on beef carcasses, half-carcasses and beef quarters in the slaughterhouse.[79] The EU still prohibits the use of other types of PRTs and antimicrobial washes when shipping to beef and poultry the EU.[80]

Finally, some meat-exporting countries, including Argentina, Brazil, India, New Zealand, Nicaragua, Paraguay, and Uruguay, have argued that the TRQ should be available to all MFN ("most favored nation") countries.[81] Some of these countries claim the U.S.-EU agreement is "discriminatory" and inconsistent with WTO rules since it allows for an increase in the U.S. quota but does not make similar concessions to other countries.[82] Brazil, for example, is reported to be considering asking the WTO to investigate whether the EU sets different rules for beef from Brazil than those for competing supplies from the United States and Canada.[83] By invoking MFN status, these countries argue that equal treatment and trade advantages should be accorded to all MFN trading partners, and that all should have access to export products under the quota.

Opposition by U.S. Importers

Some U.S. importers have actively contested higher tariffs on U.S. imports on the retaliation list. For example, Gilda Industries, an importer of Spanish toasted breads, filed a series of protests with U.S. Customs against higher tariffs on toasted breads.[84] Gilda Industries later brought a lawsuit against the United States in the U.S. Court of International Trade (CIT), seeking to force USTR to remove toasted breads from its retaliation list. For years, the United States and Canada have refused to remove their trade sanctions on grounds that the scientific evidence claimed by the EU does not provide new information and does not establish a risk to consumers from eating hormone-treated meat. In the original case, the CIT ordered a refund of all punitive duties paid on affected goods imported after July 29, 2007. The United States appealed the decision.[85] Toasted breads were subsequently removed from the "revised" retaliation list (**Appendix C**).

Following proposed changes in January 2009 adding imported waters to the list of EU products subject to higher U.S. tariffs, Nestle Waters of North America, Inc., also filed a preliminary injunction order in the CIT against the action.[86] The suit claimed that retaliation is not authorized because there was no request for changes in the product mix within the most recent deadline for such a request.[87] In addition, Gilda Industries, along with several other importing companies, sought a partial refund of retaliatory duties that the United States has imposed under the dispute.[88] In October 2010, the U.S. Court of Appeals for the Federal Circuit issued a decision in the Gilda Industries case, which could make importers of certain foods from the EU eligible for refunds for retaliatory duties paid since July 29, 2007.[89] The current status of this case is not known.

Trade Effects for Selected Products

U.S. Exports to the EU

Recent Trends

Initially, lost U.S. beef exports because of the EU's ban were estimated at about $100 million annually, and valued approximately equal to retaliatory trade sanctions against selected EU food product exports. Currently, U.S. exports do not account for a sizable share of the EU beef import market. Under the ban, eligible U.S. beef exports to the EU must be certified as not having been treated with hormones and are further subject to quotas that limit the total amount of beef imported under preferential tariffs. The U.S. beef industry claims that, absent the ban, U.S. beef exports to the European Union would be much greater.

Evaluating actual trade trends is complicated by large discrepancies between the U.S.-reported export data and the EU-reported import data for beef. Because of concerns that the U.S. beef export data may not reflect actual trade conditions, in part due to possible transshipments via certain EU port destinations and/or trade data inaccuracies, this report examines available EU import data.[90] These data are available only back to 1999 and do not allow for a full evaluation of how the ban has affected U.S. beef exports over the time period. These data indicate that EU beef imports from the United States were lower during the 2000-2006 period, compared to 1999, and averaged between $5 million and $6 million per year (**Figure 1**). During this period, U.S. beef accounted for less than 1% of the EU beef import market. The majority (more than 90%) of EU beef imports were supplied by Brazil, Argentina, and Uruguay, among other countries. Available U.S. export data for the 10-year period from 1989 to 1998 indicate that U.S. exports to the EU of fresh/chilled and frozen beef averaged between $11 million and $13 million annually.[91] The U.S. Meat Export Federation (USMEF) reports that in 2010, U.S. beef exports to EU were valued at an estimated $165 million.[92]

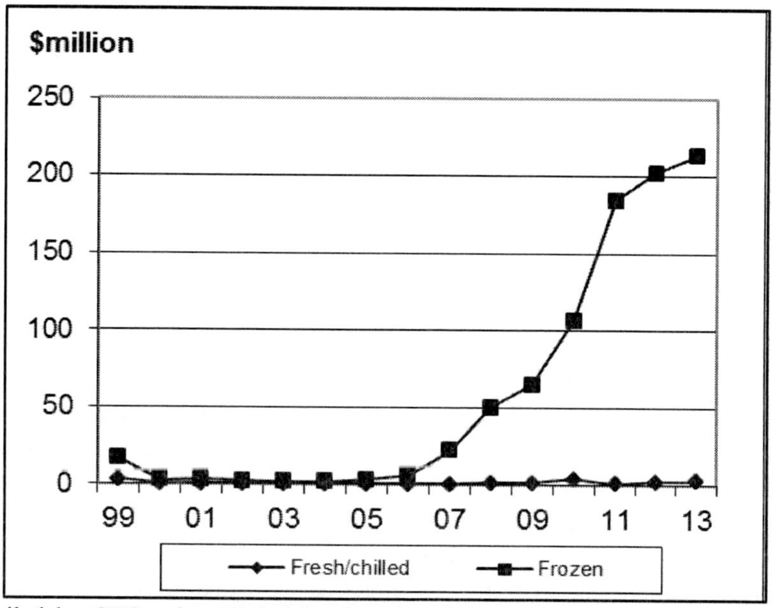

Source: Compiled by CRS using Global Trade Atlas data. EU-reported product imports to EU-27 countries, HTS 0201 (fresh/chilled beef) and HTS 0202 (frozen beef), nominal U.S. dollars.

Notes: There are considerable differences in the reported trade statistics between U.S.-reported beef exports to the European Union and EU-reported beef imports from the United States for HTS 0201 and 0202.

Figure 1. EU-Reported Beef Imports from the United States,1999-2013 (beef imports reported under trade categories HTS 0201 and 0202).

The EU import data also indicate that in the past couple of years, U.S. beef exports have risen, particularly for fresh and chilled beef products, which reached nearly $220 million in 2013 (**Figure 1**). According to EU import data, as a share of the EU import market, U.S. beef accounted for nearly 15% of EU fresh/chilled beef imports, up from about 4% in 2008.[93] U.S. exports still accounted for less than 1% of EU imports of frozen beef and offal products. Despite potential questions surrounding the available trade data, the USMEF acknowledges that U.S. beef exports to the European Union have risen in the past couple of years,[94] and that the rise may be attributable to the approval of additional, larger U.S. beef plants to export to the EU under USDA's Non-Hormone Treated Cattle (NHTC) Program (see discussion in next section).

Volume shipments for most beef products are limited by the EU's so-called "Hilton quota" for high-quality beef (HQB), a tariff rate quota that has been in effect since 1997 and allows only a fixed amount of fresh/chilled beef to be imported from selected countries before being subject to higher tariffs.[95] This quota allows for North American beef exports (which also covers Canadian beef exports) to the EU of 11,500 metric tons at a 20% tariff. The quota covers exports of fresh/chilled beef (HTS 0201); however, the EU also imports accredited frozen meat (HTS 0202) and offal products (HTS 0206), which are outside the quota. Currently the EU has extended an annual TRQ for 45,000 metric tons of hormone-free beef from certain countries, including the United States.

U.S. beef shipments to the European Union have increased sharply in recent years. In 2008, a reported 4,900 metric tons of U.S. beef was shipped to the EU under the previous quota, a roughly twofold increase compared to 2007.[96] In 2009, the United States shipped a reported 12,000 metric tons under the revised quota—another doubling compared to shipments in 2008.[97] According to EU import data, U.S. beef shipments to the EU-27 countries were between 16,000-17,000 metric tons during 2011-2013 under its existing quota.[98]

USDA's Non-Hormone Treated Cattle (NHTC) Program

Only U.S. beef from cattle raised under control measures specified in USDA's NHTC Program is eligible for export to the EU. (See box, below, for information on this program.) The program was initiated in 1989 when the United States and the EU agreed to control measures to facilitate the trade of non-hormone treated bovine meat, including veal. As of 2014, more than a dozen farms, ranches, feedlots, and cattle management groups have been audited and approved as sources of non-hormone treated cattle and are eligible for further evaluation by USDA's Food Safety and Inspection Service (FSIS).[99]

All export shipments must also be accompanied by a health certificate issued by FSIS under the non-hormone treated cattle program, certifying that all meat must originate from animals that have never been treated with growth hormones. Import licenses are issued by authorities in the EU member states, and the quantity available is published every month by the European Union.[100]

Initially, few U.S. plants were approved for export to the EU, and U.S. volume exports were low and often well below the allowable quota limit.[101] Because, historically, the U.S. quota had not been filled, this caused some to conclude that increasing the quota would not likely offer any benefit to U.S. beef exporters, particularly given additional costs of raising and shipping untreated beef.[102] In the past, negotiations between the United States and the EU to increase the quota have not been successful. However, recently some larger facilities have been approved and volume exports have been higher, approaching or possibly exceeding the quota limit, and there is renewed interest in increasing U.S. market access under the quota.[103]

Other Compensation Efforts

Prior to 2009, EU offers of compensation or trade concessions for lost U.S. meat exports were rejected by the United States. In lieu of lifting the ban, the EU has considered offering the United States compensation in the form of an expanded quota for hormone-free beef and reducing the 20% in-quota tariff. In January 2009, the EU offered to expand access for U.S. beef by 58,000 metric tons—well below what the United States initially requested.[104] However, there were unresolved issues in these negotiations, including the timing of the United States' lifting of its current trade sanctions against the European Union. The United States also asked for changes to the program, including simplifying the current system and requirements for plants, and reducing the number of chemical residues U.S. inspectors must test for before clearing shipments.[105] In addition, the United States wanted its beef exports to be allowed to be treated with antimicrobial washes to ensure cleanliness. The EU objects to such washes unless accompanied by adequate labeling, which the United States has resisted.[106] The U.S. beef industry claims its beef exporters do not use antimicrobial washes on beef destined to the EU, but that it is often difficult to set-aside or segment production within individual plants.[107] Previously, negotiations had been slowed by related disputes over detection of the presence of EU-listed hormones in U.S. shipments of presumably non-hormone treated beef.

NON-HORMONE-TREATED CATTLE (NHTC) PROGRAM

The NHTC program is a Quality Systems Assessment (QSA) program, whereby the USDA certifies the processes and procedures in place for a specific marketing claim. The program has three principal components:

- Cattle are to be grown in approved farms/feedlots and delivered to the slaughter establishment with a copy of a signed producer affidavit certifying that the animals have never been treated with hormonal growth promoters.
- Non-treated cattle and beef are segregated at the slaughter establishment and handled in a fashion that ensures that they are not commingled with other animals or meat.
- Tissue samples from non-hormone treated cattle are collected at slaughter and analyzed by accredited independent laboratories for residual levels of restricted compounds.

Each phase of the production, from birth through slaughter, must receive third-party verification prior to FSIS certifying NHTC to the EU. All cattle must be slaughtered and processed in a federally inspected establishment approved for production of products destined for the EU.

The NHTC program allows for treatment with antibiotics and ionophores, but prohibits the use of implants, growth promotants, and oral steroids. Individual animal identification and traceability are key components of the program. Certification and annual on-site audits function as verification steps for each facility's protocols.

Shipments must be accompanied by both a health certificate and a certificate of authenticity issued by USDA's Food Safety and Inspection Service (FSIS).

Other previous attempts by the United States and the EU to resolve the dispute have not been successful. In the late 1990s, the EU and the United States also discussed other options to resolve the dispute, including compensation for not lifting the ban; removal of the ban coupled with a labeling system, and conversion of the ban to a temporary measure.[108] These options were ultimately rejected by the United States—backed by most of the U.S. beef industry—preferring instead full removal of the ban and arguing that other forms of compensation would not be large enough to compensate for losses of hormone-treated exports.

U.S. Imports from the EU

The 1999 imposition of retaliatory (100%) tariffs on selected U.S. agricultural imports from EU member countries has significantly reduced imports of these products since these tariffs went into effect (**Figure 2**, **Table 1**). This graph only looks at the period from 1996-

2008, since the United States has agreed to suspend retaliatory import tariffs on selected EU products under the terms of the MOU signed in May 2009 (see section titled "2009 Memorandum of Understanding").

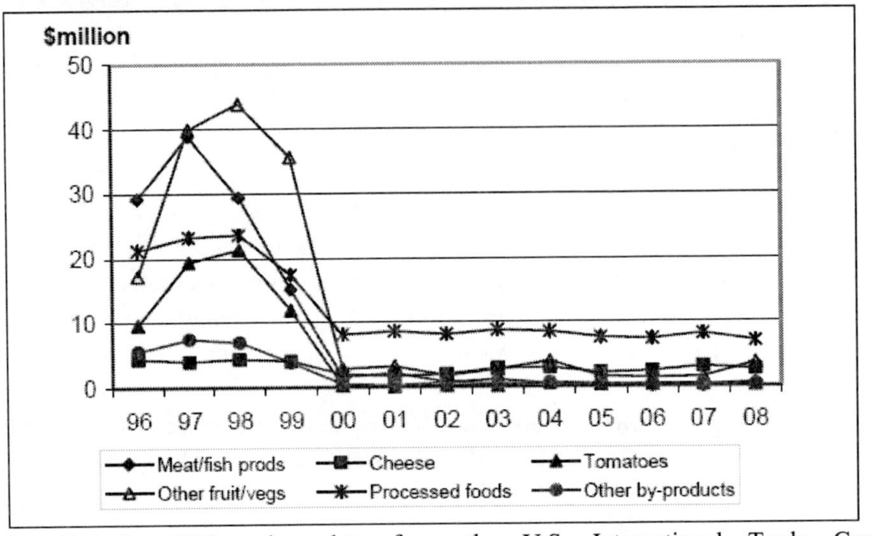

Source: Compiled by CRS using data from the U.S. International Trade Commission http://dataweb.usitc.gov. Imports for consumption (U.S. dollars). Nominal U.S. dollars. Selected products and countries (**Appendix A**).

Figure 2. U.S. Imports, Selected Products and Countries,1996-2008 (products subject to higher U.S. tariffs under the U.S.-EU beef hormone dispute).

Table 1. U.S. Imports,Selected Products and Countries, 1996-2008 ($ millions; products subject to higher U.S. tariffs under the U.S.-EU beef hormone dispute)

Products	1996	1998	2000	2002	2004	2006	2008
Meat products	16.7	20.9	1.1	0.6	0.5	0.1	0.3
Fish products	12.5	8.5	0.6	0.2	0.0	0.2	0.3
Cheese	4.4	4.4	2.1	2.0	3.0	2.4	2.7
Proc. Tomatoes	9.6	21.3	0.3	0.3	0.6	0.4	0.3
Fruit juice	10.0	25.4	0.7	0.7	3.3	0.8	3.5
Other fruit/veg.	7.2	18.3	2.2	0.9	0.7	0.6	0.2
Coffee prods.	4.4	3.8	1.1	1.1	1.2	1.2	1.0
Mustard	5.5	5.3	3.5	3.7	4.5	3.9	3.9
Soups/broths	2.3	5.2	1.3	1.3	0.5	0.1	0.0
Toasted breads	8.7	7.9	2.1	2.0	2.2	2.1	2.0
Cocoa prods.	0.4	1.5	0.1	0.2	0.1	0.1	0.1
Non-food	5.6	7.0	0.5	0.7	0.7	0.1	0.2
Total	**87.3**	**129.5**	**15.5**	**13.7**	**17.3**	**12.0**	**14.5**

Source: Compiled by CRS using data from the U.S. International Trade Commission http://dataweb.usitc.gov. Imports for consumption (U.S. dollars). Selected products and countries (**Appendix A**).

Notes: "Other fruit/veg." includes onions, dried carrots, berry jams, and truffles.

Overall, U.S. imports of these products dropped from about $130 million in 1997-1998 to under $15 million in 2008.[109] Products with the most significant decline in imports include meat and fish products, fruit juices, other fruit and vegetable products, processed foods, chocolate products, yarns, and other agriculture-based byproducts. Imports of some products, such as Roquefort cheese, mustard, and coffee products, also are lower, but less so. During this period, these EU products were still being imported to the United States and presumably sold at a higher price, given the need to cover higher importing costs due to higher tariffs.

Congressional Interest

Many in Congress have long maintained an interest in the U.S.-EU hormone dispute in support of the U.S. beef industry and its concern that the EU ban may be a disguised trade barrier, intended to protect EU domestic beef producers by restricting imports. As discussed, Congress enacted the carousel retaliation provision as part of the Trade and Development Act of 2000 (P.L. 106-200), largely in response to the dispute. In addition, over the years, the dispute has been invoked at various congressional hearings and has been a subject of introduced legislation, mostly as a means to illustrate how sanitary and phytosanitary (SPS) measures and non-tariff barriers are often used to unjustifiably restrict trade.[110] Also, in 2000, former Senator Max Baucus introduced the Trade Injury Compensation Act (S. 2709), intended to establish a Beef Industry Compensation Trust Fund with the duties imposed on products of countries that do not comply with certain WTO dispute resolution decisions; a Senate Agriculture subcommittee hearing was held on this matter.[111]

There also have been resolutions intended to express the sense of Congress that the Administration should continue to take action against the European Union under the dispute.[112] The dispute is regularly noted in USTR's annual trade policy reports as an example of the EU's continued use of non-tariff trade barriers to limit or prevent U.S. beef exports, despite the United States' measures to ensure the safety of the food supply.

Some in Congress, however, have maintained an interest in the U.S.-EU hormone dispute because of the concerns raised by some U.S. importers that have been affected by the United States' active and ongoing trade sanctions against the European Union, which have effectively restricted U.S. imports of selected EU products. Previously, in 1999 and 2000, then-Representative Menendez introduced two bills that would exempt certain small importing businesses from higher tariffs imposed against EU products under the U.S.-EU beef hormone dispute.[113]

In addition, the dispute continues to be raised as an issue under current negotiations between the United States and EU seeking to establish a free trade area as part of the Transatlantic Trade and Investment Partnership (TTIP). Some Members of Congress have expressed the expectation that the negotiations might resolve some long-standing trade disputes regarding SPS rules between the two trading blocs, including the the beef hormone dispute. However, early indications are that the EU is not likely to change its regulations prohibiting imports of meat raised with growth promotants (see discussion in section "2009 Memorandum of Understanding").[114]

Final resolution of the hormone dispute could remove a critical irritant to the overall U.S.-EU trade relationship.[115] In addition, the way in which this dispute is ultimately resolved could have important implications for future WTO disputes involving the use of SPS measures to restrict trade. The 1997 WTO meat hormone decision was the first to deal with SPS measures and, along with subsequent decisions, it provided an affirmation of the SPS Agreement and its requirements that countries base SPS measures on scientific justification and risk assessment. Beyond that, the case is a critical test of the durability of internationally agreed-upon rules and procedures for resolving disputes that are in conflict with popular concerns and national political decisions.

APPENDIX A. INITIAL RETALIATION LIST (JULY 1999)

HTS	Articles the product of Austria, Belgium, Denmark, Finland, France, Germany, Greece, Ireland, Italy, Luxembourg, the Netherlands, Portugal, Spain, or Sweden	Duty
9903.02.21	Meat of bovine animals, fresh or chilled (provided for in heading 0201); Articles of subheading 0201.10.05, 0201.10.10, 0201.20.02, 0201.20.04, 0201.20.06, 0201.20.10, 0201.20.30, 0201.20.50, 0201.30.02, 0201.30.04, 0201.30.06, 0201.30.10, 0201.30.30 or 0201.30.50	100%
9903.02.22	Articles of subheading 0201.10.50, 0201.20.80 or 0201.30.80	100%
9903.02.23	Meat of bovine animals, frozen (provided for in heading 0202); Articles of subheading 0202.10.05, 0202.10.10, 0202.20.02, 0202.20.04, 0202.20.06, 0202.20.10, 0202.20.30, 0202.20.50, 0202.30.02, 0202.30.04, 0202.30.06, 0202.30.10, 0202.30.30 or 0202.30.50	100%
9903.02.24	Articles of subheading 0202.10.50, 0202.20.80 or 0202.30.80.	100%
9903.02.25	Meat of swine, fresh or chilled (provided for in subheading 0203.11, 0203.12, or 0203.19)	100%
9903.02.26	Carcasses and half-carcasses of swine, frozen (provided for in subheading 0203.21)	100%
9903.02.27	Hams, shoulders and cuts with bone in, of swine, frozen (provided in subheading 0203.22)	100%
9903.02.28	Edible offal of bovine animals, fresh or chilled (provided for in subheading 0206.10)	100%
9903.02.29	Edible offal of bovine animals, frozen (provided for in subheading 0206.21, 0206.22 or 0206.29)	100%
9903.02.30	Roquefort cheese (provided for in subheading 0406.40.20 or 0406.40.40)	100%
9903.02.31	Onions (other than onion sets or pearl onions not over 16 mm in diameter) and shallots, fresh or chilled (provided for in subheading 0703.10.40)	100%
9903.02.32	Truffles, fresh or chilled (provided for in subheading 0709.52)	100%
9903.02.33	Dried carrots, whole, cut, sliced, broken or in powder, but not further prepared (provided for in subheading 0712.90.10)	100%
9903.02.34	Other prepared or preserved meat, meat offal or blood, of liver of any animal (provided for in subheading 1602.20)	100%
9903.02.35	Rusks, toasted bread and similar toasted products (provided for in subheading 1905.40)	100%
9903.02.36	Juices of any other single fruit, not elsewhere specified or included, not fortified with vitamins or minerals, unfermented and not containing added spirit, whether or not containing added sugar or other sweetening matter (provided for in subheading 2009.80.60)	100%

HTS	Articles the product of Austria, Belgium, Denmark, Finland, France, Germany, Greece, Ireland, Italy, Luxembourg, the Netherlands, Portugal, Spain, or Sweden	Duty
9903.02.37	Roasted chicory and other roasted coffee substitutes and extracts, essences and concentrates thereof (provided for in subheading 2101.30)	100%
9903.02.38	Prepared mustard (provided for in subheading 2103.30.40)	100%
HTS	**Articles the product of France, Germany, or Italy**	**Duty**
9903.02.39	Tomatoes prepared or preserved otherwise than by vinegar or acetic acid, whole or in pieces (provided for in subheading 2002.10)	100%
HTS	**Articles the product of France and Germany**	**Duty**
9903.02.40	Guts, bladders and stomachs of animals (other than fish), whole and pieces thereof, fresh, chilled, frozen, salted, in brine, dried or smoked (provided for in heading 0504)	100%
9903.02.41	Soups and broths and preparations (provided for in subheading 2104.10)	100%
9903.02.42	Single yarn (other than sewing thread), not put up for retail sale, containing 85% or more by weight of artificial staple fibers (provided for in subheading 5510.11)	100%
HTS	**Articles the product of France**	**Duty**
9903.02.43	Hams, shoulders and cuts of meat with of swine, with bone in, salted, in brine, dried or smoked (provided for in subheading 0210.11)	100%
9903.02.44	Wool grease (other than crude wool grease) and fatty substances derived from wool grease (including lanolin) (provided for in subheading 1505.90)	100%
9903.02.45	Chocolate and other food preparations containing cocoa, in blocks, slabs or bars, filled, weighing 2 kg or less each (provided for in subheading 1806.31)	100%
9903.02.46	Lingonberry and raspberry jams (provided for in subheading 2007.99.05)	100%
9903.02.47	Products suitable for use as glues or adhesives (other than animal glue, including casein glue, but not including fish glue) put up for retail sale as glues or adhesives, not exceeding a net weight of 1 kg (provided for in subheading 3506.10.50)	100%

Source: 64 *Federal Register* 40638, July 27, 1999. Does not include the United Kingdom. In May 2011, USTR announced it was terminating higher duties for these imported products (76 *Federal Register* 30989, May 27, 2011).

APPENDIX B. REVISED RETALIATION LIST (JANUARY 2009)

HTS	Articles the product of Austria, Belgium, Denmark, Finland, France, Germany, Greece, Ireland, Italy, Luxembourg, the Netherlands, Portugal, Spain, or Sweden (added: Bulgaria, Cyprus, Czech Republic, Estonia, Hungary, Latvia, Lithuania, Malta, Poland, Romania, Slovakia, Slovenia)	Duty
9903.02.48	Meat of bovine animals, fresh or chilled (provided for in heading 0201); Articles of subheading 0201.10.05, 0201.10.10, 0201.20.02, 0201.20.04, 0201.20.06, 0201.20.10, 0201.20.30, 0201.20.50, 0201.30.02, 0201.30.04, 0201.30.06, 0201.30.10, 0201.30.30 or 0201.30.50	100%

(Continued)

HTS	Articles the product of Austria, Belgium, Denmark, Finland, France, Germany, Greece, Ireland, Italy, Luxembourg, the Netherlands, Portugal, Spain, or Sweden (added: Bulgaria, Cyprus, Czech Republic, Estonia, Hungary, Latvia, Lithuania, Malta, Poland, Romania, Slovakia, Slovenia)	Duty
9903.02.49	Articles of subheading 0201.10.50, 0201.20.80 or 0201.30.80	100%
9903.02.50	Meat of bovine animals, frozen (provided for in heading 0202); Articles of subheading 0202.10.05, 0202.10.10, 0202.20.02, 0202.20.04, 0202.20.06, 0202.20.10, 0202.20.30, 0202.20.50, 0202.30.02, 0202.30.04, 0202.30.06, 0202.30.10, 0202.30.30 or 0202.30.50	100%
9903.02.51	Articles of subheading 0202.10.50, 0202.20.80 or 0202.30.80.	100%
9903.02.52	Meat of swine, fresh or chilled (subheading 0203.11, 0203.12, or 0203.19)	100%
9903.02.53	Carcasses and half-carcasses of swine, frozen (provided for in subheading 0203.21)	100%
9903.02.54	Hams, shoulders and cuts with bone in, of swine, frozen (subheading 0203.22)	100%
9903.02.55	Processed meat of swine, frozen, other than carcasses and half-carcasses of swine and other than hams, shoulders, and cuts thereof, with bone in (provided for in subheading 0203.29.20).	100%
9903.02.56	Edible offal of bovine animals, fresh or chilled (provided for in subheading 0206.10)	100%
9903.02.57	Edible offal of bovine animals, frozen (subheading 0206.21, 0206.22 or 0206.29)	100%
9903.02.58	Meat and edible offal, of the poultry of heading 0105, fresh, chilled or frozen (provided for in heading 0207)	100%
9903.02.59	Hams, shoulders, and cuts thereof, with bone in, of swine, salted, in brine, dried or smoked (provided for in subheading 0210.11)	100%
9903.02.60	Meat of bovine animals, salted, in brine, dried or smoked (subheading 0210.20)	100%
9903.02.61	Meat of poultry of heading 0105, salted, in brine, dried or smoked (provided for in subheading 0210.99.20).	100%
9903.02.62	Roquefort cheese (provided for in subheading 0406.40.20 or 0406.40.40)	300%
9903.02.63	Foliage, branches and other parts of plants, without flowers or flower buds, and grasses, being goods of a kind suitable for bouquets or for ornamental purposes, fresh, dried or bleached (provided for in subheading 0604.91 or 0604.99.30).	100%
9903.02.64	Truffles, fresh or chilled (provided for in subheading 0709.52)	100%
9903.02.65	Rolled or flaked grains of oats (provided for in subheading 1104.12)	100%
9903.02.66	Grains of oats, hulled, pearled, sliced, kibbled or otherwise worked, not elsewhere specified or included (provided for in subheading 1104.22)	100%
9903.02.67	Sausages and similar products of beef, and food preparations based on these products, in airtight containers (provided for in subheading 1601.00.40)	100%
9903.02.68	Other prepared or preserved meat, meat offal or blood, of liver of any animal (provided for in subheading 1602.20)	100%
9903.02.69	Other prepared or preserved meat, meat offal or blood, of poultry of heading 0105 (provided for in subheading 1602.31, 1602.32, 1602.39)	100%
9903.02.70	Other prepared or preserved meat, meat offal or blood, of bovine animals (provided for in subheading 1602.50)	100%

HTS	Articles the product of Austria, Belgium, Denmark, Finland, France, Germany, Greece, Ireland, Italy, Luxembourg, the Netherlands, Portugal, Spain, or Sweden (added: Bulgaria, Cyprus, Czech Republic, Estonia, Hungary, Latvia, Lithuania, Malta, Poland, Romania, Slovakia, Slovenia)	Duty
9903.02.71	Chewing gum, whether or not sugar-coated, not containing cocoa (provided for in subheading 1704.10)	100%
9903.02.72	Chocolate and other food preparations containing cocoa, in blocks, slabs or bars, filled, weighing 2 kg or less each (provided for in subheading 1806.31)	100%
9903.02.73	Lingonberry and raspberry jams (provided for in subheading 2007.99.05)	100%
9903.02.74	Pears, otherwise prepared or preserved, whether or not containing added sugar or other sweetening matter or spirit, nesi (provided for in subheading 2008.40)	100%
9903.02.75	Peaches, excl. nectarines, otherwise prepared/preserved, whether or not containing added sugar or other sweetening matter or spirit, nesi (subheading 2008.70.20)	100%
HTS	**Articles the product of Finland, France, Ireland, the Netherlands, Sweden**	**Duty**
9903.02.76	Meat of swine, frozen, not processed, other than carcasses and half-carcasses of swine and other than hams, shoulders, and cuts thereof, with bone in (provided for in subheading 0203.29.40)	100%
HTS	**Articles the product of France**	**Duty**
9903.02.77	Chestnuts (*Castanea* spp.), fresh or dried, whether or not shelled or peeled (provided for in subheading 0802.40)	100%
9903.02.78	Wool grease (other than crude wool grease) and fatty substances derived from wool grease (including lanolin) (provided for in subheading 1505.00.90)	100%
HTS	**Articles the product of Austria, Cyprus, France or Poland**	**Duty**
9903.02.79	Grape juice (including grape must), not fortified with vitamins or minerals, unfermented and not containing added spirit, whether or not containing added sugar or other sweetening matter (provided for in subheading 2009.61 or 2009.69)	100%
9903.02.80	Juices of any other single fruit, nesi, not fortified with vitamins or minerals, unfermented and not containing added spirit, whether or not containing added sugar or other sweetening matter (provided for in subheading 2009.80.60)	100%
9903.02.81	Mixtures of juices, other than mixtures of vegetable juices, not fortified with vitamins or minerals, unfermented and not containing added spirit, whether or not containing added sugar or other sweetening matter (provided for in subheading 2009.90.40)	100%
HTS	**Articles the product of Italy**	**Duty**
9903.02.81	Mineral waters and aerated waters, not containing added sugar or other sweetening matter nor flavored (provided for in subheading 2201.10).	100%

Source: 74 *Federal Register* 4264, January 23, 2009. In September 2009, USTR announced it was officially terminating its plan to rotate the list of products (74 *Federal Register* 48808, September 24, 2009).

APPENDIX C. "REDUCED" PRODUCT LIST (MARCH 2009)

Articles the product of Austria, Belgium, Denmark, Finland, France, Germany, Greece, Ireland, Italy, Luxembourg, the Netherlands, Portugal, Spain, or Sweden	Duty
Meat of bovine animals, fresh or chilled (provided for in heading 0201); Articles of subheading 0201.10.05, 0201.10.10, 0201.20.02, 0201.20.04, 0201.20.06, 0201.20.10, 0201.20.30, 0201.20.50, 0201.30.02, 0201.30.04, 0201.30.06, 0201.30.10, 0201.30.30 or 0201.30.50	100%
Articles of subheading 0201.10.50, 0201.20.80 or 0201.30.80	100%
Meat of bovine animals, frozen (provided for in heading 0202); Articles of subheading 0202.10.05, 0202.10.10, 0202.20.02, 0202.20.04, 0202.20.06, 0202.20.10, 0202.20.30, 0202.20.50, 0202.30.02, 0202.30.04, 0202.30.06, 0202.30.10, 0202.30.30 or 0202.30.50	100%
Articles of subheading 0202.10.50, 0202.20.80 or 0202.30.80.	100%
Meat of swine, fresh or chilled (provided for in subheading 0203.11, 0203.12, or 0203.19)	100%
Carcasses and half-carcasses of swine, frozen (provided for in subheading 0203.21)	100%
Hams, shoulders and cuts with bone in, of swine, frozen (provided in subheading 0203.22)	100%
Edible offal of bovine animals, fresh or chilled (provided for in subheading 0206.10)	100%
Edible offal of bovine animals, frozen (provided for in subheading 0206.21, 0206.22 or 0206.29)	100%
Roquefort cheese (provided for in subheading 0406.40.20 or 0406.40.40)	100%
Truffles, fresh or chilled (provided for in subheading 0709.52)	100%
Other prepared or preserved meat, meat offal or blood, of liver of any animal (provided for in subheading 1602.20)	100%
Articles the product of Austria and France	**Duty**
Juices of any other single fruit, not elsewhere specified or included, not fortified with vitamins or minerals, unfermented and not containing added spirit, whether or not containing added sugar or other sweetening matter (provided for in subheading 2009.80.60)	100%
Articles the product of France	**Duty**
Hams, shoulders and cuts of meat with of swine, with bone in, salted, in brine, dried or smoked (provided for in subheading 0210.11)	100%
Wool grease (other than crude wool grease) and fatty substances derived from wool grease (including lanolin) (provided for in subheading 1505.90)	100%
Chocolate and other food preparations containing cocoa, in blocks, slabs or bars, filled, weighing 2 kg or less each (provided for in subheading 1806.31)	100%
Lingonberry and raspberry jams (provided for in subheading 2007.99.05)	100%

Source: 74 *Federal Register* 40864, August 13, 2009; and 74 *Federal Register* 48808, September 24, 2009. Trade sanctions were to remain in effect on certain EU exports (listed in **Appendix C**) until the final phase of the MOU; however, in May 2011, USTR announced it was terminating higher duties for imported products under the dispute (76 *Federal Register* 30989, May 27, 2011).

Appendix D. Chronology of the U.S.-EU Beef Hormone Dispute

1981-1988—The European Commission institutes a series of restrictions on livestock production (Directives 81/602, 88/146, and 88/299) limiting the use of natural hormones to therapeutic purposes, banning the use of synthetic hormones, and prohibiting imports of animals and meat from animals that have been administered with hormones.

Between 1986-1987, the United States raises the EU hormone ban in the Committee on Technical Barriers to Trade ("Standards Code"), and invokes dispute settlement under the Tokyo Round Agreement on Technical Barriers to Trade in the General Agreement on Tariffs and Trade (GATT). The EU delays implementing its ban until January 1, 1989. In late 1987, President Reagan announces, and suspends, retaliatory tariffs (100% *ad valorem*) on about $100 million worth of EU imports.

Also during this time, various scientific reviews are initiated, including studies by the commission, the Joint Expert Committee on Food Additives (JECFA) of the World Health Organization and the United Nations Food and Agriculture Organization, the Committee on Veterinary Drugs of the Codex Alimentarius Commission ("Codex"), and the U.S. Food and Drug Administration and comparable institutions in other countries.

1989—The EU fully implements its ban on meat and meat product imports from animals treated with six growth promotants, three of which are naturally occurring—estradiol-17β, progesterone and testosterone—and three of which are synthetic—zeranol, trenbolone, and melengestrol. These six hormones are approved for use in the United States. The EU's ban effectively cuts off U.S. beef exports to the European Union. The United States institutes retaliatory tariffs (100% *ad valorem*) on EU imports valued at $93 million, which remain in effect until May 1996, when the EU seeks a WTO panel against the U.S. action.

1995—The GATT Uruguay Round Agreement, including the Sanitary and Phytosanitary (SPS) Agreement, enters into force. Codex decides Maximum Residue Limits (MRLs) are not necessary for the three natural hormones and adopts MRLs for the two synthetics. The EU concludes that there is no evidence of health risk from the five hormones approved for use in the United States.

1996—The EU votes to maintain the ban. The United States requests a WTO dispute settlement panel case against the EU, claiming the ban is inconsistent with the EU's WTO obligations. Australia, Canada, and New Zealand join the United States in the complaint. The commission issues a new Directive 96/22, which repeals the 1981 and 1988 directives, and confirms and extends the prohibitions. The law becomes effective July 1, 1997.

1997—AWTO dispute settlement panel releases its report, ruling that the EU ban on the use of hormones to promote the growth of cattle is inconsistent with its obligations under the SPS Agreement (specifically, Articles 3.1, 5.1, and 5.5), in that the ban is not based on science, that is, on an adequate risk assessment or according to relevant international standards. The EU appeals the dispute panel's decision and also initiates a series of scientific studies on these six hormones.

1998—The WTO Appellate Body (AB) upholds the dispute panel's decision but overrules some panel findings. The AB decides the EU had not scientifically proven that the hormones in question posed a cancer risk to consumers; the AB also acknowledges that countries may adopt stricter standards, if supported by an adequate risk assessment. The AB rules the EU ban does not constitute a hidden barrier to international trade. The WTO Dispute Settlement Body (DSB) adopts the panel decision and the AB rulings on the ban. The EU says it will implement the WTO ruling in "as short a time as possible." Neither party is able to agree on a "reasonable period of time" for implementation; the arbitrator decides the EU needs 15 months (until May 13, 1999).

1999—In February, the EU outlines three options to resolve the dispute: (1) compensation, (2) removal of the ban coupled with a suitable labeling system, and (3) the conversion of the ban to a temporary measure. The United States sends a letter to EC Commissioners of Agriculture and of Trade outlining a possible labeling system. The United States backed by most of the U.S. beef industry, decides against various compensation measures, preferring instead removal of the ban. The EU decides it wants to conduct additional risk reviews before considering removing the ban. In March, the U.S. announces it will consider trade sanctions against the EU and publishes a preliminary list of products that could be subject to increased tariffs if the dispute is not resolved.

In April, the EU issues its first review and opinion based on studies by the EU's Scientific Committee on Veterinary Measures relating to Public Health (SCVPH) on the potential human health risks associated with consumption of hormone-treated beef. The SCVPH opinion states that it has evidence to show that a growth hormone (estradiol-17β) used in U.S. cattle production is carcinogenic, among other potential health risks to consumers. The report draws criticism from the United Kingdom's Veterinary Products Committee, as outlined in a report.

The EU deadline for implementing the AB ruling expires on May 13. In July, the United States and Canada seek WTO authorization to suspend tariff concessions and retaliate against the European Union. The WTO sets the levels at $116.8 million (United States) and C$11.3 million (Canada). The Office of the U.S. Trade Representative (USTR) announces its decision to impose a 100% *ad valorem* rate of duty on a specified list of products from certain EU member states, effective July 29. The product list includes beef, pork, goose livers, cheese, truffles, onions, carrots, preserved tomatoes, sausage casings, soups, yarn, mustard, juice, chicory, toasted breads, chocolate, jams, glue, and wool grease. The U.S. list targets France, Germany, Italy, and Denmark, but excludes the United Kingdom.

2000—In May, the EU issues its second review and opinion based on studies by the EU's SCVPH on the potential human health risks associated with consumption of hormone-treated beef. The review concludes that the new information does "not provide convincing data and arguments demanding revision of the conclusions" of the SCVPH April 1999 opinion on the "potential risks to human health from hormone residues in bovine meat and meat products."

Congress passes legislation as part of the Trade and Development Act of 2000 (P.L. 106-200), requiring the USTR to review and periodically revise the list of products subject to retaliation when another country fails to implement a WTO dispute decision. This periodic revision of the product list has become known as "carousel retaliation."

2001—The commission provides documentation of studies and journals for publications. The United States and European Union initiate compensation discussions.

2002—In April, the EU issues its third review and opinion based on studies by the EU's SCVPH on the potential human health risks associated with consumption of hormone-treated beef. The review concludes its review of the 17 studies initiated in 1998, and again confirms the previous findings of the two earlier reviews (1999 and 2000).

2003—In September, the commission issues Directive 2003/74, amending 96/22. The new law permanently bans the use of estradiol in farm animals and provisionally bans use of the five other hormones, while it seeks more complete scientific information. The EU declares its effort to replace its original ban with a provisional ban is in compliance with its WTO obligations, citing Article 5.7 of the SPS Agreement (allows for provisional measures when there is insufficient scientific evidence, provided that a risk assessment is conducted within a reasonable time).

In October, the EU issues a press release claiming its ban is supported by the 1999 and 2002 SCVPH reviews, which constitute "a thorough risk assessment based on current scientific knowledge" and thus fulfill its WTO obligations. The United States questions whether the SCVPH studies constitute a risk assessment. The EU claims the United States and Canada have no legal basis for continuing trade sanctions against the EU. In December, the EU refers the dispute to the WTO for a multilateral decision.

2004-2005—The EU initiates a new dispute claiming that because it has modified its ban, the United States (and Canada) should remove its trade sanctions against the EU, as the continued retaliation by the United States and Canada is no longer consistent with WTO rules. The United States and Canada cases are effectively merged under the one panel cases, given largely identical substance, even though they are technically separate. Australia and Mexico join the consultations. The EU requests that a new WTO panel be established and the substantive panel meeting takes place in September 2005. It is the first WTP panel open for observation by the public.

2006—The WTO panel announces that due to the complexity of the dispute, and the administrative and procedural matters involved, the panel will not complete its work until October 2006.

The United Kingdom's Veterinary Products Committee issues a second report criticizing the SCVPH findings.

In October, USTR decides against revising the list of EU products subject to higher U.S. import tariffs under the dispute. This decision is supported by the National Cattlemen's Beef Association and the U.S. Meat Export Federation. The U.S. Court of International Trade determines this action meets requirements under "carousel retaliation."

2007—The WTO panel again announces that due to the complexity of the scientific issues involved and scheduling difficulties, the panel's final report is delayed until June 2007.

In June, the European Food Safety Authority (EFSA) adopts an opinion related to hormone residues in bovine meat and meat products based on its review of the scientific data. EFSA concludes that the new publicly available data do not provide quantitative information for a risk assessment and therefore do not call for a revision of previous risk assessments.

In July, the WTO panel issues its interim report, including findings and conclusions. The expected final report date is delayed until October 2007, and eventually is issued in December.

2008—In March, the WTO panel report is circulated to members. The panel announces that it found fault with all three parties (EU, United States, and Canada) on various substantive and procedural aspects of the dispute. The panel report claims the EU had not presented sufficient scientific evidence to justify the import ban, including the EU's 2003 risk assessment report. The panel report faults the United States and Canada for maintaining its trade sanctions. Both parties file appeals citing procedural errors and disagreements with the panel findings.

In October, the WTO's AB issues a mixed ruling that allows for continued imposition of trade sanctions on the EU by the United States and Canada, but also grants that the EU can continue to ban imports of hormone-treated beef from the United States and Canada. The AB reverses the dispute panel decision by stating that the EU's ban is not incompatible with WTO law, thus granting the EU more deference in deciding the basis for its food safety regulations.

The USTR announces in October that it is seeking comment on possible modification of the list of EU products subject to increased tariffs under the dispute. In December 2008, the EU requests consultations under Article 21.5 of the DSU to determine whether it is in compliance with its WTO obligations in the underlying beef hormone dispute.

2009—In January, USTR announces changes to the list of EU products subject to increased tariffs under the dispute, adding countries and raising the tariff on select products, effective March 23, 2009. The EU claims USTR's action constitutes an "escalation" of the dispute, and is "more punitive" than the current trade sanctions. In May 2009, following a series of negotiations, the United States and the EU sign a memorandum of understanding (MOU) in an attempt to resolve this long-standing dispute by further opening up the EU market to non-hormone treated beef. The terms of this agreement are to be phased in over the next few years.

As part of Phase 1 of the MOU, the EC adopted regulations opening a tariff quota for 20,000 metric tons imports of high-quality beef (HQB), effective August 2009. The United States agreed not to implement its January 2009 revised ("carousel") sanctions, which would have resulted in higher retaliatory duties on selected EU exports to the United States. Trade sanctions would remain in effect on certain EU exports until the final phase of the agreement.

2010—In October 2010, a U.S. Court of Appeals issued a decision in a case regarding duties paid by importers from the EU under the dispute, which could make them eligible for refunds.

2011—In May 2011, USTR announced it was suspending higher duties for imported products listed under the dispute, ahead of the scheduled date under the MOU.

2012—As part of Phase 2 of the MOU, in June 2012, the EU issued regulations increasing the HQB quota to 48,200 MT and changing the quota management system to a "first come, first served" basis, fully effective by August 2012.

2013—In October 2013, the EU approved a two-year extension of Phase 2 of the MOU, allowing for access of U.S. beef raised without the use of growth promotants in exchange for continued U.S. suspension of retaliatory import duties on some EU food products. The extension will remain in place until August 2015.

Sources: Compiled by CRS from various USDA and WTO documents, and other information.

End Notes

[1] National Cattlemen's Beef Association (NCBA), "Fact Sheet: Growth Promotant Use in Cattle Production."

[2] USDA, Food Safety and Inspection Service, "Beef ... from Farm to Table." The implanted hormone is time-released and is effective for 90 to 120 days.

[3] Information on approved hormone products is at 21 CFR Parts 522, 556, and 558. For information on FDA requirements for the review and approval of new animal drug applications, see http://www.fda.gov/ AnimalVeterinary/ DevelopmentApprovalProcess/NewAnimalDrugApplications/ default. htm. Also see FDA's online "Green Book," http://www.fda.gov/animalveterinary/products/ approvedanimaldrugproducts/ default.htm.

[4] Council Directives 81/602 (July 1981), 88/146 (7 March 1988), 88/299 (17 May 1988).

[5] Directive 2003/74 (Sept. 22, 2003), amending Council Directive 96/22 concerning the prohibition on the use in stockfarming of certain substances having a hormonal or thyrostatic action and of beta-agonists. Directive 96/22 repealed the original regulations (81/602, 88/146 and 88/299).

[6] See WTO, "SPS Agreement Training Module, Chapter 8: The Precautionary Principle," http://www.wto.org/ english/ tratop_e/sps_e/sps_agreement_cbt_e/c8s2p1_e.htm.

[7] T. Josling, D. Roberts, and A. Hassan, "The Beef-Hormone Dispute and its Implications for Trade Policy," Stanford University, 2000. DES use in cattle production is also banned in the United States.

[8] See CRS Report RL32199, *Bovine Spongiform Encephalopathy (BSE, or "Mad Cow Disease"): Current and Proposed Safeguards*, and CRS Report RS21709, *Mad Cow Disease and U.S. Beef Trade*.

[9] See CRS Report RS21556, *Agricultural Biotechnology: The U.S.-EU Dispute*, and CRS Report RL33334, *Biotechnology in Animal Agriculture: Status and Current Issues*.

[10] In the 1980s, observers suggested that EU beef surpluses were so large that policy makers were likely to support any measure that might limit imports likely to compete with domestic production and interfere with operating the CAP.

[11] See CRS Report RL31860, *U.S.-European Union Disputes in the World Trade Organization*.

[12] In 1999 the commission voted unanimously to continue its ban, with only the Agriculture Minister of the United Kingdom voting to end the ban.

[13] WTO, "European Communities—Measures Concerning Meat and Meat Products (Hormones)," Dispute DS26. Canada initiated a similar action (Dispute DS48).

[14] WTO, "The WTO Agreement on the Application of Sanitary and Phytosanitary Measures (SPS Agreement)."

[15] Delegation of the European Commission to the USA, "EU complies with WTO ruling on Hormone beef, calls on US and Canada to lift trade sanctions," Press Release EU/NR 61/03, October 15, 2003.

[16] Article 5.7 of the SPS Agreement provides that "Members shall seek to obtain the additional information necessary for a more objective assessment of the risk, and review the sanitary and phytosanitary measures accordingly within a reasonable period of time." See http://www.wto.int/english/tratop_e/sps_e/spsagr_e.htm.

[17] See, for example, "United States—Continued Suspension of Obligations in the EC-Hormones Dispute," WT/DS320, First Written Submission of the United States of America, August 8, 2005.

[18] EC, "EU complies with WTO ruling on hormone beef and calls on USA and Canada to lift trade sanctions," October 15, 2003.

[19] WTO, "United States—Continued Suspension of Obligations in the EC-Hormones Dispute," Dispute DS320. Canada requested to join the consultations, along with Australia and Mexico. The case against Canada is under Dispute DS321.

[20] There were separate panel reports and separate Appellate Body reports for Canada and the United States.

[21] For information on Article 21.5, see http://www.wto.org/english/res_e/booksp_e/analytic_index_e/dsu_08_e.htm.

[22] "Burden of Proof in Compliance Cases Unclear in Hormone Ruling," *Inside US Trade*, October 31, 2008.

[23] SCVPH is one of the scientific committees providing the EC with scientific advice on food safety on issues transferred to the European Food Safety Authority (EFSA).

[24] EC, *Opinion of the Scientific Committee on Veterinary Measures Relating to Public Health Assessment of Potential Risks to Human Health from Hormone Residues in Bovine Meat and Meat Products*, April 30, 1999. Also see EC summary, "Hormones In Bovine Meat," http://ec.europa.eu/dgs/health_consumer/library/press/press57_en.pdf.

[25] EC, *Review of Specific Documents Relating to the SCVPH Opinion of 30 April 99 on the Potential Risks to Human Health from Hormone Residues in Bovine Meat and Meat Products*, May 3, 2000.

[26] EC, *Opinion of the Scientific Committee on Veterinary Measures Relating to Public Health On Review of Previous SCVPH Opinions of 30 April 1999 and 3 May 2000 on the Potential Risks to Human Health from Hormone Residues in Bovine Meat and Meat Products*, April 10, 2002.

[27] EFSA was created in January 2002 as part of a comprehensive program to improve EU food safety and ensure consumer protection and confidence, providing scientific advice and communication on food-borne risks.

[28] EFSA, *Opinion of the Scientific Panel on Contaminants in the Food Chain On a Request from the European Commission Related to Hormone Residues in Bovine Meat and Meat Products*, EFSA-Q-2005-048, June 12, 2007.

[29] Ibid.

[30] EFSA, "EFSA Concludes Review of New Scientific Data on Potential Risks to Human Health from Certain Hormone Residues in Beef," Press Release dated July 18, 2007.

[31] USDA, Foreign Agriculture Service, *Historic Overview and Chronology of EU's Hormone Ban*, GAIN Report E23206, November 7, 2003.

[32] "United States – Continued Suspension of Obligations in the EC-Hormones Dispute," WT/DS320, First Written Submission of the United States of America, August 8, 2005.

[33] World Health Organization (WHO), *Evaluation of certain veterinary drug residues in food* (32nd JECFA report), WHO Technical Report Series, No. 763, 1988 (et seq.), http://whqlibdoc.who.int/trs/WHO_TRS_763.pdf. JECFA is an international scientific expert committee that is administered jointly by the United Nations Food and Agriculture Organization (FAO) and WHO. Its mission is to evaluate the safety of food additives, contaminants, naturally occurring toxicants, and residues of veterinary drugs in food.

[34] Codex Alimentarius Commission (CAC), *Report of the 8th Session of the Codex Committee on Residues of Veterinary Drugs in Foods*, July 1995. CAC develops food standards, guidelines and codes of practice under the Joint FAO/WHO Food Standards Programme.

[35] European Commission, Proceedings of the Scientific Conference on Growth Promotion in Meat Production, November 29, 1995 (Office for Official Publications for the European Communities, Brussels).

[36] A subcommittee of the European Medicines Agency (EMEA), which coordinates the evaluation and supervision of medicinal products throughout the European Union.

[37] UK's Veterinary Products Committee, "VPC Report - Risk Associated with the Use of Hormonal Substances in Food Producing Animals," July 2006, and "Sub Group on Hormonal Growth Promoters" October 1999. Also see USDA, *UK scientific report questions EU position on beef hormones*, GAIN Report UK6022, July 7, 2006.

[38] Australian Pesticides and Veterinary Medicines Authority, "A Review to Update Australia's Position on the Human Safety of Residues of Hormone Growth Promotants (HGPs) Used in Cattle," July 2003.

[39] As reported in "United States – Continued Suspension of Obligations in the EC-Hormones Dispute," WT/DS320, First Written Submission of the United States of America, August 8, 2005. The EU-commissioned group also concluded that that limitations on the use of such hormones "are a reasonable safeguard of public health."

[40] WTO, "EC Measures Concerning Meat and Meat Products (Hormones) - Complaint by the United States - Report of the Panel," WT/DS26/R/USA, August 18, 1987.

[41] USDA's Foreign Agricultural Service (FAS), U.S. Mission to the European Union, "WTO Hormone Case."

[42] FAS, *EU Presentation on Hormone Ban Directive (2003/74/EC)*, GAIN Report E23217, November 13, 2003.

[43] NCBA, NCBA Statement On WTO Report On EU Ban of Hormone-Treated Beef, October 16, 2008.

[44] See, for example, "Coalition Statement on EU's Latest Pronouncement on Hormones," May 14, 2002 by AFBF, AHI, AMI, and NCBA, http://www.meatami.com/ht/d/sp/i/1482/pid/1482.

[45] FAS, *Historic Overview and Chronology of EU's Hormone Ban*, GAIN Report E23206, November 7, 2003.

[46]WTO, "European Communities - Measures Concerning Meat And Meat Products (Hormones)," WT/DS26/21, July 15, 1999.

[47] 64 *Federal Register* 40638, July 27, 1999.

[48] USTR, "WTO's Appellate Body Vindicates Continued U.S. Imposition of Sanctions after the EU Claimed Compliance in the EU-Hormones Dispute," October 16, 2008.

[49] See, for example, Clemens, Roxanne, "The EU-U.S. Hormone Dispute: The Negotiations Continue," *Iowa Ag Review*, Center for Agricultural and Rural Development, Spring 2002.

[50] *Cattlenetwork*, "Cattlemen's Capitol Concerns," September 2005.

[51] See, for example, letter from Senator Grassley to Pascal Lamy of the European Commission, November 18, 2004.

[52] The 2003 law permanently banned one hormone and provisionally banned the other five hormones, pending more detailed scientific assessments.

[53] It is aimed primarily at maintaining pressure on the EU to resolve the meat hormone dispute (and another U.S.-EU dispute over banana trade) by penalizing a wider range of foreign products and countries.

[54] USTR, *President's 2008 Policy Agenda*, Trade Enforcement Activities, March 2008. Section 306(b)(2) of the Trade Act provides that the USTR is not required to revise a retaliation list if the USTR, together with the affected United States industry, agrees that it is unnecessary to revise the retaliation list.

[55] Based on responses from food and textile groups, and some non-agricultural stakeholders.

[56] 74 *Federal Register* 4264, January 23, 2009.

[57] 73 *Federal Register* 66066, November 6, 2008, Annex I and Annex II list of products; and USTR, "USTR Seeks Public Comments on Possible Changes to Product List in EU-Beef Hormones Dispute," October 31, 2008.

[58] European Commission, "WTO Dispute Settlement: EU Prepares WTO Action over Trade Sanction Law," *Trade Issues*, January 15, 2009.

[59] U.S. Mission to the EU, "U.S. Announces Delay of Trade Action in Beef Hormones Dispute," March 13, 2009; USTR, "USTR Ron Kirk Announces Delay of Trade Action in Beef Hormones Dispute," April 22, 2009.

[60] "Two Major Hurdles Remain For U.S.-EU Beef Hormones Deal," *World Trade Online*, April 24, 2009.

[61] 74 *Federal Register* 40864, August 13, 2009.

[62] WTO, European Communities—Measures Concerning Meat And Meat Products (Hormones), Joint Communication from the European Communities and the United States, WT/DS26/28, September 30, 2009; 74 *Federal Register* 40864, August 13, 2009; 74 *Federal Register* 48808, September 24, 2009; and USTR press releases.

[63] See text box on next page for explanation of definition.

[64] ICTSD, "EU, U.S. Strike Provisional Deal to End 13-Year-Old Beef Dispute," May 13, 2009; and AFBF, statement by Bob Stallman, American Farm Bureau Federation, regarding the EU beef hormone agreement, May 7, 2009.

[65] Council Regulations No 617/2009 of 13 July 2009 opening an autonomous tariff quota for imports of high-quality beef.

[66] 74 *Federal Register* 48808, September 24, 2009.

[67] 76 *Federal Register* 30989, March 27, 2011.

[68] "U.S. to end retaliation in EU beef hormone dispute due to court ruling," *World Trade Online*, March 26, 2011.

[69] EU Regulation (EU) No 464/2012, increasing the high-quality beef (HQB) quota, and EU Regulation (EU) No 481/2012, changing the quota management system to a first come, first served system.

[70] USDA, FAS, *Changes to the EU High Quality Beef Quota Published*, GAIN Report E70024, June 12, 2012.

[71] European Communities—Measures Concerning Meat And Meat Products (Hormones), Joint Communication From the European Union and the United States, WT/DS26/29, April 17, 2014.

[72] U.S., EU Officials Sign Two-Year Extension of Non-Hormone Beef Quota," *World Trade Online*, October 24, 2013.

[73] See CRS Report R43450, *Sanitary and Phytosanitary (SPS) and Related Non-Tariff Barriers to Agricultural Trade*. For more general information about TTIP, see CRS Report R43387, *Transatlantic Trade and Investment Partnership (TTIP) Negotiations*.

[74] "High Bar for SPS Issues in U.S.-EU Talks," *World Trade Online*, November 6, 2013.

[75] "U.S. Says 'Successful' TTIP Deal Will Eliminate EU Barriers to Meat Exports," *Inside U.S. Trade*, March 11, 2014. Ractopamine is a feed additive that results in more lean meat production in animal raised for meat.

[76] "In Trade Talks, EU Says it Won't Budge on Hormones in Beef," *Agri-Pulse*, February 19, 2014.

[77] "EU Agriculture Council Approves TRQ for Hormone Beef Deal," *World Trade Online*, July 14, 2009; "EU-U.S. Beef Dispute: Talks Inching Towards Deal?" *AgraFacts*, March 18, 2009.

[78] "U.S., EU Explore Basis of Possible Beef Hormone Settlement," *Inside U.S. Trade*, February 27, 2009.

[79] Commission Regulation (EU) No 101/2013, published in the Official Journal on February 5, 2013. Also see EFSA, "Scientific Opinion on the evaluation of the safety and efficacy of lactic acid for the removal of microbial surface contamination of beef carcasses, cuts and trimmings," EFSA Journal 2011; 9(7):2317.

[80] For more information, see CRS Report R40199, *U.S.-EU Poultry Dispute on the Use of Pathogen Reduction Treatments (PRTs).*

[81] Invoking MFN status implies that level treatment or equal trade advantages should be accorded to all "most favored nation" trading partners.

[82] "A Challenge Over EU-US Beef Accord," *Washington Trade Daily*, June 22, 2009; and ICTSD, "New Issues Arise in EU-US Beef Trade Dispute," June 24, 2009. Also see comments by Uruguay at a WTO meeting: see WTO, "Minutes of Meeting" (meeting held June 19, 2009), WT/DSB/M/270, August 28, 2009.

[83] "Brazil eyes WTO challenge to EU beef quota rules," *Food Chemical News*, July 29, 2011.

[84] See CIT, *Gilda Industries Inc., v. the United States*, Slip Op 08-51, May 14, 2008, and other related case reports since 2004 at CIT's website (http://www.cit.uscourts.gov/). Toasted breads are imported to the U.S. under U.S. Harmonized Tariff Schedule (HTS) code 1905.40.

[85] "U.S. Appeals CIT Decision Ordering Refund of Duties Paid in Hormone Dispute," *International Trade Daily*, August 19, 2009.

[86] "U.S., EU Explore Basis of Possible Beef Hormone Settlement," *Inside U.S. Trade*, February 27, 2009.

[87] See CRS Report RS20088, *Dispute Settlement in the World Trade Organization (WTO): An Overview*.

[88] "U.S. Appeal Brief in Hormone Retaliation Case Due Next Month," Inside U.S. Trade, September 11, 2009; and "Importers File Suits Refund of Retaliatory Duties Paid Under Beef Hormone Dispute," *World Trade Online*, August 14, 2009. See also U.S. CIT, *Cheeseworks v. United States*, Court No. 09-00298, Case 1:09-cv-00298-N/A.

[89] "Federal Circuit Court Strikes Down Beef Hormone Dispute Retaliatory Tariffs," *Global Trade Alert*, October 2010.

[90] This is consistent with the approach recommended by the U.S. Meat Export Federation. See, for example, "USMEF: U.S. Pork, Beef Exports Defy Expectations," *High Plain Midwest Ag Journal*, December 16, 2008.

[91] Based on trade data reported by the U.S. International Trade Commission. U.S.-reported product exports to EU-27 countries, U.S. Harmonized Tariff Schedule (HTS) 0201 (fresh/chilled beef) and HTS 0202 (frozen beef).

[92] "U.S. hopes to ramp up beef import agreement ahead of schedule," *Agri-Pulse*, June 29, 2011.

[93] Global Trade Atlas data.

[94] "USMEF: U.S. Pork, Beef Exports Defy Expectations," *High Plain Midwest Ag Journal*, December 16, 2008.

[95] EC, Commission Regulation (EC) No 936/97 of 27 May 1997, opening and providing for the administration of tariff quotas for high-quality fresh, chilled, and frozen beef and for frozen buffalo meat, Official Journal L 137, May 28, 1997. Other affected country suppliers are Argentina, Australia, Brazil, Canada, New Zealand, Paraguay, and Uruguay.

[96] "U.S., EU reach provisional deal in beef dispute," *Meatingplace Online*, May 6, 2009.

[97] USMEF, "New EU Quota Has Positive Impact," *Cattle Buyers Weekly*, September 21, 2009.

[98] Global Trade Atlas data, EU-reported imports of HTS 0201 (fresh/chilled beef) and HTS 0202 (frozen beef).

[99] USDA, Agricultural Marketing Service, "Official Listing of Approved Sources of Non-Hormone Treated Cattle," http://www.ams.usda.gov/AMSv1.0/getfile?dDocName=STELPRD3107503. Last updated April 2014. Cattle management groups may include approved farms, ranches, and feedlots.

[100] USDA, Foreign Agricultural Service, U.S. Mission to European Union, "High Quality Beef Quota."

[101] USDA, FAS, EU-25 Livestock and Products, U.S. beef faces strong competition on the European market, *GAIN Report* E35178, September 8, 2005.

[102] See, for example, Clemens, Roxanne, "The EU-U.S. Hormone Dispute: The Negotiations Continue," *Iowa Ag Review*, Center for Agricultural and Rural Development, Spring 2002.

[103] "U.S., EU Look to Resolve Beef Fight by Increasing Hormone-free TRQ," *Inside U.S. Trade*, October 13, 2006.

[104] "U.S., EU Moved Closer to Beef Market Access Deal Last Year," *Inside U.S. Trade*, January 23, 2009.

[105] "U.S., EU Explore Basis of Possible Beef Hormone Settlement," *Inside U.S. Trade*, February 27, 2009; and "U.S., EU Look to Resolve Beef Fight by Increasing Hormone-free TRQ," *Inside U.S. Trade*, October 13, 2006.

[106] Ibid. In a different but related case, the U.S. also has a long-standing dispute with the EU over its refusal to accept U.S. imports of poultry treated with antimicrobial rinses (see CRS Report R40199, *U.S.-EU Poultry Dispute on the Use of Pathogen Reduction Treatments (PRTs)*).

[107] "U.S., EU Explore Basis of Possible Beef Hormone Settlement," *Inside U.S. Trade*, February 27, 2009.

[108] "EU Outlines Three Options for Compliance in WTO Hormone Dispute," *Inside U.S. Trade*, February 12, 1999.

[109] CRS calculations from USITC trade data for U.S. imports for selected products and countries subject to retaliatory tariffs due to U.S.-EU beef hormone dispute (**Appendix B**).

[110] See, for example, hearing of the House Committee on Ways and Means on the Implementation of the United States-Australia Free Trade Agreement, June 16, 2004, Statement of Leo McDonnell, Ranchers-Cattlemen Action Legal Fund-United Stockgrowers of America. Also see related bills S. 2328 and H.R. 4288 (Agriculture Export Enhancement Act of 1998, 105th Congress), H.R. 4761 (Uruguay Round Agreements

Compliance Act of 1998, 105th Congress), and H.R. 3050 (To prohibit imports into the United States of meat products from the European Union until certain unfair trade barriers are removed, 104th Congress).

[111] Subcommittee on Forestry, Conservation and Rural Revitalization, U.S. Senate Committee on Agriculture, Nutrition and Forestry, hearing on S. 2709, Trade Injury Compensation Act of 2000, September 25, 2000.

[112] For example, see H.J.Res. 80 and H.Con.Res. 26 (101st Congress) and S.Res. 277 (104th Congress).

[113] Two 106th Congress bills were H.R. 2106 and H.R. 4478 (as part of the Small Business Trade Protection Act).

[114] Additional information is in CRS Report R43450, *Sanitary and Phytosanitary (SPS) and Related Non-Tariff Barriers to Agricultural Trade.*

[115] See CRS Report RL30732, *Trade Conflict and the U.S.-European Union Economic Relationship*, and CRS Report RL34381, *European Union-U.S. Trade and Investment Relations: Key Issues, European Union-U.S. Trade and Investment Relations: Key Issues*.

In: Agricultural Trade
Editor: Rowan Stroud

ISBN: 978-1-63321-888-8

Chapter 3

U.S.-EU POULTRY DISPUTE ON THE USE OF PATHOGEN REDUCTION TREATMENTS (PRTS)*

Renée Johnson

SUMMARY

In January 2009, the outgoing Bush Administration escalated a long-running dispute with the European Union (EU) over its refusal to accept imports of U.S. poultry processed with certain pathogen reduction treatments (PRTs). Bush officials requested World Trade Organization (WTO) consultations with the EU on the matter, a prerequisite first step toward the establishment of a formal WTO dispute settlement panel. The U.S. poultry industry supported the WTO filing by the U.S. Trade Representative (USTR) and encouraged the Obama Administration to continue to pursue the case.

PRTs are antimicrobial rinses—including chlorine dioxide, acidified sodium chlorite, trisodium phosphate, and peroxyacids, among others—that have been approved by the U.S. Department of Agriculture (USDA) for use in poultry processing to reduce the amount of microbes on meat. Meat and poultry products processed with PRTs are judged safe by the United States and also by European food safety authorities. Nevertheless, the EU prohibits the use of PRTs and the importation of poultry treated with these substances. The EU generally opposes such chemical interventions and believes that stronger sanitary practices during production and processing are more appropriate for pathogen control than what it views as U.S. overreliance on PRTs.

As PRTs are widely used in U.S. poultry processing, the EU's ban on their use effectively prohibits U.S. poultry meat from entering EU countries. Prior to 1997, when the prohibition took effect, U.S. exports of broiler and turkey meat to the 15 countries that then constituted the EU totaled nearly 38,000 metric tons (MT), valued at $58 million. In 2011, U.S. exports to the same 15 countries were reported to be nearly 9,000 MT, valued at $13 million. USDA analysts believe that almost all of these U.S. exports represent "transshipments," meaning that Europe is not the intended final destination and that virtually no U.S. poultry meat is being purchased for the EU market. Now that the EU consists of 27 countries, it currently imports worldwide about $500 million of fresh, chilled, and frozen poultry meat annually (excluding intra-EU trade), most of which is

---

* This is an edited, reformatted and augmented version of a Congressional Research Service publication R40199, prepared for Members and Committees of Congress, dated January 9, 2014.

supplied by Brazil and other Latin American countries. Some estimate the U.S. loss of the EU poultry market at between $200 million and $300 million annually. Still, other foreign buyers continue to make the United States the second-largest exporter of poultry meat in the world, after Brazil.

Despite initial consultations between the United States and the EU, in October 2009, the USTR asked the WTO to establish a dispute settlement panel regarding the EU restrictions on imports of U.S. poultry. The United States has asked the panel to review whether the EU's ban on the import and marketing of poultry meat and poultry meat products processed with PRTs violates the EU's WTO obligations. USTR claims that PRTs are judged safe by U.S. and other public health authorities, citing European scientific opinions indicating that PRTs pose no risk to human health. The latest scientific opinion of the European Food Safety Authority (EFSA) states that "chemical substances in poultry are unlikely to pose an immediate or acute health risk for consumers." In addition, in 2011, the international food safety organization Codex Alimentarius Commission (Codex) issued guidelines for the control of Campylobacter and Salmonella in chicken meat that covers the use of certain hazard-based control measures, including acidified sodium chlorite and trisodium phosphate, among other rinses and oxidants. Some believe the Codex guidelines should effectively resolve concerns about the use of these substances in poultry processing. Nevertheless, USTR and the U.S. poultry industry remain actively engaged in this case, and the United States and EU continue to maintain widely divergent views not only on the poultry issue but on some aspects of their basic approach to food safety regulation.

Overview

In January 2009, the outgoing Bush Administration escalated a long-running dispute with the European Union (EU) over its refusal to accept imports of U.S. poultry treated with certain pathogen reduction treatments (PRTs). PRTs are antimicrobial rinses that have been approved for use by the U.S. Department of Agriculture (USDA) in poultry production to reduce the amount of microbes on meat. Meat and poultry products processed with PRTs are judged safe by the United States and also by European food safety authorities. Nevertheless, the EU prohibits the use of PRTs and the importation of poultry treated with these substances. The EU generally opposes such chemical interventions and asserts that its own poultry producers follow much stricter production and processing rules that are more effective in reducing microbiological contamination than simply washing products at the end of the process.

This dispute dates to 1997, when the EU first banned the use of PRTs on poultry, effectively shutting out virtually all imports from the United States since then. Such treatments are routinely used in U.S. chicken and turkey plants. The United States views the EU ban as a trade barrier that is not based on scientific evidence showing that such treatments are harmful. EU interests believe that stronger sanitary practices during production and processing are more appropriate for pathogen control than what they view as U.S. overreliance on PRTs.

Bush officials requested World Trade Organization (WTO) consultations with the EU on the matter, a prerequisite first step toward the establishment of a formal WTO dispute settlement panel. The U.S. poultry industry supported the WTO filing by the U.S. Trade

Representative (USTR) and encouraged the Obama Administration to continue to pursue the case. The Administration and the U.S. poultry industry remain actively engaged in this case.

U.S.-EU Poultry Trade

Trailing only Brazil, the United States is the second leading exporter of poultry meat (broiler and turkey) in the world. Together these two countries account for nearly 70% of all world poultry meat exports.[1] Although the U.S. accounts for about one-third of all world poultry trade, virtually no U.S. exports go to EU countries, the world's second largest importer of poultry meat. The EU accounted for about 9% of all world poultry imports in 2011.

Prior to 1997, when the EU began to prohibit U.S. poultry because of the PRT rule, U.S. exports of broiler and turkey meat to the 15 countries that then constituted the EU were reported to total nearly 38,000 metric tons (MT) with a value of $52 million. By 2011, U.S. exports to the same 15 countries were reported to be nearly 9,000 MT with a value of $13 million.[2] Furthermore, these annually reported data likely include "transshipments," meaning that Europe was not their final destination. According to USDA, virtually no U.S. poultry meat is being purchased for consumption in the EU.[3] Moreover, as additional countries have joined the EU, the United States has lost markets in Europe. After Bulgaria and Romania joined the EU under the 2007 enlargement (to 27 countries), total U.S. poultry meat exports to the two countries dropped to zero, compared with about 54,000 MT, valued at $34 million, during the prior year. The 27 countries that now comprise the European Union (EU-27) imported an estimated 175,000 MT of fresh, chilled or frozen poultry meat from outside the EU in 2011, which was valued at $503 million.[4] Some estimate that the combined effects of the ban and the growth of the EU market may have led to $200 million to $300 million in lost U.S. sales annually.[5]

EU Prohibitions on Use of PRTs

The EU began to prohibit the use of PRTs for both domestic and imported poultry in 1997. Key language in the regulations reads, in part, "[f]ood business operators shall not use any substance other than potable water"—or, when otherwise permitted, "clean water—to remove surface contamination from products of animal origin," unless use of another substance has specifically been approved by the EU.[6]

In 2002, the United States asked the EU to approve the use of four PRTs on poultry destined for export there. These included chlorine dioxide, acidified sodium chlorate, trisodium phosphate, and peroxyacids. Each is approved for use in poultry processing by both USDA and the U.S. Food and Drug Administration (FDA).[7] More specifically, after birds are slaughtered and the carcasses eviscerated, a USDA inspector examines them for fecal contamination or other problems. They then enter a final washing procedure, where the PRTs may be applied, either as a spray or wash on the processing line, or as an addition to the water used to lower the carcass temperature (the chiller tank). Federal regulations further specify PRT concentration levels and other usage requirements.

Following the U.S. request for use of these four PRTs, several key European opinions on PRT use were issued. These opinions helped form the basis for the U.S. request to allow them. For example, the European Food Safety Authority (EFSA), in December 2005, adopted an opinion that use of the four PRTs under described conditions "does not present any risk to public health" but that "the use of antimicrobial solutions does not replace the need for good hygienic practices during processing of poultry carcasses, particularly during handling." A second EFSA opinion that month also pointed out that information on one of the substances, peroxyacids, indicated limited effectiveness, requiring that specific conditions of use should be defined.[8]

In April 2008, EFSA published another scientific opinion which found that "there are currently no published data to conclude in whatever way" that these substances, when applied on poultry carcasses, cause "acquired reduced susceptibility" (a buildup in resistance to the PRTs), or cause resistance to therapeutic antimicrobials.[9] Around the same time, two other scientific committees under the auspices of the Health and Consumer Protection Directorate-General of the European Commission (EC)[10] issued a joint opinion which essentially found that there appeared to be low environmental risk associated with residues on carcasses, but that there was not enough data for it to make a comprehensive assessment, particularly with regard to post-processing environmental risk.[11]

On December 18, 2008, the EU rejected the U.S. request of approval for use of four PRTs on poultry destined for export to the EU—six years after the U.S. request was submitted.[12] This followed a U.S.-EU economic summit in May 2008, where the EC committed to proposed EU regulatory changes that would permit PRT-treated poultry meat to be imported or produced in EU member states. Changes to the EU's Food Hygiene Regulation were offered, in June 2008, to the Standing Committee on the Food Chain and Animal Health but were overwhelmingly rejected (316-0, with 29 abstentions). The same proposal was considered in December 2008, by the EU Agricultural and Fisheries Council, representing the agricultural ministers of the EU member states. They too rejected it by the same vote margin.[13]

U.S. Filing with WTO

In response to the EC's explicit prohibition of these four PRTs and the importation of poultry treated with such substances, the United States requested WTO consultations in January 2009. The outgoing Bush Administration expressed its frustration with the EU's decision not to allow U.S. poultry processed using these PRTs, given what it characterized as several favorable European scientific opinions that PRTs pose no risk to human health. The Bush Administration expressed concern that even the rejected changes represented a "heavily conditioned" proposal, including requirements for labeling, a limitation on PRT use to carcasses, not parts, and a limitation to use of a single PRT (not a combination of them) to be followed by potable water rinses. USTR concluded that this issue could not be resolved through further negotiation and initiated its request to establish a WTO panel to determine whether the EU is acting consistently with its WTO obligations.[14] The U.S. poultry industry supported the WTO filing by the USTR and encouraged the Obama Administration to continue to pursue the case. The United States and the EU continued to hold consultations starting again in February 2009.

The U.S. request for WTO consultations on the poultry matter was filed on January 16, 2009.[15] It states that the EU ban on PRTs in poultry processing violates the EU's WTO obligations under both the Agreement on the Application of Sanitary and Phytosanitary (SPS) Measures and the Agreement on Technical Barriers to Trade (TBTs). (For more information on these two agreements, see text box on next page.) Specifically, the U.S. filing states that the ban by the EU on PRTs for poultry appears to violate the following WTO obligations:

- Article 2.2 of the SPS agreement, which permits only those measures necessary to protect human, animal, and plant life or health and that are based on scientific principles;
- SPS Article 5, which governs risk assessment and determination of the appropriate level of SPS protection, with the objective of minimizing trade impacts;
- SPS Article 8, on control, inspection, and approval procedures, which are aimed at treating imports no less favorably than domestic products; and
- Article 2 of the TBT Agreement, which is intended to assure that TBT measures do not discriminate against imports or create unjustified barriers to trade.

In October 2009, despite initial consultations between the United States and the EU, the USTR asked the WTO to establish a dispute settlement panel regarding the EU's restrictions on imports of U.S. poultry. The United States has asked the panel to review whether the EU's ban on the import and marketing of poultry meat and poultry meat products processed with PRTs violates the EU's WTO obligations. USTR and the U.S. poultry industry remain actively engaged in this case. A panel was established in November 2009, and USTR and poultry industry officials remain interested in moving forward.

Formal WTO cases can take many years to be resolved to the satisfaction of either party. A case in point is the long-running U.S.-EU dispute over the use of hormones in beef, which the EU prohibits and which has kept beef from the United States, where they are used, out of the EU market for many years.[16] Several WTO dispute panel rulings concluded that the EU hormone ban is scientifically unjustified and inconsistent with WTO rules, and the United States imposed WTO-approved retaliatory tariffs on some EU imports. However, the EU continued to enforce the hormone ban. Decades later, the United States and the EU signed a memorandum of understanding (MOU) implementing an agreement that could eventually resolve this longstanding dispute. Meanwhile, as EU officials have pointed out, the United States is permitted to, and does, export hormone-free beef to the EU; likewise, U.S. poultry meat not treated with PRTs likely would be accepted.

Role of the World Trade Organization (WTO)

Multilateral trade rules allow governments to adopt measures to protect human, animal, or plant life or health, provided that they do not discriminate or use them as disguised protectionism. This principle was clarified in 1994 by WTO members' approval, along with the other so-called Uruguay Round Agreements, of the Agreement on the Application of Sanitary and Phytosanitary (SPS) Measures ("SPS Agreement").

A separate accord, the Agreement on Technical Barriers to Trade (TBTs, the "TBT Agreement") covers other government measures (including but not limited to food and agriculture) to regulate markets and protect consumers and the environment.

Both the United States and the EU are parties to these WTO agreements.

SPS Agreement

The Agreement on Sanitary and Phytosanitary (SPS) Measures (or "SPS Agreement") prescribes rules requiring a scientific basis for measures that restrict imports on the basis of health or safety concerns, and sets out the basic rules for ensuring that each country's food safety and animal and plant health laws and regulations are transparent, scientifically defensible, and fair. The agreement was entered into force on January 1, 1995, as one of the agreements in the Uruguay Round of the General Agreement on Tariffs and Trade (GATT), the multilateral trade negotiations administered by the WTO. It is designed to protect animals and plants from diseases and pests, and to protect humans from animal- and plant-borne diseases and pests, and foodborne risks. Examples include specific product or processing standards, requirements for products to be produced in disease-free areas, quarantine and inspection procedures, sampling and testing requirements, residue limits for pesticides and drugs in foods, and prohibitions on certain food additives. The SPS Agreement provides that dispute settlement procedures under the WTO apply also to disputes about food safety and health measures.

TBT Agreement

The Agreement on Technical Barriers to Trade ("TBT Agreement") addresses the growing number of technical regulations and standards adopted by countries that might restrict trade. The agreement resulted from the Tokyo Round in 1979, when members signed a so-called Standards Code. The agreement sets down rules for regulations and standards concerning specific characteristics of a product such as its size, shape, design, functions and performance, or the manner in which a product is labeled or packaged. The TBT Agreement covers the preparation, adoption, and application of technical regulations, product standards, and conformity assessment procedures, as well as environmental regulations and voluntary procedures relating to health, sanitary concerns, and animal welfare. Examples include trademarks and patents, geographical indications (GIs), labeling and packaging requirements, certification and inspection procedures, product specifications, and approval and marketing of biotechnology. The TBT Agreement also provides for WTO dispute settlement procedures.

For more information, see the WTO's website, http://www.wto.org/english/tratop_e/sps_e/sps_e.htm, and also CRS Report RL33472, Sanitary and Phytosanitary (SPS) Concerns in Agricultural Trade.

Current Status and Issues

The United States and the EU maintain widely divergent views not only on the poultry issue but on some aspects of their basic approach to food safety regulation. A widely held European view appears to be that the U.S. use of these treatments compensates for poor sanitary standards earlier in the production process. European poultry producers assert that they follow much stricter production and processing rules that are more successful in reducing microbiological contamination than simply washing products at the end of the process.

In its June 2008 resolution, the European Parliament claimed that the European industry had made "considerable investments ... in accordance with Community legislation, with a view to reducing pathogen contamination by implementing a total food chain approach."[17] The resolution also argued, among other things, that to allow the use of PRTs given the lack of evidence supporting their safety "is out of step with both the European public's food safety and hygiene expectations and the demand for production models—both within and outside Europe—which ensure that high hygiene standards are maintained throughout the production and distribution process," and would likely "undermine European consumer confidence in foodstuffs sold within the European Union, which remains fragile following the food safety problems that have arisen within the Union over recent years."[18]

Nevertheless, a 2012 scientific opinion by European Food Safety Authority (EFSA) recommends changes to the EU's own meat inspection procedures, criticizing its efforts for detecting and controlling *Campylobacter* and *Salmonella* in chicken meat. Regarding chemical intervention, the opinion further states that "chemical substances in poultry are unlikely to pose an immediate or acute health risk for consumers."[19]

This followed the release of 2011 guidelines issued by the international food safety organization Codex Alimentarius Commission (Codex) for the control of *Campylobacter* and *Salmonella* in chicken meat.[20] These Codex guidelines cover, among other types of production controls, the use of certain hazard-based control measures, including acidified sodium chlorite and trisodium phosphate, among other antimicrobial rinses and oxidants. Some believe the Codex guidelines might effectively resolve concerns about the use of these substances in poultry processing.[21]

The USTR and the U.S. poultry industry remain actively engaged in this case.

End Notes

[1] USDA, Livestock and Poultry: World Markets and Trade, October 2012, http://www.fas.usda.gov/psdonline/circulars/livestock_poultry.pdf.

[2] Compiled by CRS from data in the U.S. International Trade Commission's Trade DataWeb database, HTS 0207 (Meat and Edible Offal of Poultry (Chickens, Ducks, Geese, Turkeys and Guineas), Fresh, Chilled or Frozen).

[3] CRS communications with USDA staff, February 2, 2009 (FAS) and February 4, 2009 (ERS).

[4] Compiled by CRS from Global Trade Atlas data, HTS 0207 (Meat and Edible Offal of Poultry (Chickens, Ducks, Geese, Turkeys and Guineas), Fresh, Chilled or Frozen). Data exclude intra-EU shipments.

[5] "USTR Requests Formal WTO Consultations in EU Poultry Dispute," Inside U.S. Trade, January 23, 2009.

[6] EC Reg. No. 853/2004, http://eur-lex.europa.eu/LexUriServ/LexUriServ.do?uri=OJ:L:2004:139:0055: 0205: EN:PDF.

[7] 21 CFR Part 173, Subpart D ("Specific Usage Additives"). See also, for example, FSIS Directive 7120.1, "Safe and Suitable Ingredients used in the production of meat, poultry, and egg products," July 2012; USDA/FSIS, "Guidance on Ingredients and Sources of Radiation Used to Reduce Microorganisms on Carcasses, Ground Beef, and Beef Trimmings;" and University of Georgia, Cooperative Extension, "Processing Tip: Chlorine is still the most popular sanitizer in the poultry industry," November 2007.

[8] Explanatory Memorandum to accompany the EC "Proposal for a Council Regulation implementing Regulation (EC) No 853/2004 of the European Parliament and of the Council as regards the use of antimicrobial substances to remove surface contamination from poultry carcasses," Brussels, October 29, 2008.

[9] Scientific Option of the Panel on Biological Hazards on a Request from DG SANCO on the assessment of the possible effect of the four antimicrobial treatment substances on the emergence of antimicrobial resistance, EFSA Journal (2008) 659, 1-26.

[10] The European Commission (EC) represents the interests of the EU, and is responsible for proposing and applying laws, implementing regulations and other decision, and other activities within the EU.

[11] Scientific Committee on Health and Environmental Risks and Scientific Committee on Emerging and Newly Identified Health Risks, scientific opinion on the environmental impact and effect on antimicrobial resistance of four substances used for the removal of microbial surface contamination of poultry carcasses, April 2008.

[12] Council Decision 2009/121/EC of 18 December 2008 rejecting the proposal from the Commission for a Council Regulation implementing Regulation (EC) No 853/2004 of the European Parliament and of the Council as regards the use of antimicrobial substances to remove surface contamination from poultry carcasses, 2009/121/EC.

[13] "Parliament opposes sale of chlorinated chicken in EU," June 19, 2008. Earlier, in June 2008, the European Parliament, which has a more limited role in this phase of the process, had approved a resolution urging the Commission to reject the food hygiene changes (526-27, with 11 abstentions).

[14] USTR, "U.S. Files WTO Case Challenging EU Restrictions on U.S. Poultry Exports," January 16, 2009.

[15] WTO, European Communities—Certain Measures Affecting Poultry Meat and Poultry Meat Products from the United States—Request for Consultations by the United States (WT/DS389/1, January 20, 2009. The document and current status of the dispute is available at http://www.wto.org/english/tratop_e/ dispu_e /cases_e/ds389_e.htm.

[16] For more information on this case, see CRS Report R40449, The U.S.-EU Beef Hormone Dispute.

[17] "European Parliament resolution of 19 June 2008 on imports of poultry carcasses," http://www.europarl. europa.eu/sides/getDoc.do?pubRef=-//EP//TEXT+TA+P6-TA-2008-0307+0+DOC+ XML+V0//EN&language=EN.

[18] Ibid.

[19] EFSA, "Scientific Opinion on the public health hazards to be covered by inspection of meat (poultry)," Appendix B, EFSA Journal 10(6):2741, 2012, http://www.efsa.europa.eu/en/efsajournal/pub/2741.htm.

[20] Joint FAO/WHO Food Standards Programme Codex Committee on Food Hygiene, "Guideline for the Control of Camplyobacter and Salmonella spp. in Chicken Meat," CAC/GL 78-2011, http://www.codexalimentarius.org/.

[21] D. Pisanello, "Happy end for US-EC dispute on poultry SPS measures," Lex Alimentaria, August 24, 2011, http://www.lexalimentaria.eu/ing/news/46-happy-end-for-us-ec-dispute-on-poultry-sps-measures.html.

In: Agricultural Trade
Editor: Rowan Stroud

ISBN: 978-1-63321-888-8

Chapter 4

COUNTRY-OF-ORIGIN LABELING FOR FOODS AND THE WTO TRADE DISPUTE ON MEAT LABELING*

Remy Jurenas and Joel L. Greene

SUMMARY

Most retail food stores are now required to inform consumers about the country of origin of fresh fruits and vegetables, fish, shellfish, peanuts, pecans, macadamia nuts, ginseng, and ground and muscle cuts of beef, pork, lamb, chicken, and goat. The rules are required by the 2002 farm bill (P.L. 107-171) as amended by the 2008 farm bill (P.L. 110-246). Other U.S. laws have required such labeling, but only for imported food products already pre-packaged for consumers. The final rule to implement country-of-origin labeling (COOL) took effect on March 16, 2009.

Both the authorization and implementation of COOL by the U.S. Department ofAgriculture (USDA) have been controversial, particularly the labeling rules for meat and meat products.A number of livestock and food industry groups continue to oppose COOL as costly and unnecessary, and they and the main livestock exporters to the United States—Canada and Mexico—view the requirement as trade-distorting. Others, including some cattle and consumer groups, maintain thatAmericans want and deserve to know the origin of their foods.

Less than one year after the COOL rules took effect, Canada and Mexico challenged them in the World Trade Organization (WTO), arguing that COOL has a trade-distorting impact by reducing the value and number of cattle and hogs shipped to the U.S. market, thus violating WTO trade commitments agreed to by the United States. In November 2011, the WTO dispute settlement (DS) panel found that (1) COOL treats imported livestock less favorably than like U.S. livestock (particularly in the labeling of beef and pork muscle cuts), and (2) COOL does not meet its objective to provide complete information to consumers on the origin of meat products.

In March 2012, the United States appealed the WTO ruling. In June 2012 the WTO's Appellate Body (AB) upheld the DS panel's finding that the COOL measure treats imported Canadian cattle and hogs, and imported Mexican cattle, less favorably than like domestic livestock. But the AB reversed the finding that COOL does not fulfill its

* This is an edited, reformatted and augmented version of a Congressional Research Service publication RS22955, prepared for Members and Committees of Congress dated January 28, 2014.

legitimate objective to provide consumers with information on origin. The Obama Administration welcomed the AB's affirmation of the U.S. right to adopt labeling requirements to inform consumers on the origin of the meat they purchase. Participants in the U.S. livestock sector had mixed reactions, reflecting the ongoing heated debate on COOL.

AWTO arbitrator set May 23, 2013, as the deadline for the United States to comply with the WTO findings. To comply, USDA issued a final rule requiring that labels show where each production step (i.e., born, raised, slaughtered) occurs and prohibiting the commingling of muscle-cut meat from different origins. COOL's supporters applauded the final rule for providing consumers with specific and more useful information on origin.

Opponents of COOL argue that the new rule is more discriminatory than the previous rule and imposes additional recordkeeping burdens on processors and retailers, and in turn, additional costs on consumers. In July 2013, opponents filed suit to stop USDA from implementing the final COOL rule, but in September 2013 they were denied their request for a preliminary injunction against the rule. COOL opponents appealed and await a court ruling.

Opponents of COOL lobbied the farm bill conference committee to either repeal or modify the COOL law to resolve the WTO dispute. However, the conference report to H.R. 2642 did not make such changes.

Canada and Mexico expressed disappointment with USDA's final rule, and argued that it does not bring the United States into compliance with its WTO obligations. In September 2013, Canada and Mexico secured the establishment of a compliance panel to determine if the final COOL rule complies with WTO findings. This panel will hear the COOL case on February 18-19, 2014. Depending on the outcome of the compliance report, any possible appeal, procedural timelines, and whether or not the case progresses to the retaliation phase and arbitration, the WTO COOL case may not be concluded before 2015.

OVERVIEW

Since the 1930s, U.S. tariff law has required almost all imports to carry labels so that the "ultimate purchaser," usually the retail consumer, can determine their country of origin. However, certain products, including a number of agricultural commodities in their "natural" state, such as meats, fruits, and vegetables, were excluded (see **Appendix A** for a description of this and two other food labeling laws dealing with the display of country of origin on imported products). For almost as many decades, various farm and consumer groups have pressed Congress to end one or more of these exceptions, arguing that U.S. consumers have a right to know where all of their food comes from and that given a choice they would purchase the domestic version. This would strengthen demand and prices for U.S. farmers and ranchers, it was argued.

Opponents of ending these exceptions to country-of-origin labeling (COOL) contended that there was little or no real evidence that consumers want such information and that industry compliance costs would far outweigh any potential benefits to producers or consumers. Such opponents, including some farm and food marketing groups, argued that mandatory COOL for meats, produce, or other agricultural commodities was a form of protectionism that would undermine U.S. efforts to reduce foreign barriers to trade in the global economy. COOL supporters countered that it was unfair to exempt agricultural commodities from the labeling requirements that U.S. importers of almost all other products already must meet, and that major U.S. trading partners impose their own COOL requirements for imported meats, produce, and other foods.

Legislation

With passage of the 2002 farm bill, retail-level COOL was to become mandatory for fresh fruits and vegetables, beef, pork, lamb, seafood, and peanuts, starting September 30, 2004 (P.L. 107-171, §10816). Continuing controversy over the new requirements within the food and agricultural industry led Congress to postpone full implementation. The FY2004 Omnibus Appropriations Act (P.L. 108-199) postponed COOL—except for seafood—until September 30, 2006; the FY2006 Agriculture Appropriations Act (P.L. 109-97) further postponed it until September 30, 2008.

During deliberations on the 2008 farm bill, the interest groups most affected by COOL reached consensus on various changes intended to ease what they viewed to be some of the more onerous provisions of the 2002 COOL law. Provisions dealing with record-keeping requirements, the factors to be considered for labeling U.S. and non-U.S. origin products, and penalties for noncompliance were modified. These amendments were incorporated into P.L. 110-246, Section 11002. The enacted 2008 farm bill required that COOL take effect on September 30, 2008, and added goat meat, chicken, macadamia nuts, pecans, and ginseng as commodities covered by mandatory COOL. (See **Appendix B** for a timeline of key COOL developments.)

USDA Regulations and Secretary's Statement to Implement COOL

The final rule to implement the COOL requirements for all covered commodities was issued by the U.S. Department of Agriculture's (USDA's) Agricultural Marketing Service (AMS) during the final days of the Bush Administration in January 2009.[1] It included changes to the interim rule published in August 2008 that some had criticized as watering down the COOL statute (see "Changes Made from Interim Rule to Final Rule"). In February 2009, the Secretary of Agriculture announced that the final rule would take effect as planned on March 16, 2009.[2] At the same time, he also urged affected industries to voluntarily adopt additional changes that, he asserted, would provide more specific origin information to consumers and more closely adhere to the intent of the COOL law (see sections "Vilsack Letter" and "Vilsack Letter Is Not a Technical Regulation" for details).

Costs and Benefits

COOL supporters argued that numerous studies show that consumers want country-of-origin labeling and would pay extra for it. Analysis accompanying USDA's interim and final rules concluded that, while benefits are difficult to quantify, it appears they will be small and will accrue mainly to consumers who desire such information. A Colorado State University economist suggested that consumers might be willing to pay a premium for "COOL meat" from the United States, but only if they perceive U.S. meat to be safer and of higher quality than foreign meat.[3] USDA earlier had estimated that purchases of (i.e., demand for) covered commodities would have to increase by 1% to 5% for benefits to cover COOL costs, but added that such increases were not anticipated. Data from several economic studies that aimed to model COOL impacts appear to fall within this range.[4]

Critics of mandatory COOL argued that large compliance costs will more than offset any consumer benefits. USDA's analysis of its final rule estimated first-year implementation costs to be approximately $2.6 billion for those affected. Of the total, each commodity producer would bear an average estimated cost of $370, intermediary firms (such as wholesalers or processors) $48,219 each, and retailers $254,685 each. The USDA analysis also included estimates of record-keeping costs and of food sector economic losses due to the rule.[5]

COOL's Meat Labeling Challenged in the WTO

Meat labeling proved to be the most contentious of COOL requirements, leading Canada and Mexico to challenge COOL using the World Trade Organization's (WTO's) dispute settlement process. They expressed concerns that normal livestock trade flows would be disrupted in response to the COOL regulations and questioned COOL's legality under international trade rules. In November 2011, a WTO dispute settlement panel found that COOL discriminated against foreign livestock and was not consistent with WTO rules. After weighing available options, the Obama Administration decided to appeal the WTO panel's adverse findings. In June 2012, WTO's appellate body upheld one of the panel's findings that favored Canada's and Mexico's positions, and overturned another. Under a ruling since made by a WTO arbitrator, the United States must bring those features of COOL addressed by the appellate body's findings into compliance by May 23, 2013.

KEY PROVISIONS OF COOL

Mandatory country-of-origin labeling:

- *applies* to ground and muscle cuts of beef (including veal), lamb, and pork, fish and shellfish, peanuts, "perishable agricultural commodities" as defined by the Perishable Agricultural Commodities Act (i.e., fresh and frozen fruits and vegetables), goat meat, chicken, pecans, macadamia nuts, and ginseng (these are referred to as "covered commodities");[6]
- *requires* method of production information (farm-raised or wild-caught) for fish and shellfish to be noted at the final point of sale to consumers;
- *exempts* these items if they are an ingredient in a processed food;
- *covers* only those retailers that annually purchase at least $230,000 of perishable agricultural commodities,[7] and requires them to inform consumers of origin "by means of a label, stamp, mark, placard, or other clear and visible sign on the covered

commodity or on the package, display, holding unit, or bin containing the commodity at the final point of sale"; and

- *exempts* from these labeling requirements such "food service establishments" as restaurants, cafeterias, bars, and similar facilities that prepare and sell foods to the public.

Defining and Labeling Origin for Meats

In designating country of origin, difficulties arise when products—particularly meats—are produced in multiple countries. For example, beef might be from an animal that was born and fed in Canada, but slaughtered and processed in the United States. Likewise, products from several different countries often are mixed, such as for ground beef. For covered red meats and chicken, the COOL law:[8]

- *permits* the U.S. origin label to be used only on meats from animals that were exclusively born, raised, and slaughtered in the United States, with an exception for those animals present here before July 15, 2008;
- *permits* meats or chicken with multiple countries of origin to be labeled as being from all of the countries in which the animals may have been born, raised, or slaughtered;
- *requires* meat or chicken from animals imported for immediate U.S. slaughter to be labeled as from both the country the animal came from and the United States;
- *requires* products from animals not born, raised, or slaughtered in the United States to be labeled with their correct country(ies) of origin; and
- *requires*, for ground meat and chicken products, that the label list all countries of origin, or all "reasonably possible" countries of origin.

Because these statutory requirements are at the heart of the ongoing WTO dispute case, **Table 1** traces the progression of statutory language from the initial implementing regulations to the retail labels to be used for each of these five categories. Subsequent changes to these rules as now seen at the retail level are shown in **Table 2**.

Changes Made from Interim Rule to Final Rule

The meat labeling requirements have proven to be among the most complex and controversial areas of rulemaking, in large part because of the steps that U.S. feeding operations and packing plants must adopt to segregate, hold, and slaughter foreign-origin livestock separately from U.S. livestock. After AMS issued the interim rules in August 2008, many retailers and meat processors reportedly planned to use the "catch-all" multiple countries of origin label on as much meat as possible—even products that would qualify for the U.S.-only label, because it was both permitted and the easiest requirement to meet. COOL supporters objected that the label would be overused, undermining the intent of COOL (i.e., to distinguish between U.S. and non-U.S. meats).[9] In an effort to balance the concerns of both sides, USDA issued a statement attempting to clarify its August 2008 interim rule, stating that meats derived from both U.S.- and non-U.S.-origin animals may carry a mixed-origin claim (e.g., "Product of U.S., Canada, and Mexico"), but that the mixed-origin label cannot be used if only U.S.-origin meat was produced on a production day.[10]

The final (January 2009) rule attempted to further clarify the "multiple countries of origin" language. For example, muscle cut products of exclusively U.S. origin along with those from foreign-born animals, if commingled for slaughter on a single production day, can continue to qualify for a combined U.S. and non-U.S. label. "It was never the intent of the Agency [AMS] for the majority of product eligible to bear a U.S. origin declaration to bear a multiple origin destination. The Agency made additional modifications for clarity," AMS stated in material accompanying the rule.[11]

The clarifying changes failed to mollify some. The National Farmers Union continued to view this portion of the rule as a "loophole that would allow meat packers to use a multiple countries, or NAFTA [North American Free Trade Agreement] label, rather than labeling U.S. products as products of the United States" and stated "[t]his is misleading to consumers."[12] Seven Senators highlighted similar concerns, stating that it would allow "meatpackers to put a multiple country of origin label on products that are exclusively U.S. products as well as those that are foreign." They characterized the final rule as defeating COOL's primary purpose to provide "clear, accurate and truthful information" to U.S. consumers, and hoped the rules will be revised "to close these loopholes."[13]

Vilsack Letter

To address these views to comply with an Obama White House directive that all agencies review recent regulations issued by the outgoing Administration, Secretary of Agriculture Vilsack in a February 20, 2009, letter urged industry representatives to voluntarily adopt three suggested labeling changes in order to provide more useful information to consumers than the final rule itself might imply, and to better meet congressional intent. These dealt with the labeling of meat products with multiple countries of origin, a reduction in the time allowance for labeling ground meat held in inventory, and exemptions to the rules for processed products.

On labeling for multiple countries of origin, he stated that

> processors should voluntarily include information about what production step occurred in each country when multiple countries appear on the label. For example, animals born and raised in Country X and slaughtered in Country Y might be labeled as "Born and Raised in Country X and Slaughtered in Country Y." Animals born in Country X but raised and slaughtered in Country Y might be labeled as "Born in Country X and Raised and Slaughtered in Country Y."

Vilsack's letter noted that the final rule allows a label for ground meat to bear the name of a country even if the meat from that country was not present in a processor's inventory in the preceding 60-day period. Noting that this allows for labeling this product "in a way that does not clearly indicate [its] country of origin," the Secretary asked processors to reduce this time allowance to 10 days, stating that this "would enhance the credibility of the label." (See also "Scope of Coverage.")

Secretary Vilsack also stated that USDA would closely monitor industry compliance to determine whether "additional rulemaking may be necessary to provide consumers with adequate information."[14] His letter was widely viewed as an effort to address the concerns of COOL adherents without reopening the rule and thereby attracting renewed criticism from the meat industry and U.S. trading partners.

Defining Origin for Other Covered Commodities

For perishable agricultural commodities, ginseng, peanuts, pecans, and macadamia nuts, retailers may only claim U.S. origin if the product was exclusively produced in the United States. However, a U.S. state, region, or locality designation is a sufficient U.S. identifier (e.g., Idaho potatoes). For farm-raised fish and shellfish, a U.S.-labeled product must be derived exclusively from fish or shellfish hatched, raised, harvested, and processed in the United States; wild fish and shellfish must be derived exclusively from those harvested either in U.S. waters or by a U.S. flagged vessel, and processed in the United States or on a U.S. vessel. Also, labels must differentiate between wild and farm-raised fish and shellfish.

Scope of Coverage

Consumers may not find country-of-origin labels on much more of the food they buy, due to COOL's statutory and regulatory exemptions. First, as noted, all restaurants and other food service providers are exempt, as are all retail grocery stores that buy less than $230,000 a year in fresh fruits and vegetables. Second, "processed food items" derived from the covered commodities are exempt, and USDA, in its final rule, defined this term broadly (at 7 C.F.R. §65.220). Essentially, any time a covered commodity is subjected to a change that alters its basic character, it is considered to be processed. Although adding salt, water, or sugar do not, under USDA's definition, change the basic character, virtually any sort of cooking, curing, or mixing apparently does. For example, roasting a peanut or pecan, mixing peas with carrots, or breading a piece of meat or chicken all count as processing. As a result, only about 30% of the U.S. beef supply, 11% of all pork, 39% of chicken, and 40% of all fruit and vegetable supplies may be covered by COOL requirements at the retail level.[15] Whole peanuts are almost always purchased in roasted form, and will not have to be labeled. Some critics argued that AMS overstepped its authority, and congressional intent, by excepting such minimally processed commodities.

AMS countered that in fact many imported items still must carry COOL under provisions of the Tariff Act of 1930. "For example, while a bag of frozen peas and carrots is considered a processed food item under the COOL final rule, if the peas and carrots are of foreign origin, the Tariff Act requires that the country of origin be marked on the bag," AMS argued, citing similar regulatory situations for roasted nuts and for a variety of seafood items.[16]

Vilsack's letter, however, acknowledged that the "processed foods" definition in the final rule "may be too broadly drafted. Even if products are subject to curing, smoking, broiling, grilling, or steaming, voluntary labeling would be appropriate," he wrote.

Record-Keeping, Verification, and Penalties

The COOL law prohibits USDA from using a mandatory animal identification (ID) system,[17] but the original 2002 version stated that the Secretary "may require that any person that prepares, stores, handles, or distributes a covered commodity for retail sale maintain a verifiable record-keeping audit trail that will permit the Secretary to verify compliance." Verification immediately became one of the most contentious issues, particularly for livestock producers, in part because of the potential complications and costs to affected industries of tracking animals and their products from birth through retail sale. Producers of plant-based commodities, as well as food retailers and others, also expressed concern about the cost and difficulty of maintaining records for commodities that are highly fungible and often widely sourced. The 2008 law eased these requirements somewhat by stating that USDA "may conduct an audit of any person that prepares, stores, handles, or distributes a covered commodity" in order to verify compliance. Such persons must provide verification, but USDA may not ask for any additional records beyond those maintained "in the course of the normal conduct of business."

In its final rule, AMS stated that covered persons generally would have to keep records for one year that can identify both the immediate previous source and the immediate subsequent recipient of a covered commodity; certain exceptions are provided for pre-labeled products. Also, a slaughter facility can accept a producer affidavit as sufficient evidence for animal origin claims.

Also, potential fines for willful noncompliance are set for retailers and other persons at no more than $1,000 per violation. The 2002 law had set the fine at no more than $10,000 (and for retailers only), but the 2008 farm bill lowered this amount.

ADMINISTRATIVE ENFORCEMENT AND AUDITS

USDA's Agricultural Marketing Service implements COOL through cooperative agreements with all 50 states.[18] In 2012, state agencies conducted 3,836 retail surveillance reviews (out of the 37,000 individual retail stores subject to COOL), and 521 follow-up retail reviews, to ensure compliance with COOL requirements. These reviews involved the auditing of 225 products as they moved from initial suppliers to retail shelves. AMS resources (i.e., appropriated funding of $5.0 million and 16 staff years in FY2013) were available to train federal and state employees on enforcement responsibilities, conduct supply chain audits, analyze and respond to formal complaints, and develop educational and outreach activities for retailers, suppliers, and other interested parties. In June 2012, AMS began to implement a real-time database to track the findings of federal-state retail reviews, enforcement actions taken, and other information viewed as critical to COOL operations.[19]

USDA's Office of Inspector General (OIG) audited the operations of the COOL program during 2010. Its report noted that "AMS made significant strides implementing the final rule" but found the need for improvements in its controls and processes to ensure that retailers and suppliers fully comply with COOL regulations. The OIG identified the need for AMS to strengthen its process to select retailers to be reviewed and the review process itself, and to more quickly evaluate the documentation kept by retailers and issue noncompliance letters.

Auditors also pointed out that AMS needs to be more vigorous in enforcing COOL requirements, provide better oversight of the state agencies that conduct retailer reviews, and improve how it communicates with and provides program guidance to retailers. AMS agreed with all of the OIG recommendations, and by late 2012, had incorporated 11 of them into program operations. The remaining three were anticipated to be put into effect in March 2013, according to AMS.[20]

In reviews conducted during 2012 in retail stores, AMS found that overall retail compliance (based on the average of covered commodities sold in a store) was about 96%, but that only 19% of the stores reviewed were in full compliance. Findings of noncompliance with COOL were due to the lack of labeling on covered commodities (72%), followed by inaccurate labeling (10%), the absence of a label showing method of production on covered fish and shellfish commodities (7%), and non-compliance with recordkeeping requirements (5%). Of the 536 suppliers selected for traceback audits, AMS reported 21 findings of noncompliance. Nine suppliers were cited for providing inaccurate country-of-origin information to the immediate subsequent recipient of a covered commodity; five suppliers did not provide records within the required five business days.[21]

COOL Challenged by Canada and Mexico in WTO

Canada and Mexico are major suppliers of live cattle and hogs that are fed in U.S. feeding facilities and/or processed into beef and pork in U.S. meat packing plants. As the U.S. meat processing sector geared up to implement COOL in mid-2008, Canada and Mexico expressed concern that COOL would adversely impact their livestock sectors. Indeed, U.S. cattle imports from Canada and Mexico and hog imports from Canada dropped in both 2008 and 2009 from year-earlier levels. Some analyses supported claims that COOL hampered livestock imports. Other analyses pointed out that factors such as exchange rates and inventory levels were also affecting import levels and that declines could not be entirely attributed to COOL (see **Appendix C** for background on livestock trade in North America).

Canada and Mexico requested consultations with the United States in December 2008 and June 2009 about their concerns. Not satisfied with the outcome of these consultations with U.S. officials, both countries in early October 2009 requested the establishment of a WTO dispute settlement (DS) panel to consider their case. In response, the U.S. Trade Representative (USTR) and the Secretary of Agriculture commented that they "regretted that the formal consultations" did not resolve concerns, and stated their belief that U.S. implementation of COOL provides consumers with information that is consistent with WTO commitments. They noted that countries worldwide had agreed that the principle of country-of-origin labeling was legitimate policy long before the WTO was created, and that other countries also require goods to be labeled with their origin.[22]

Both the Canadian and Mexican governments, in requesting a panel, asserted that COOL is inconsistent with U.S. obligations under certain WTO agreements—the General Agreement on Tariffs and Trade 1994, the Agreement on Technical Barriers to Trade, and the Agreement on Rules of Origin. These obligations include treating imports no less favorably than like products of domestic origin; making sure that product-related requirements are not more trade-restrictive than necessary to fulfill a legitimate public policy objective; ensuring that compliance with laws on marks of origin does not result in damaging imports, reducing their value, or unreasonably increasing their cost; and ensuring that laws, rules, and procedures on country of origin do not "themselves create restrictive, distorting, or disruptive" international trade, among others.

On November 19, 2009, the WTO's Dispute Settlement Body (DSB)[23] established a panel to consider both countries' complaints. In proceeding with this WTO case, Canadian officials stated that the COOL requirements are "so onerous" that when they were implemented, Canadian exporters of cattle and hogs were discriminated against in the U.S. market. The Canadian beef and pork industries, led by the Canadian Cattlemen's Association (CCA) and the Canadian Pork Council, actively pushed their government to initiate a WTO challenge. The CCA argued that COOL cost its producers C$92 million over the two months following the publication of the interim rule in August 2008, and could cost C$500 million per year. CCA estimated that slaughter steers and heifers were losing C$90 per head, because U.S. meat establishments did not want to assume the increased costs of complying with new labeling requirements by segregating, holding, and then slaughtering Canadian cattle separately from U.S. cattle. The losses included lower prices for all Canadian cattle due to decreased U.S. demand, as well as the cost of shipping those that are sold further distances to the fewer number of U.S. plants willing to take them. Canadian pork producers expressed similar concerns.[24]

USTR's request for public comment on this pending WTO case generated responses that reflected the heated debate on mandatory COOL seen earlier among key players in the livestock sector. The American Meat Institute (AMI), representing U.S. meat processors and packers, stated that the U.S. law, in addition to violating WTO commitments, also violates NAFTA commitments. AMI argued that COOL discriminates against imports in favor of domestic meat.[25]

In opposition, the U.S. Cattlemen's Association (USCA) and the National Farmers Union argued that COOL is "fully consistent" with the General Agreement on Tariffs and Trade and the Agreement on Technical Barriers to Trade (key WTO commitments). Both stated that COOL "does not discriminate between domestic and imported beef ... [and] operates neutrally in the market place," and noted that COOL does not impose any domestic content requirements (i.e., does not stipulate what share of value or quantity determines country of origin).[26] The Ranchers-Cattlemen Action Legal Fund, United Stockgrowers of America (R-CALF), presented similar comments.[27]

The National Cattlemen's Beef Association (NCBA) expressed concern that Canada's decision to pursue its case against U.S. COOL rules has the potential for retaliatory action to be taken against U.S. beef. It noted that "COOL has damaged critically important trading relationships [i.e., the import of Canadian and Mexican livestock, the value added as they pass through U.S. feedlots and are processed into meat, and the export of finished meat products back to Mexican and Canadian consumers], and is not putting additional money into the pockets of cattlemen."[28]

Dispute Settlement Panel Ruling

On November 18, 2011, the WTO dispute settlement (DS) panel ruled that certain COOL requirements violate two articles of the WTOAgreement on Technical Barriers to Trade (TBT) and the requirement for impartial administration of regulations laid out in the General Agreement on Tariffs and Trade 1994 (GATT 1994). The panel first concluded that the COOL "measure"— the statute and the final rule—constituted a "technical regulation" under the TBTAgreement and was thus subject to TBT obligations. It then found that the COOL measure (1) treated imported livestock less favorably than "like domestic livestock," particularly in the labeling of muscle cut meats (beef and pork), in violation of the national treatment obligation in the TBT's Article 2.1; and (2) failed to meet the legitimate objective of providing information to consumers on the origin of meat products, and thus violated the TBT's Article 2.2. The panel also found that the Vilsack letter's "suggestions for voluntary action" went beyond COOL's obligations and, while not a "technical regulation," constitute unreasonable administration of COOL itself, thus violating Article X:3(a) of the GATT 1994.[29] The panel concluded that the United States has "nullified or impaired benefits" to which Canada and Mexico are entitled, and recommended that the WTO's DSB request the United States to conform these "inconsistent measures" with its obligations under the TBT Agreement and GATT 1994.[30]

U.S. Appeal of the WTO Panel Ruling

Under WTO rules, the United States had various options available to respond to the dispute panel's adverse ruling on certain aspects of U.S. COOL. One was to accept the decision and make changes to the COOL statute and/or regulations to comply with the WTO findings. Another was to appeal the panel report on legal issues.

On March 23, 2012, the United States appealed two findings of the DS panel's report to the WTO Appellate Body (AB).[31] A USTR spokeswoman restated its position that the report had confirmed the U.S. right to adopt rules to inform consumers of the country of origin in their purchasing decisions, but expressed disappointment that the panel "disagreed with the way that the United States designed its COOL requirements" for beef and pork. USTR's chief counsel stated that the U.S. appeal is "a signal of our commitment" to ensure that consumers "are provided with accurate and relevant information" on the origin of beef and pork, and "to fight for the interests of U.S. consumers at the WTO."[32]

Appellate Body's Report Determinations

On June 29, 2012, the WTO's AB upheld the DS panel's finding that the COOL measure treats imported Canadian cattle and hogs, and imported Mexican cattle, less favorably than like domestic livestock, due to its record-keeping and verification requirements. The AB, however, reversed the DS panel's finding that COOL does not completely fulfill its legitimate objective to provide consumers with information on origin.

WTO Adoption of Dispute Settlement Reports

On July 23, 2012, the Dispute Settlement Body (DSB) adopted the AB's report and the DS panel's report, as modified by the AB, under the reverse consensus rule. Under this rule, both reports are adopted unless all WTO member countries present at the meeting vote not to do so. This rule makes adoption virtually automatic.[33] In turn, the United States, Canada, and Mexico were required to unconditionally accept the AB's decision. The DSB, as is the practice, did not specify what the United States must do to comply with these reports' findings.

WTO Procedures for the United States to Comply with Reports' Findings

The WTO's Dispute Settlement Understanding (DSU) lays out a multi-step process for a country to comply with the adopted WTO findings.[34] Once WTO findings are adopted by the DSB, a compliance deadline is established. If a party or parties to a dispute believe compliance measures fail to meet WTO obligations, the process may move into a compliance panel phase. If that does not resolve disagreements among parties, the dispute could move into a retaliation phase. A resolution to a WTO case may be delayed for months as the parties work through the compliance and/or retaliation processes.

Timetable to Comply; Arbitrator's Role

After the adoption of the dispute settlement reports, the United States had up to 30 days to inform the DSB of its plans to implement the WTO findings. If a country is unable to comply immediately, the DSU allows for a "reasonable period of time" for this to occur. Often, WTO members are given approximately one year from the date of adoption of the panel report to comply. If the disputing countries fail to agree on a compliance deadline, as occurred in this case, an arbitrator may determine the deadline. Because the three countries could not agree on a timetable or an arbitrator, the WTO Director-General appointed one. In the arbitration hearing, the United States argued that 18 months were needed to pursue the steps required to adopt a regulatory response. Canada argued that six months would be sufficient. Mexico argued for an eight-month compliance period, but would welcome six. On December 4, 2012, the arbitrator determined that 10 months from the reports' adoption (i.e., July 23, 2012) was a reasonable period of time for the United States to comply. The United States was given until May 23, 2013, to bring COOL into WTO compliance.

Form of Compliance

Facing the deadline of May 23, 2013, the United States began the process of deciding how to modify those features of COOL targeted by the WTO panels' findings to bring them into compliance. This continued USTR's reported engagement in late 2012 and early 2013 with Congress and interest groups on how to proceed (see "Options to Bring COOL into Compliance" for discussion). On March 12, 2013, USDA published a proposed rule in the *Federal Register* that modifies COOL labeling regulations. The proposed rule had a 30-day comment period. USDA published the final rule in the *Federal Register* on May 24, 2013, making it effective May 23, 2013 (see "USDA's Final COOL Rule ").

Ratification of Substance of Compliance; Consequences If Not Ratified

Canada and Mexico had the right under WTO rules to confirm whether or not they accept the substance of compliance taken by the United States on May 23, 2013. If either or both countries asserted that the United States had not complied or had only partially complied with the WTO's findings, Canada and Mexico could request that a compliance panel investigate whether the United States had in fact adopted a compliance measure or whether any measure that it had adopted was consistent with the WTO decision. Because WTO dispute settlement rules provide conflicting timetables in the event that a party requests both authorization to retaliate and a compliance panel, disputing parties often enter into so-called "sequencing" agreements that accommodate both procedures.[35]

Both Canada and Mexico argued that USDA's May 23 COOL rule fails to bring the United States into compliance with its WTO obligations.[36] On June 10, 2013, Canada, Mexico, and the United States provided the DSB with sequencing agreements that each agreed they would follow as the COOL case moves forward.[37] On August 19, 2013, Canada and Mexico informed the WTO that they would request a compliance panel to rule on whether or not USDA's final COOL rule complies with the WTO findings (see "Compliance Panel").[38] On September 25, 2013, the DSB agreed to establish a compliance panel, and referred the request to the original dispute settlement panel. The panel will hear the COOL case on February 18-19, 2014.

Consequences of Non-Compliance: Compensation or Retaliation

If the United States is found to not be in compliance with the WTO decision, Canada and Mexico can request that the United States negotiate a compensation agreement. If such an agreement is not requested, or if an agreement is not reached on a request, Canada and Mexico can request authorization from WTO's DSB to retaliate. The retaliation request would need to be made within 30 days after the compliance period ends. Retaliation can involve the suspension of concessions or obligations owed by Canada and Mexico to the United States under a WTO agreement. One permitted action could involve Canada and Mexico increasing tariffs on products imported from the United States.[39] The United States may object to the retaliation request, in which case it would be automatically sent to arbitration (see "Canada's Preliminary Retaliation List"). At the same time, the WTO DSU provides that a country cannot suspend WTO concessions or other obligations as retaliatory measures in a particular dispute unless authorized by the WTO Dispute Settlement Body. If unauthorized retaliation were to occur, the United States could challenge such retaliation in a separate WTO dispute settlement proceeding. But if Canada and Mexico felt that the United States was making progress toward compliance, they could agree to extend the original compliance deadline.

WTO FINDINGS

COOL Treats Imported Livestock Less Favorably than Domestic Livestock

Dispute Panel

The DS panel found that Canada and Mexico demonstrated that COOL is a technical regulation governed by, and in violation of, Article 2.1 of the TBT. The AB upheld this finding, but for different reasons (see below). This TBT article states: "Members shall ensure that in respect of technical regulations, products imported from the territory of any Member shall be accorded treatment no less favourable than that accorded to like products of national origin and to like products originating in any other country." The panel first found that the COOL statute and the final rule (but not the Vilsack letter) are a "technical regulation" because they are legally enforceable requirements governing the labeling of meat products offered for sale.[40] The panel further found that Canadian and U.S. cattle, Canadian and U.S. hogs, and Mexican and U.S. cattle are "like products," and the muscle cut labels used to implement COOL affect competitive conditions for these products in the U.S. market to the detriment of imported livestock. According to the panel, COOL creates this "competitive advantage" by creating an incentive for "processing exclusively domestic livestock and a disincentive against handling imported livestock." More specifically, the panel found that to comply with COOL, processors need to segregate imported from domestic livestock to an extent that discourages them from using imported livestock at all. In turn, this reduces the competitive opportunities for imported livestock relative to those for domestic livestock.

The panel based this conclusion on its assessment of the compliance requirements of COOL. It first reviewed the four statutory definitions used to label the origin of beef and pork muscle cuts (**Table 1**), noting that "origin is determined by the country in which specific livestock production and processing steps took place (i.e., birth, raising and slaughtering)," and highlighted the distinctions between the exclusive U.S. origin label and the other three labels that identified livestock with an imported element (i.e., at least one step took place outside the United States). It observed that "there was ... major flexibility" under COOL's interim final rule (August 2008) to use "multiple countries of origin" (Category B) for muscle cuts eligible for the U.S.-origin only label (Category A) "without limitations." However, in response to public comment, COOL's final rule (January 2009) ended this flexibility, allowing the multiple countries declaration (Category B) to be used to label U.S.-origin meat only if U.S. and foreign livestock were commingled for slaughter "on a single production day."

The panel then examined what is involved in segregating livestock and meat between domestic and foreign origin under five business scenarios. It determined that "the least costly way" to comply with COOL "is to rely on exclusively domestic livestock" rather than imported livestock. Accepting evidence provided by Canada and Mexico that major U.S. slaughterhouses are "applying a considerable COOL discount of [US$] 40-60 per head for imported livestock" but not to domestic livestock, the panel observed that COOL creates an incentive to process domestic rather than imported livestock because it is less costly to do so. It pointed out that several U.S. meat processors indicated they plan to move to use Category A (U.S. origin) "for the vast majority of their beef and pork products" and to ensure segregation by origin (i.e., minimize commingling). Other evidence presented confirmed that the U.S.-origin label accounts for a large share of the meat marketed. The United States indicated that 71% of the beef, and 70% of the pork, sold at the retail level carries the exclusive U.S. label. Canada showed that close to 90% of meat sold at retail carries this U.S. label.

Table 1. COOL for Beef and Pork: From Statute to Label

Muscle Cuts & Ground Meat Categories	COOL Statutory Definition	AMS Final Rule (January 2009)	COOL Label at Retail Level under 2009 Rule[a]
UNITED STATES COUNTRY OF ORIGIN [Category A or Label A]	"beef [or] ... pork ... derived from an animal that was ... exclusively born, raised, and slaughtered in the United States"	For beef and pork, means: "(1) From animals *exclusivelyborn, raised, and slaughtered in the United States;* (2) From animals born and raised in Alaska or Hawaii and transported for a period of not more than 60 days through Canada to the United States and slaughtered in the United States; ..."	Product of the US(A)
MULTIPLE COUNTRIES OF ORIGIN [Category B or Label B]	""beef [or] ... pork... derived from an animal that is— (i) not exclusively born, raised and slaughtered in the United States; (ii) born, raised or slaughtered in the United States; and (iii) not imported into the United States for immediate slaughter	For muscle cuts of beef and pork "derived from animals that were born in Country X or (as applicable) Country Y, raised and slaughtered in the United States, and were not derived from animals imported for immediate slaughter [defined as "consignment directly from the port of entry to a recognized slaughtering establishment and slaughtered within 2 weeks from the date of entry"], the origin may be designated as Product of the United States, Country X, and (as applicable) Country Y." For muscle cuts of beef and pork "derived from animals born, raised, and slaughtered in the U.S. that are commingled during a production day with muscle cuts [of beef and pork from animals born outside the U.S., raised and slaughtered in the U.S., and not imported for immediate slaughter], the origin may be designated as Product of the United States, Country X, and (as applicable) Country Y." For muscle cuts of beef and pork "derived from animals that are *born in Country* X or Country Y, *raised and slaughtered in the United States, that are commingled during a production day with muscle cut[s of beef and pork] derived from animals that are imported into the United States for immediate slaughter ...,* the origin may be designated as Product of the United States, Country X, and (as applicable) Country Y." "In each case, the countries may be listed in any order. In addition,	Product of the US, Country X, and (as applicable) Country Y

Table 1. (Continued)

Muscle Cuts & Ground Meat Categories	COOL Statutory Definition	AMS Final Rule (January 2009)	COOL Label at Retail Level under 2009 Rule[a]
		the origin declaration may include more specific information related to production steps provided records to substantiate the claims are maintained and the claim is consistent with other applicable Federal legal requirements."	
IMPORTED FOR IMMEDIATE SLAUGHTER [Category C or Label C]	"beef [or] ... pork ... derived from an animal that is imported into the United States for immediate slaughter"	"If an animal was imported into the United States *for immediate slaughter* [defined as "consignment directly from the port of entry to a recognized slaughtering establishment and slaughtered within 2 weeks from the date of entry"], the origin of the resulting [beef and pork] derived from that animal shall be designated as Product of Country X and the United States."	Product of Country X, US
FOREIGN COUNTRY OF ORIGIN [Category D or Label D]	"beef [or] ... pork... derived from an animal ... not born, raised, or slaughtered in the United States"	"Imported [beef and pork] for which origin has already been established as defined by this law (e.g., born, raised, and slaughtered or produced) and for which *no production steps have occurred in the United States*, shall retain their origin, as declared to U.S. Customs and Border Protection at the time the product entered the UnitedStates, through retail sale."	Product of Country X
GROUND BEEF OR PORK	"notice ... for ground beef, ground pork ... shall include a list of all [or] ... all reasonably possible countries of origin of such ground beef, ground pork, ..."	"The declaration for ground beef, ground pork,... shall *list all countries of origin contained therein or that may be reasonably contained* therein. In determining what is considered reasonable, when a raw material from a specific origin is not in a processor's inventory for more than 60 days, that country shall no longer be included as a possible country of origin."	Product of US, Country X, (and as applicable) Country Y, Country Z,...

Source: 7 U.S.C. §§1638a(a)(2)(A)-(D), Section 282 of Agricultural Marketing Act of 1946, as amended by 2008 farm bill (§10816 of P.L. 107-171); 7 CFR 65.260(a)(1), 65.300(e)(1)-(4) and 65.300(h), as published in the Federal Register, January 15, 2009, p. 2706; Agricultural Marketing Service, "Labeling Options," p. 2, http://www.ams.usda.gov/AMSv1.0/getfile?dDocName= STELPRDC5074845.

Notes: Key terms are in italics. These same designations also apply to other covered meats (lamb, chicken, and goat meat), but they were not the subject of complaints filed by Canada and Mexico in the WTO case.

a. See **Table 2** for retail-level labeling changes made by the May 2013 revised rule to comply with WTO panel findings.

Based on the above, the panel "preliminarily" concluded that COOL "creates an incentive to use domestic livestock—and a disincentive to handle imported livestock—by imposing higher segregation costs on imported livestock than on domestic livestock." The panel's report also showed that some U.S. plants and companies "are simply refusing to process any imported livestock anymore," and that fewer U.S. processing plants are accepting cattle and hog imports than before. It also noted that certain suppliers had to transport imported livestock longer distances than before COOL, and that they also faced logistical problems and additional costs for timing delivery to specific times or days when processing is scheduled. Although the panel took these into account, it decided it also was important to make findings on COOL's actual trade effects. To do this, it considered data, economic analyses, and econometric studies submitted by Canada, Mexico, and the United States.

In reviewing two economic studies on COOL's livestock segregation costs submitted by Canada, the panel stated "both studies shed some light on the different types of segregation and compliance costs encountered at different stages of the supply chain." Noting that such costs need to be absorbed somewhere in the marketing system, it concluded that "economic competition pressure" will dictate how these costs are allocated. Whether this involves processing only U.S.-origin livestock because it is the cheapest way to comply with COOL and because many U.S. consumers are not willing to pay a price premium for country-of-origin labeling, or incurring the additional costs associated with segregating imported livestock before processing, either option "is likely to cause a decrease in the volume and price of imported livestock."

The panel also reviewed econometric analyses[41] submitted by Canada and the United States that purported to assess COOL's impacts on prices and shares of imported livestock. Whereas the Canadian study concluded that COOL caused reduced competitive opportunities for Canadian livestock in the U.S. market, the U.S. study concluded that the economic recession was the primary cause. Rather than seeking to reconcile these disparate conclusions, the panel instead assessed "the robustness of each study." It considered Canada's study to be "sufficiently robust" because it included other economic variables that confirmed that COOL—not the economic recession that began in 2008, the 2004-2005 U.S. import ban due to the discovery of BSE in Canada's cattle herds, or transport costs—"had a negative and significant impact on Canadian import shares and price basis." Conversely, the panel found the U.S. study did not sufficiently show that the economic recession rather than COOL accounted for the negative impacts experienced in the cattle sector, did not fully analyze what occurred in both countries' hog sectors, and thus did not refute what Canada's study laid out.

Appellate Body

The United States appealed the DS panel's finding that COOL treats imported livestock less favorably than domestic livestock (i.e., that COOL is inconsistent with TBT's Article 2.1). Its main argument was that COOL did not change the "conditions of competition" to the detriment of Canadian and Mexican cattle and hog producers. The U.S. legal brief acknowledged that though private market participants incur costs in complying with COOL, "any country of origin labeling will necessarily introduce compliance costs" and governments cannot control how participants respond to these costs. The brief argued that market forces, rather than the COOL measure in and of itself, increased the cost of selling Canadian and Mexican livestock into the U.S. market, and that COOL cannot be faulted for being discriminatory.[42]

In reviewing the U.S. appeal, the Appellate Body found that the panel's analysis of the finding of unfavorable treatment was incomplete in not considering whether or not the detrimental impact on imports was due exclusively to a "legitimate regulatory distinction" (i.e., a legally valid reason for similar products to be treated differently), which the TBT allows. The AB found that the COOL measure:

> lacks even-handedness because its recordkeeping and verification requirements impose a disproportionate burden on upstream producers and processors of livestock as compared to the information conveyed to consumers through the mandatory labelling requirements for meat sold at the retail level. That is, although a large amount of information must be tracked and transmitted by upstream producers for purposes of providing consumers with information on origin, only a small amount of this information is actually communicated to consumers in an understandable or accurate manner, including because a considerable proportion of meat sold in the United States is not subject to the COOL measure's labelling requirements at all.[43]

Based on these findings, the AB concluded that COOL's "regulatory distinctions" (i.e., the prescribed labels and labeling exemptions) "amount to arbitrary and unjustifiable discrimination against imported livestock, such that they cannot be said to be applied in an even-handed manner," rather than being based upon a "legitimate regulatory distinction." It thus upheld the DS panel's finding, but for different reasons, that COOL's requirements on labeling beef and pork accord "less favorable treatment to imported livestock than to domestic livestock."

COOL Does Not Meet Objective of Providing Consumers with Information on Origin of Meats

Dispute Panel

Canada and Mexico also alleged that COOL violates Article 2.2 of the TBT by being more trade-restrictive than necessary to fulfill a legitimate policy objective. Article 2.2 reads:

> Members shall ensure that technical regulations are not prepared, adopted or applied with a view to or with the effect of creating unnecessary obstacles to international trade. For this purpose, technical regulations *shall not be more trade-restrictive than necessary to fulfil a legitimate objective*, taking account of the risks non-fulfillment would create. Such legitimate objectives are, *inter alia*: national security requirements; the prevention of deceptive practices; protection of human health or safety, animal or plant life or health, or the environment. In assessing such risks, relevant elements of consideration are, *inter alia*: available scientific and technical information, related processing technology or intended end-uses of products. (italics added for emphasis)

The panel accepted the U.S. position that COOL's objective is to inform consumers of the country of origin of meat products,[44] and it agreed with the United States that this is a "legitimate" policy objective under TBT's Article 2.2 to pursue. However, it concluded that COOL's implementation is more trade restrictive than is necessary to fulfill its objective because it does not meaningfully inform consumers about the countries of origin of meat products.

In reaching its conclusion that COOL does not achieve its objective, the DS panel agreed with Canada and Mexico that the labels identifying multiple countries of origin could confuse or mislead, rather than inform, consumers. It noted that a consumer could not readily distinguish the origins of meat products listed on a Category B label as coming from multiple countries, from the origins of meat products shown on a Category C label as coming from those same multiple countries (e.g., Product of the United States, Canada [Category B], compared to Product of Canada, United States [Category C]—see **Table 1**). The panel added that because processors have the flexibility to use both types of labels interchangeably for commingled meat (i.e., meat processed from animals of different origins on the same day), the labels not only fail to inform the average consumer of the distinction between them but could also mislead a fully informed consumer about the precise origins of some meat products.

Appellate Body

The United States appealed the DS panel's finding that COOL does not meet the objective of providing consumers with meaningful information on the origin of meats. It challenged the two-step approach the panel followed to determine whether COOL is consistent with TBT's Article 2.2. Its brief pointed out that the panel first looked at whether COOL fulfills a legitimate policy objective, and if it had been found to do so, would have examined whether COOL is more trade-restrictive than necessary compared to other possible less trade-restrictive measures that could have just as well met the policy objective. The United States argued that the panel took the wrong approach and instead should have focused only on whether COOL is more trade-restrictive than necessary. It argued that the panel went beyond the scope of Article 2.2 to make an "intrusive and far-ranging judgment" on whether COOL "is effective public policy."

In its analysis, the Appellate Body found that the DS panel erred in interpreting and applying Article 2.2. Although it agreed with the panel that COOL's objective is to provide consumers with information on origin and that this is a legitimate objective, the AB viewed the panel's finding as too narrow. The AB found that the panel

> appeared to have considered, incorrectly, that a measure could be consistent with Article 2.2 only if it fulfilled its objective completely or exceeded some minimum level of fulfilment, and to have ignored its own findings, which demonstrated that the COOL measure does contribute, at least to some extent, to achieving its objective.

The AB reversed the panel's finding that COOL is inconsistent with Article 2.2, but was not able to determine whether COOL is more trade-restrictive than necessary to meet the TBT requirement that it be a legitimate objective.[45]

Since the United States won its appeal on this finding, no U.S. response is required.

Ground Meat Label Does Not Result in Less Favorable Treatment for Imported Livestock

Dispute Panel

The DS panel determined that, unlike the muscle cut labels, the ground meat labels were consistent with Article 2.1 of the TBT. It found that the 60-day "inventory allowance" gives significant flexibility to processors (e.g., beef grinders) in labeling country of origin. This rule is based on the statutory requirement that ground meat labels list all actual or "reasonably possible" countries of origin. In practice, the rule allows a processor to use the same label for all of its ground meat so long as the label lists all countries of origin of the meat in the processor's inventory for the last 60 days. Moreover, the 60-day "inventory allowance" flexibility is available not only for meat processors, but for market participants at every stage of meat supply and distribution. The panel determined that, contrary to Canada and Mexico's assertions, the rule's flexibility "limits any additional costs of implementing" the ground meat labeling requirements. It noted that Canada and Mexico did not present any evidence that, *despite* this flexibility, compliance with COOL for ground meat affected imported livestock less favorably than domestic livestock.

Appeal Status

Canada and Mexico did not appeal the DS panel's finding to the AB.

Vilsack Letter Is Not a Technical Regulation

Dispute Panel

Although the panel recognized that the Vilsack letter is not a technical regulation within the scope of the TBT Agreement, the panel agreed with Canada and Mexico that the Vilsack letter constitutes "unreasonable administration" of COOL and thus violates Article X:3(a) of GATT 1994 (see "Vilsack Letter" for details). This article states that "[e]ach contracting party shall administer in a uniform, impartial and reasonable manner all its laws, regulations, decisions and rulings ..." Specifically, the panel found that the letter is an unreasonable act of administering COOL because (1) it could not find any "justifiable rationale" for simultaneously permitting the final rule to enter into force and suggesting stricter practices than the ones the rule requires, (2) the language of the letter may have caused uncertainty and confusion as to its force and effect, and (3) its timing relative to the final rule's entry into force may have caused confusion about whether processors should comply with the final rule or the Vilsack letter. The letter, it wrote, did not meet the minimum standards for transparency and procedural fairness in the administration of trade regulations.

Appeal Activity

The United States did not appeal this finding. Canada, in its appeal, requested that the AB make certain rulings on the Vilsack letter. Subsequently, Canada stated that it no longer sought a finding on this matter because the United States asserted that this measure had been withdrawn on April 5, 2012.

Reaction to WTO DS Panel and Appellate Body Reports

United States

With the WTO's release of the DS panel's report, USTR welcomed its affirmation of "the right of the United States to require country of origin labeling for meat products." Acknowledging that the panel disagreed with the details on how the U.S. COOL requirements were designed, it expressed the U.S. commitment to provide "consumers with accurate and relevant information [on] the origin of meat products that they buy at the retail level." USTR stated that it would consider all options going forward, including an appeal.[46]

The U.S. meat sector expressed mixed reactions. Those in favor of making changes to COOL to address the panel's conclusions include the National Cattlemen's Beef Association (NCBA), the National Pork Producers Council (NPPC), and the American Meat Institute (AMI). The NCBA advised against appealing this ruling. Instead, it urged USTR to work "to apply pressure on Congress to bring the United States into WTO compliance across the board" and to act quickly before Canada and Mexico—two important trading partners—impose "unnecessary and unfortunate tariffs" on U.S. agricultural exports. The NPPC "will be working with lawmakers to craft a legislative fix so that [COOL] is WTO-compliant" to avoid risking "retaliation from and a trade war with Canada and Mexico." AMI commented that the ruling "was not surprising," stating that it had "contended for years ... that [COOL] was not just costly and cumbersome, but a violation of our country's WTO obligations."[47]

Livestock groups that support COOL as now implemented include the Ranchers-Cattlemen Action Legal Fund (R-CALF) and the U.S. Cattlemen's Association (USCA). R-CALF responded that "the WTO is trying to usurp our nation's sovereignty," questioning "when do we allow an international tribunal to dictate to our U.S. Congress what is or is not a legitimate objective of providing information to United States' citizens?" The USCA strongly disagreed with the panel's findings, but was pleased that the report "affirmed the right of the U.S. to label meat for consumers." Its president expressed support for USTR's efforts to defend U.S. rights, pledging to assist "with the appeal process" and to work "with our allies in the Administration and Congress to ensure that COOL continues."[48]

Other groups that had participated in the debate leading up to COOL's enactment also weighed in. The Food Marketing Institute (FMI) agreed with the panel's conclusion that COOL "fails to provide information in a meaningful way" and highlighted that "COOL enforcement has become more burdensome than ever ... for retailers." Its spokesman stated that COOL "will need to be repealed or rewritten for the U.S. to meet its [trade obligations]" and that FMI will work with Congress and USDA "to develop an alternative system" that informs consumers with useful information.[49] Among those supporting COOL, the National Farmers Union (NFU) responded that it will work with USTR and USDA "to ensure that COOL is implemented to the fullest extent of the law and in accordance with WTO." Its statement concluded that "if these results are unsatisfactory, then NFU will push to appeal the decision and continue to fight ... to ensure COOL is allowed to continue for as long as it takes to get this done." Public Citizen commented that the WTO's ruling against COOL for meats "make[s] it increasingly clear to the public that the WTO is leading a race to the bottom in consumer protection" by its second-guessing "the U.S. Congress, courts and public by elevating the goal of maximizing trade flows over consumer and environmental protection." Food and Water Watch urged the Administration to appeal the ruling, noting that the WTO "should not get to decide what U.S. consumers get to know about their food and should not be able to undermine rules put in place by U.S. elected officials."[50]

Members of Congress also hold diverse views on COOL's future. Some did not expect the WTO panel's decision on COOL to be favorable and view more "unwinnable" WTO cases as not in the "best interest" of U.S. agricultural producers. Senator Pat Roberts, ranking Member of the Senate Agriculture Committee, at a regional livestock meeting stated that he does not know of any market study that "shows American consumers will buy more American products with labels in the store" and hoped "we can change people's minds."[51] By contrast, 19 Senators requested that the Obama Administration appeal the panel's ruling and "work to ensure that our COOL program both meets our international trade obligations while continuing to provide such information to consumers." Their letter expressed concern about the ruling's impact "on our ability to continue providing [COOL] information to consumers" and noted that congressional intent behind the 2008 statutory changes was for "such labeling [to] be nondiscriminatory in its treatment of imported products by requiring the labeling of both domestic as well as imported products." The letter further stated that the final COOL rule "appropriately establishes a labeling system which provides important and useful information to consumers while not placing an undue burden on the industry" and which "continues to provide the same opportunity for imported livestock to compete in the domestic marketplace as was the case prior to USDA's implementation of COOL."[52]

Canada

The Canadian government welcomed the panel's ruling as a "clear victory for Canada's livestock industry." Its Minister of Agriculture stated that the WTO decision "recognizes the integrated nature of the North American supply chain in this vitally important industry" and that "[r]emoving onerous labelling measures and unfair, unnecessary costs will improve competitiveness, boost growth and help strengthen the prosperity of Canadian and American producers alike." He expressed the hope this ruling "will open the door to a negotiated settlement of the dispute" and stressed Canada's commitment to work with the United States to "create a stronger more profitable livestock industry on both sides of the 49th parallel."[53]

The Canadian Pork Council (CPC) stated that the panel's report "vindicates [the] objections" the pork industry had to COOL legislation, which it believes restricts market access (i.e., the movement of live swine to the U.S. market) and constitutes a technical barrier. The CPC plans to work "with like-minded groups in the U.S. to find a meaningful solution without further litigation" (referring to a possible U.S. appeal and the process that would follow). The Canadian Cattlemen's Association (CCA) stated the ruling confirms Canada's position that COOL discriminates against live cattle shipped to the United States to the detriment of Canadian cattle producers. In particular, it noted that since taking effect, COOL "has increased costs for U.S. companies that import live Canadian cattle," which has reduced "the competiveness of those Canadian cattle in the U.S. market." The CCA plans to continue working with the U.S. industry "not ... for the outright repeal of COOL but [to] seek only those regulatory and statutory changes necessary to eliminate the discrimination that COOL has imposed to the comparative disadvantage of livestock imported into the U.S. vis-a-vis U.S. livestock."[54]

Reactions to the USTR Decision to Appeal

Interest groups that had urged the Obama Administration to appeal the WTO report (R-CALF, NCA, NFU, Food and Water Watch, Public Citizen) supported this decision.[55] Those that advocated resolving this dispute (NCBA, NPPC) expressed disappointment, and noted that the appeal jeopardizes strong trading relationships with Canada and Mexico and invites the prospect of retaliation by these two countries against U.S. meat exports.[56] (For background on all of these groups' positions, see "Reaction to WTO Panel Ruling, United States," above.)

Canada's Agriculture Minister expressed disappointment that the United States appealed, stating his confidence that the WTO findings "will be upheld so that trade can move more freely, benefiting producers and processors on both sides of the border." Mexico's Economic Ministry declared that it would defend Mexico's interests in the appeal process, and that it plans to file its own notice of appeal seeking a review of some issues in the panel's report that it says reflect inadequate legal analysis.[57]

Options to Bring COOL into Compliance

With the WTO arbitrator establishing May 23, 2013, as the deadline for the United States to comply with the findings of the dispute settlement (DS) panel and appellate body (AB) reports, the case moves to the compliance stage (see "WTO Procedures for the United States to Comply with Reports' Findings"). The WTO found that the COOL regulations treated imported livestock in an unfavorable manner by altering the conditions of competition in a way that favored domestic livestock over imported livestock (see "WTO Findings"). The United States has said it will bring COOL into compliance with its WTO obligations.[58] Stakeholders have two views about how the United States should comply with the WTO findings. One is to amend the COOL legislation; the other is to change the COOL regulations to bring the United States into compliance.

Legislative Approach

Some U.S. stakeholders have argued that, for the United States to comply with the WTO findings, the COOL law would have to be changed, because the law requires that meat derived from foreign-born, or foreign-born and -raised, animals has to have a different label than meat from animals born, raised, and slaughtered in the United States.[59] The National Cattlemen's Beef Association (NCBA), the National Pork Producers Council (NPPC), the American Meat Institute (AMI), and the Food Marketing Institute (FMI) have opposed mandatory COOL from its inception. They have advocated that Congress change the law to enable the United States to meet its WTO obligations, and warn that retaliation by Canada and Mexico will harm U.S. livestock and meat markets.[60]

These industry groups point to research conducted by Kansas State University, which found that consumers valued meat with a "Product of North America" label about the same as meat with a "Product of the United States" label.[61] A "Product of North America" label could apply to any meat from imported livestock from Canada and Mexico that is substantially altered through slaughtering and processing in a U.S. meatpacking plant. A single label for meat that is from any animal slaughtered in the United States could eliminate the extra cost associated with segregating and recordkeeping for imported livestock, thus ending discriminatory pricing of imported livestock. Some in the meat industry argue that the "Product of the United States" label should apply to any meat being processed in a U.S. meatpacking plant.[62] This approach would require a change in the COOL legislation.

Canadian stakeholders have consistently contended that a change in legislation will be required. According to the Canadian Pork Council (CPC):

> for the U.S. to come into compliance with the WTO ruling will require legislative action to eliminate the conditions that give rise to the discrimination against live animals born outside of the U.S.—the discrimination arising from the requirement of COOL that there be different labels for animals processed in a U.S. plant (that are) born, raised and slaughtered in the U.S. from those not born raised and slaughtered in the U.S. Those labeling requirements are explicit in the legislation; thus, a legislative or statutory change will be needed.

A representative from the Canadian Cattlemen Association (CCA) agreed with the CPC assessment. In the view of the CPC and CCA, mandatory COOL labels are acceptable, but the law would have to be amended to require that all meat processed from imported livestock in a U.S. meatpacking plant be labeled the same as meat processed from domestic livestock.[63]

During the WTO arbitration process over the compliance timeline, Canada expressed the view that a regulatory change is unlikely to bring the United States into compliance and that a legislative change could be necessary.[64] In presenting their arguments for quicker compliance, Canada and Mexico argued that the United States had adequate time to take a legislative approach to compliance, especially because the ongoing 2012 farm bill debate would have provided a legislative vehicle for addressing COOL. Some U.S. stakeholders also have suggested that the farm bill would be an appropriate vehicle to legislatively comply with WTO obligations.[65] Taking advantage of the placeholder provision inserted into the House-passed farm bill (Section 11105 of H.R. 2642), COOL was one of the outstanding issues placed on the agenda of farm bill conferees. The conference agreement sent to the floor did not include any major changes to COOL (see "Congressional Interest").

Regulatory Approach

Other stakeholders advocated that USDA rework the COOL regulations to bring the United States into compliance with the WTO ruling. Reportedly, at the beginning of 2012, USTR considered but did not follow through with making changes to COOL regulations. The change would have allowed for more flexibility for commingling imported and domestic cattle and using a multi-country label. This approach was dropped as supporters of COOL believed such a change would undermine the COOL law. Others argued that the change would not go far enough.[66]

Interest Group Support for Regulatory Fix

In August 2012, the Ranchers-Cattlemen Action Legal Fund, United Stock growers of America (R-CALF) sent a letter to Secretary Vilsack and U.S. Trade Representative Kirk that proposed regulatory changes to simplify the recordkeeping requirements of COOL.[67] Because U.S. animal health regulations[68] require that imported cattle have a foreign mark and that cattle imported for immediate slaughter be shipped in sealed conveyances to slaughter plants, R-CALF proposed that any cattle arriving at a slaughter plant without a mark or seal be considered U.S. cattle. The WTO found that more information was collected on imported cattle compared with what was passed on to consumers on labels. According to R-CALF, its proposed presumption for U.S. cattle would reduce additional documentation and recordkeeping for imported cattle. Currently, hogs are exempt from a country-of-origin mark under the Tariff Act of 1930.[69] R-CALF suggested that this livestock exemption be removed, thus requiring a country-of-origin mark on hogs. Once the exemption is lifted, the presumption of domestic hogs would become workable.

R-CALF also called on USDA to eliminate the use of a mixed label (Labels B or C; see **Table 1**) on meat from an animal that is exclusively of U.S. origin. R-CALF also suggested that ground beef labeling be revised to not allow for a country to be listed on a label if meat from that country is not included in the ground product (see Ground Beef label, **Table 1**). Lastly, R-CALF's proposal calls for the expanded coverage of minimally processed products, such as cooked, smoked, or cured meats, that are currently exempt from COOL regulations.

On February 4, 2013, the National Farmers Union (NFU) and the United States Cattlemen's Association (USCA) released an analysis of proposed options to bring COOL into WTO compliance.[70] This analysis laid out their case for how the United States could comply with its WTO obligations if USDA required more information to be added to labels about where cattle were born, raised, and slaughtered. The proposal also called for USDA to halt the commingling of meat from animals of different origin. For minimally processed products, such as smoked, cured, or cooked products, which are exempt from labeling, USDA could revise the regulations to require that these products be labeled. The proposal also suggested that COOL should be extended to food service, which the COOL statute currently exempts. The proposal noted this would require a change in law and could not be accomplished through a change in regulations.

Congressional Support for a Regulatory Fix

Some Members of Congress have expressed the view that USDA and USTR should bring the United States into WTO compliance through regulatory means. In a January 31, 2013, letter to the Secretary of Agriculture and the U.S. Trade Representative, 31 Senators asked that USDA and USTR find a regulatory solution.[71] The Senators asked that a regulatory fix make the COOL regulations consistent with WTO rules, provide accurate origin information for all meat cuts to consumers, engage industry stakeholders in the rulemaking process, and keep Congress informed.

USDA's Final COOL Rule

On March 12, 2013, USDA released its proposed rule to amend COOL regulations. According to USDA, the proposed rule would improve the operation of the COOL program and bring it into compliance with WTO trade obligations.[72] There was a 30-day public comment period. The department issued the final rule on May 23, 2013, and published it in the *Federal Register* on May 24, 2013.[73] The final rule was not significantly different from the proposed rule issued in March. On May 24, 2013, the United States notified the WTO Dispute Settlement Body (DSB) that it had complied with the WTO findings on COOL.

Table 2. COOL Retail Labels for Muscle Cuts of Meat: Original Rule Compared with Revised Rule

Animal Origin of Muscle Cuts	Original COOL Label (January 2009)	Revised COOL Label (May 2013)
Muscle cuts from animals exclusively born, raised, and slaughtered in the U.S.; and animals born and raised in Alaska or Hawaii and transported for a period of not more than 60 days through Canada to the U.S. and slaughtered in the U.S.	Product of the U.S.	Born, Raised, and Slaughtered in the U.S.
(1) Muscle cuts from animals born in Country X and (as applicable) Country Y, and raised and slaughtered in the U.S., excluding animals imported for immediate slaughter. (2) Muscle cuts from animals born, raised, and slaughtered in the U.S. that are commingled during a production day with muscle cuts from animals born outside the U.S., raised and slaughtered in the U.S., and not imported for immediate slaughter. (3) Muscle cuts from animals born in Country X, and (as applicable) Country Y, raised and slaughtered in the U.S., that are commingled during a production day with muscle cut derived from animals that are imported into the U.S. for immediate slaughter.	(1) Product of the U.S., Country X and (as applicable) Country Y (2) Product of the U.S., Country X and (as applicable) Country Y (3) Product of the U.S., Country X and (as applicable) Country Y	(1) Born in Country X, Raised and Slaughtered in the U.S. (2) Not applicable because commingling is no longer allowed (3) Not applicable because commingling is no longer allowed
Muscle cuts from animals imported into the United States for immediate slaughter.	Product of Country X, U.S.	Born and Raised in Country X, Slaughtered in the U.S.
Imported muscle cuts for which no production steps occurred in the United States.	Product of Country X	Unchanged

Source: **Table 1;** USDA, AMS, final rule published in Federal Register, May 24, 2013 (see footnote 73), and codified in a revision to 7 C.F.R. 65.300(d)-(f).

USDA's final rule revised labeling requirements for covered meat products and is intended to address the WTO's finding that COOL regulations are not enforced in an evenhanded manner. The WTO found that COOL requirements result in much more information being collected upstream than is passed on to consumers on labels, and that the information on labels may be confusing and incomplete.

Under the final COOL rule, the retail labeling of covered meat commodities must include the country of origin of each production step. That is, meat labels have to include where the animals were born, where raised, and where slaughtered. The rule also prohibits the practice of commingling muscle meat produced during a single production day and the use of multi-country labels for muscle meat.

Under the final COOL rule, meat from animals that are exclusively born, raised, and slaughtered in the United States has to be labeled "Born, Raised, and Slaughtered in the United States." Under the previous rule, meat exclusively from U.S. animals was labeled as "Product of the United States." (See **Table 2** for comparison of the initial labels and revised labels at the retail level.)

The final rule also eliminates the previous use of mixed origin labels, such as "Product of the United States, and Country X, and/or Country Y" and "Product of Country X, and/or Country Y and the United States." Under the rule, each production stage must be included on the label. For example, beef from cattle that were originally imported into the United States as feeder cattle require a label stating "Born in Country X, Raised and Slaughtered in the United States." For cattle that were imported for immediate slaughter, the label is required to read "Born and Raised in Country X, Slaughtered in the United States." Previously the label would have read "Product of Country X and the United States."

In addition, the final COOL rule no longer allows meat that is processed during a single production day from animals of different origins to be commingled and labeled with a mixed label such as "Product of the United States, and Country X, and/or Country Y." Meat labels, as noted above, now must include each production step (born, raised, and slaughtered) for the processed animals. The labeling requirement for imported muscle cuts of meat is unchanged; however, the labels may include the production steps if there is supporting documentation for them.

Last, the final rule also amends the definition of retailer to extend it to any person that meets the definition of retailer in the Perishable Agricultural Commodities Act of 1930 (PACA; 7 U.S.C. 499a et seq.), whether or not the retailer has a PACA license. This provision clarifies who is subject to COOL regulations.

Implementation of the COOL Rule

The final COOL rule went into effect on May 23, 2013, and did not apply to muscle cuts produced or packaged before that date. USDA recognized that meat processors would not be able to implement new labeling requirements immediately. During the first six months after the rule was published, USDA planned to conduct industry education and outreach activities. The six-month period also provided time for existing stocks of muscle meat labeled under old regulations to clear the pipeline. USDA also allowed meat processors to use their existing stock of old labels until they were completely used. However, under this allowance, retailers had to provide in-store signs or placards that notify country of origin according to the final rule.

Costs and Benefits of the Final Rule

In the proposed rule, USDA estimated the cost for implementing new labeling at $32.8 million (range of $17.0 million to $47.3 million), and estimated that 33,350 establishments owned by 7,181 firms would need to rework labels.[74] However, the proposed rule did not calculate costs from prohibiting commingling. The final rule estimated the cost of losing commingling flexibility at $90.5 million, with a range of $36.1 million to $144.8 million. When labeling costs are added to the costs of losing commingling flexibility, the total costs of implementation range from $53.1 million to $192.1 million.[75] USDA noted that it is not possible to specify how often packers use commingling flexibility, and therefore difficult to estimate. But USDA believed the cost of losing commingling flexibility would fall towards the lower end of the range, resulting in a likely total cost of $53.1 million to $137.8 million.[76]

Most of the labeling costs are expected to be borne by packing and processing facilities as they add new production steps to labels. USDA noted that it does not believe additional recordkeeping will be necessary under the new rule. As for the economic benefits of this change, USDA says it was unable to quantify benefits from adding production steps to labels, but noted they were likely "comparatively small" relative to benefits discussed in the final 2009 COOL rule.[77] In previous analysis of COOL, USDA found the economic benefits to be positive but difficult to quantify.

Reaction to the New COOL Rule

Mixed Views among Livestock Producers and Meat Processors

U.S. farm and ranch groups that have been long-time supporters of COOL responded positively to USDA's final rule. The National Farmers Union (NFU) said, "We are very pleased that the USDA has decided to stand strong and keep COOL. The decision to bring the law into compliance with the WTO's ruling is a win-win situation for all interested parties. We further applaud the administration for deciding to take a proactive approach in bringing COOL into compliance by providing more information on the origins of our food, instead of simply watering down the process."[78] The United States Cattlemen's Association (USCA) also commended USDA for finalizing the COOL rule, which "will not only strengthen the overall program, but will also bring the U.S. into compliance with our international trade obligations. Consumers will have even more information on labels with which they can make informed purchasing decisions."[79] When the proposed rule was issued, USCA, as well as NFU, noted that the rule was similar to the proposals presented in the legal analysis commissioned by USCA and NFU (see "Regulatory Approach").

R-CALF also supported USDA's final rule because it would provide accurate information to consumers about the origin of their meat. R-CALF noted that, "Without COOL it is the meatpacker and not the consumer that decides from what country cattle will be sourced to satisfy consumer demand for beef. Only with COOL can consumers trigger a demand signal for cattle sourced from U.S. farmers and ranchers, which they can do simply by consistently choosing to purchase a USA product."[80]

U.S. livestock groups that have opposed mandatory COOL requirements also weighed in on the final rule. The American Meat Institute (AMI) said, "It is incomprehensible that USDA would finalize a controversial rule that stands to harm American agriculture, when comments on the proposal made clear how deeply and negatively it will impact U.S. meat companies and livestock producers."[81] The National Cattlemen's Beef Association (NCBA) called the rule shortsighted, and said it would increase discrimination against imported product, and increase recordkeeping burdens. NCBA noted that "any retaliation against U.S. beef would be devastating for our producers."[82]

In October 2013, Tyson Foods, Inc., announced that it would stop buying direct-to-slaughter cattle from Canada. According to the company, the COOL rule raised costs due to the need for additional product codes and product segregation. Tyson Foods will continue to purchase Canadian-born cattle that are fed in U.S. feedlots.[83]

Meat Industry Lawsuit

On July 8, 2013, a group of eight meat industry organizations, led by AMI, filed a lawsuit in the U.S. District Court for the District of Columbia to block USDA's final COOL rule.[84] The plaintiffs challenged the COOL rule for three reasons. They contend first, that COOL violates the U.S. Constitution because it compels speech in the form of a label that does not advance a government interest; second, that the rule violates the COOL statute, which does not allow for detailed labels; and third, that the rule is arbitrary and capricious, violating the Administrative Procedure Act, because it is burdensome for industry but provides little or no benefit to consumers.

According to the plaintiffs, USDA's final rule is more complex and discriminatory against foreign meat and livestock than the previous rule because stricter segregation will be necessary to meet the requirements. They say that the rule would be particularly onerous for U.S. meat processors that are located near the border of Mexico or Canada who often use imported livestock. Furthermore, the plaintiffs do not believe the rule will meet U.S. WTO obligations.[85]

The National Farmers Union, which supports COOL, characterized the lawsuit as a tactic to delay the implementation of a stronger COOL rule by groups that do not support COOL.[86] In response to the lawsuit, R-CALF started a petition requesting that USDA stop NCBA, one of the plaintiffs in the lawsuit, from receiving mandated beef check off funds. R-CALF claims that it is a conflict of interest for NCBA to receive those funds while suing USDA to halt the implementation of the popular COOL program that provides U.S. consumers information about the source of their beef.[87]

On July 25, 2013, the plaintiffs requested that the U.S. District Court for the District of Columbia grant a preliminary injunction against the implementation of the final COOL rule.[88] The plaintiffs argued that they would likely succeed in challenging USDA on the final rule, and that they would suffer irreparable harm if USDA continued to implement the rule during the challenge. On August 9, 2013, supporters of COOL, led by the United States Cattlemen's Association (USCA), filed a motion to intervene in the meat industry lawsuit, and the court granted the request on August 20.[89] The district court heard the plaintiffs' arguments for a preliminary injunction on August 27.

On September 11, the court denied the plaintiffs' request.[90] The court found that the plaintiffs were unlikely to succeed on their constitutional, statutory, or arbitrary and capricious claims.

Furthermore, the court found that the plaintiffs did not demonstrate they would suffer irreparable harm if an injunction was not granted. AMI disagreed with the court's decision and appealed the decision.[91] Supporters of COOL that intervened in the case will continue to oppose AMI's court challenge to the COOL rule.[92] The plaintiffs' appeal was heard on January 9, 2014, before the U.S. Court of Appeals for the District of Columbia Circuit.

Response from Canada and Mexico

Canadian cattle and hog industry representatives have stated their belief that the final COOL rule will not bring the United States into compliance, with both groups noting that it increases discrimination. The Canadian Cattlemen's Association (CCA) said the new rule will increase the impact of COOL on Canadian cattle because it "will require additional segregation by eliminating the ability to commingle cattle of different origins."[93] The Canadian Pork Council (CPC) also issued a similar statement: "The new rule does nothing to reduce discrimination against Canadian feeder pigs and slaughter hogs.... The new rule will strip away any flexibility to commingle Canadian and US live swine at processing plants. This will make a very bad situation of the last four years much worse."[94] Both the CCA and CPC are plaintiffs on the meat industry lawsuit to halt the implementation of the COOL rule.

The governments of both Canada and Mexico have rejected the USDA final rule as a solution to the WTO dispute. Canada's Minister of International Trade and Minister of Agriculture stated: "Canada is extremely disappointed with the regulatory changes put forward by the United States today with respect to COOL. These changes will not bring the United States into compliance with its WTO obligations. These changes will increase discrimination against Canadian cattle and hogs and increase damages to industry on both sides of the border. Canada will consider all options at its disposal, including, if necessary, the use of retaliatory measures."[95] Mexico also stated that USDA's "new rule does not meet the requirements of the WTO and will further damage Mexican cattle exports. The U.S. COOL program has created severe trade distortions as it has unnecessarily increased costs for the cattle industry."[96]

Canada's Preliminary Retaliation List

On June 7, 2013, Canada's Minister of International Trade and Minister of Agriculture issued a press release stating that the final rule did not meet the WTO requirements.[97] At the same time, Canada released a list of products imported from the United States that could be targeted for retaliation. The list includes 38 harmonized tariff codes that cover a range of food and agricultural commodities and products, as well as a few manufactured products. The list was officially published in the *Canada Gazette* (Canada's *Federal Register*) for public comment.[98] The press release states that Canada expects to consult with stakeholders to resolve the COOL dispute over the next 18 to 24 months, and that the Canadian government will abide by its WTO obligations and not take retaliatory measures until the WTO provides authorization.

Damage Estimates

Should the COOL case reach the retaliation stage, the damage claims could fall between $1 billion and $2 billion, by some estimates. According to a Canadian Pork Council study, COOL harms the Canadian hog industry by $500 million per year.[99] For the Canadian cattle industry, annual losses from COOL have been estimated at $639 million.[100] Mexico's claim on damages to its cattle sector could also be substantial. In the last three years, U.S. imports from Mexico have topped more than 1 million head, and per-head discounts on imported Mexican cattle due to COOL reportedly have been estimated by some analysts at as much as $60 per head.[101] In addition, Mexico's cattle industry would likely argue that COOL has led to economic losses throughout the Mexican cattle sector beyond the discounted import prices. If the COOL dispute moves into the retaliation phase, the WTO would have to approve the level of retaliation, and the United States would be able to contest it.

Compliance Panel

On June 10, 2013, the United States, Canada, and Mexico communicated to the DSB that they have agreed to procedures for proceeding under WTO rules to establish a compliance panel and to address compensation or suspension of concessions.[102] It was agreed that Canada and Mexico could request a compliance panel at any time, and consultations with the United States are not necessary prior to the request.[103]

On August 19, 2013, Canada and Mexico informed the DSB that they would request the establishment of a compliance panel. The United States objected to Canada's and Mexico's first request at the August 30, 2013, DSB meeting. At the September 25, 2013, DSB meeting, Canada and Mexico again requested the establishment of a compliance panel.[104] The DSB accepted the request and referred the dispute to the original COOL dispute settlement panel. The compliance panel will hear the COOL dispute February 18-19, 2014.

The compliance panel could issue a report within 90 days of the hearing. According to the June 10, 2013, agreement, the compliance panel report findings could be appealed to the Appellate Body (AB), and the AB report could be issued within another 90 days. Depending on the outcome of the compliance ruling(s), procedural timelines, and whether or not the case progresses to the retaliation phase and arbitration, the WTO COOL case may not be concluded before 2015.

Congressional Interest

Observers point out that the 2008 farm bill amendments to the initial COOL statute were intended to balance the concerns of both proponents and opponents and to settle the long-standing controversy over requiring COOL for meats and other covered commodities. However, the outcome of the WTO challenge initiated by Canada and Mexico likely will influence the dynamics of COOL debate in the 113th Congress and beyond, particularly if the WTO finds that USDA's new rule is deficient in addressing the WTO findings. Some lawmakers agree with some industry groups' criticisms of mandatory COOL and could offer legislation to limit its scope and impacts. Others remain strongly supportive of COOL as enacted and oppose any rollback.

Farm Bill

In the 113th Congress, House and Senate conferees completed work on the farm bill without making any major changes to COOL's statutory language (see below).

Earlier, in May 2013, during the Senate Agriculture Committee markup of the Senate farm bill (S. 954), Senator Mike Johanns offered and then withdrew an amendment to repeal COOL for beef, lamb, and pork. Senator Johanns noted that he believed the rule USDA had proposed to address the WTO findings would be a regulatory nightmare and would not satisfy the U.S. WTO obligations. But instead of asking for a roll call vote on the amendment, he withdrew it in recognition that the committee's opinion on COOL was divided. S. 954, the Senate-passed farm bill, contains no provisions on COOL.

The House-passed farm bill (H.R. 2642, passed July 11, 2013) contained a provision (Section 11105) that would have required USDA to conduct an economic analysis of USDA's March 2013 proposed COOL rule (78 *Federal Register* 15645). The analysis was to include the impact on consumers, producers, and packers of the COOL law and rule. The report on COOL would have been due to Congress within 180 days of farm bill enactment. During the first farm bill conference meeting on October 30, 2013, several conferees from both the House and Senate raised concerns about the COOL rules. While the farm bill conference leaders worked, reports speculated that conferees would repeal the COOL law or perhaps modify it.[105] COOL opponents encouraged conferees to find a WTO-compliant resolution to the WTO COOL dispute.[106] Reportedly, one proposal considered called for a "North American" meat label, which COOL proponents strongly oppose.[107] USDA's Secretary Vilsack weighed in on COOL with the view that Congress should let the WTO process resolve the issue.[108]

The farm bill conference report to H.R. 2642, released on January 27, 2014, did not contain any language or provision to repeal or modify the COOL law. The only COOL-pertinent provision (Section 12104) includes the economic analysis provision found in the House-passed farm bill. The conference report clarifies that the economic analysis is to be of the May 2013 final rule (78 *Federal Register* 31367) instead of the March 2013 proposed rule. In addition, the COOL provision adds venison as a covered commodity. In a letter to conference leadership, COOL opponents expressed their disappointment that conferees did not alter COOL in a way that would resolve the WTO COOL dispute.[109]

Appropriations

In the explanatory statement for the Consolidated Appropriations Act, 2014 (P.L. 113-76, H.R. 3547), the House Committee on Appropriations expressed disapproval of USDA's May 2013 COOL rule (78 *Federal Register* 31367), pointing to its high costs to the livestock industry and the potential of retaliation in the WTO case. The committee recommended that USDA delay implementing the COOL rule until the WTO case is completed.[110] On January 23, 2014, Representative DeLauro, a member of the House Committee on Appropriations, sent a letter to Secretary Vilsack urging that USDA continue to implement and enforce COOL regulations.[111]

APPENDIX A. OTHER LAWS WITH FOOD LABELING PROVISIONS

The COOL provisions of the 2002 and 2008 farm bills[112] do not change the requirements of the Tariff Act or the food safety inspection statutes described below. Instead, they were incorporated into the Agricultural Marketing Act of 1946 (Sections 281-285).

Tariff Act

Under Section 304 of the Tariff Act of 1930, as amended (19 U.S.C. 1304), every imported item must be conspicuously and indelibly marked in English to indicate to the "ultimate purchaser" its country of origin. The U.S. Customs and Border Protection generally defines the "ultimate purchaser" as the last U.S. person to receive the article in the form in which it was imported. So, articles arriving at the U.S. border in retail-ready packages—including food products, such as a can of Danish ham, or a bottle of Italian olive oil—must carry such a mark. However, if the article is destined for a U.S. processor where it will undergo "substantial transformation," the processor is considered the ultimate purchaser. Over the years, numerous technical rulings by Customs have determined what is, or is not, considered "substantial transformation," depending upon the item in question.

The law has authorized exceptions to labeling requirements, including articles on a so-called "J List," named for Section 1304(a)(3)(J) of the statute. This empowered the Secretary of the Treasury to exempt classes of items that were "imported in substantial quantities during the five-year period immediately preceding January 1, 1937, and were not required during such period to be marked to indicate their origin." Among the items placed on the J List were specified agricultural products including "natural products, such as vegetables, fruits, nuts, berries, and live or dead animals, fish and birds; all the foregoing which are in their natural state or not advanced in any manner further than is necessary for their safe transportation."[113] Although J List items themselves have been exempt from the labeling requirements, Section 304 of the 1930 act has required that their "immediate container" (essentially, the box they came in) have country-of-origin labels. But, for example, when Mexican tomatoes or Chilean grapes were sold unpackaged at retail in a store bin, country labeling had not been required by the Tariff Act.

Meat and Poultry Products Inspection Acts

USDA's Food Safety and Inspection Service (FSIS) is required to ensure the safety and proper labeling of most meat and poultry products, including imports, under the Federal Meat Inspection Act, as amended (21 U.S.C. 601 *et seq.*), and the Poultry Products Inspection Act, as amended (21 U.S.C. 451 *et seq.*). Regulations issued under these laws have required that country of origin appear in English on immediate containers of all meat and poultry products entering the United States (9 C.F.R. 327.14 and 9 C.F.R. 381.205). Only plants in countries certified by USDA to have inspection systems equivalent to those of the United States are eligible to export products to the United States.

All individual, retail-ready packages of imported meat products (for example, canned hams or packages of salami) have had to carry such labeling. Imported bulk products, such as carcasses, carcass parts, or large containers of meat or poultry destined for U.S. plants for further processing also have had to bear country-of-origin marks. However, once these non-retail items have entered the country, the federal meat inspection law has deemed them to be domestic products. When they are further processed in a domestic, FSIS-inspected meat or poultry establishment—which has been considered the ultimate purchaser for purposes of country-of-origin labeling—FSIS no longer requires such labeling on either the new product or its container. FSIS has considered even minimal processing, such as cutting a larger piece of meat into smaller pieces or grinding it for hamburger, enough of a transformation so that country markings are no longer necessary.

Meat and poultry product imports must comply not only with the meat and poultry inspection laws and rules but also with Tariff Act labeling regulations. Because Customs generally requires that imports undergo more extensive changes (i.e., "substantial transformation") than required by USDA to avoid the need for labeling, a potential for conflict has existed between the two requirements.

Federal Food, Drug, and Cosmetic Act

Foods other than meat and poultry are regulated by the U.S. Department of Health and Human Services' Food and Drug Administration (FDA), primarily under the Federal Food, Drug, and Cosmetic Act (FFDCA; 21 U.S.C. 301 et seq.). This act does not expressly require COOL for foods. Section 403(e) of the FFDCA does regard a *packaged* food to be misbranded if it lacks a label containing the name and place of business of the manufacturer, packer, or distributor (among other ways a food can be misbranded). However, this name and place of business is not an indicator of the origin of the product itself.

Appendix B. Timeline of COOL

Table B-1. Major COOL Developments &WTO Dispute Settlement Case

May 13, 2002	COOL provisions are enacted in the 2002 farm bill to take effect on September 30, 2004 (P.L. 107-171, §10816).
October 30, 2003	USDA's Agricultural Marketing Service (AMS) publishes in the *Federal Register* the proposed rule on COOL. The comment period, initially to close December 29, 2003, is extended to February 27, 2004.
January 23, 2004	Implementation of COOL for covered commodities except fish and shellfish is delayed until September 30, 2006, per enactment of the FY2004 omnibus appropriations act (P.L. 108-199, Division A, §749).
October 5, 2004	AMS publishes in the *Federal Register* the interim final rule on COOL for fish and shellfish.

April 4, 2005	COOL labeling for fish and shellfish takes effect.
November 10, 2005	Implementation of COOL for all other covered commodities is delayed until September 30, 2008, per enactment of the FY2006 agriculture appropriations act (P.L. 109-97, §792).
May 22, 2008	Amendments to the 2002-enacted COOL provisions become law in the 2008 farm bill (P.L. 110-246, §11002), to take effect on September 30, 2008.
August 1, 2008	AMS publishes in the *Federal Register* the interim final rule to implement COOL for all covered commodities except fish and shellfish, to take effect on September 30, 2008.
December 16, 2008	Canada, joined by Mexico, holds consultations on COOL with the United States.
January 15, 2009	AMS publishes the final rule to implement COOL for all covered commodities, to take effect on March 16, 2009.
February 20, 2009	Secretary of Agriculture sends letter to meat and food industry representatives urging the voluntary adoption of three labeling changes.
March 16, 2009	COOL's final rule for all covered commodities takes effect.
June 5, 2009	Canada holds consultations with the United States to resolve differences on COOL.
October 7, 2009	Canada requests the establishment of a World Trade Organization (WTO) dispute settlement (DS) panel to consider its complaint on the U.S. COOL program. Mexico follows with a comparable request on October 9.
November 19, 2009	WTO establishes a DS panel to consider complaints made by Canada and Mexico on the U.S. COOL program.
November 18, 2011	WTO DS panel releases final report that concludes that some features of U.S. COOL discriminate against foreign livestock and are not consistent with U.S. WTO trade obligations.
March 23, 2012	The United States appeals the WTO DS panel's conclusions.
March 28, 2012	Canada and Mexico also appeal some of the DS panel's conclusions.
June 29, 2012	The WTO's Appellate Body (AB) issues its report, upholding the DS panel finding that U.S. COOL does not favorably treat imported livestock but reversing the other finding that COOL does not provide sufficient information to consumers on the origin of meat products.
July 10, 2012	Canada, Mexico, and the United States withdraw consideration of the AB report from the Dispute Settlement Body (DSB) agenda to provide more time to consult on the 90-day reporting requirement that was missed by the AB.
July 23, 2012	WTO's DSB adopts the AB report and the DS panel report, as modified by the AB report.
August 22, 2012	30-day deadline for the United States to inform the DSB about how it plans to implement the WTO findings.
August 31, 2012	United States informs the DSB that it intends to comply with the WTO recommendations and rulings, and states its need for a "reasonable period of time" to do so.
October 4, 2012	With Canada, Mexico, and United States unable to agree on what a reasonable period of time should be and on who the arbitrator should be, the WTO's Director appoints an arbitrator to determine this.
December 4, 2012	WTO's arbitrator announces his determination that the "reasonable amount of time" for the United States to implement the DSB's recommendations

	and rulings is 10 months from when the AB and DS panel reports were adopted (i.e., May 23, 2013).
March 12, 2013	AMS issues a proposed rule to modify certain COOL labeling requirements for muscle-cut commodities to bring them into compliance with WTO's findings and to improve the COOL program's overall operation.
April 11, 2013	Deadline for interested parties to submit comments to AMS on proposed COOL rule.
May 23, 2013	Deadline for the United States to comply with the WTO's findings on U.S. COOL.
May 24, 2013	At the DSB meeting, the United States notifies that it had complied with the WTO findings on COOL by issuing a final rule on May 23. No compliance proceeding was initiated by Canada or Mexico.
June 7, 2013	Canada releases an itemized tariff list of products that could be targeted in a retaliatory action against the United States.
July, August, September 2013	In July, U.S., Canadian, and Mexican meat industry organizations file suit against USDA to block the May 2013 COOL rule. They file a motion for a preliminary injunction against implementing the rule in August. In September, the District Court for the District of Columbia denies the group's request to halt the implementation of the COOL rule. The plaintiffs appeal the ruling.
August 19, 2013	Canada and Mexico notify the DSB that they will request the establishment of a compliance panel at the August 30 meeting of the DSB.
August 30, 2013	The United States objects to the establishment of a compliance panel. The request will be made again at the September DSB meeting on September 25, and the United States will not be able to object to its formation.
September 27, 2013	The DSB selects the members of the compliance panel to be the same members that served earlier on the COOL dispute settlement panel.
January 9, 2014	The U.S. Court of Appeals for the District of Columbia Circuit hears the meat industry's appeal of the September denial of the preliminary injunction halting COOL.
February 18-19, 2014	The WTO's compliance panel is scheduled to hear the COOL case.

APPENDIX C. NORTH AMERICAN LIVESTOCK TRADE

Overview

After COOL took full effect in March 2009, Canada and Mexico continued to question the trade legality of mandatory COOL, and claimed that COOL disrupted normal live cattle and hog trade patterns and caused large financial losses to their livestock industries. Canada and Mexico were concerned that labeling requirements and the need to segregate imported and domestic animals to assure proper labeling would raise the cost of handling and processing imported animals. The increased cost would ultimately lead U.S. livestock buyers to reduce live animal imports or to offer lower prices for imported animals.

The cattle and hog industries of Canada, Mexico, and the United States have become increasingly integrated over the last two decades, particularly after NAFTA took effect in 1994 and, before that, the Canada-U.S. Free Trade Agreement in 1988. These agreements, along with the global Uruguay Round Agreements under the WTO that reduced tariff and non-tariff barriers to trade, have enabled animals and animal products to move across borders more freely, based on market demand.

A number of animal health incidents have disrupted this market integration from time to time. The most significant event was the discovery of *bovine spongiform encephalopathy* (BSE or mad cow disease) in 2003, first in Canada and later in the United States, which halted most cross-border movement of cattle from Canada to the United States from mid-2003 through mid-2005. The predominance of BSE cases in Canada rather than in the United States may have contributed to wider support for the mandatory COOL law, some analysts believe, although government officials assert that both countries now have strong, scientifically defensible safeguards in place to ensure that BSE is controlled and that its infectious agent does not enter the human food supply.

Table C-1. Value of U.S. Cattle and Hog Trade

($ million)					
EXPORTS					
	2008	**2009**	**2010**	**2011**	**2012**
Canada					
Cattle	9.7	13.5	19.7	42.3	31.6
Hogs	1.0	1.4	1.6	2.1	1.7
Mexico					
Cattle	51.5	25.8	30.8	20.8	8.1
Hogs	9.0	1.0	2.0	2.9	6.4
Cattle and Hogs Total	71.2	41.6	54.1	68.1	47.9
World					
Cattle	108.1	58.8	132.7	378.9	403.3
Hogs	27.9	9.6	8.6	24.1	33.3
Cattle and Hogs Total	136.0	68.4	141.4	403.0	436.7
IMPORTS					
Canada					
Cattle	1,462.6	917.7	1,051.9	832.3	1,044.0
Hogs	482.3	295.2	363.3	362.9	330.4
Mexico					
Cattle	298.3	381.0	522.8	616.9	716.9
Hogs	0.0	0.0	0.0	0.0	0.0
Cattle and Hogs Total	2,243.1	1,593.9	1,938.0	1,812.1	2,091.4
World					
Cattle	1,760.8	1,298.7	1,574.6	1,449.2	1,761.0
Hogs	482.3	295.2	363.5	362.9	330.4
Cattle and Hogs Total	2,243.1	1,593.9	1,938.1	1,812.1	2,091.4

Proximity, abundant feed supplies, and established feeding operations in the United States have resulted in an increase in live cattle and hog imports from Canada and Mexico. Imports may fluctuate year to year as factors such as relative animal and feed prices, inventory levels, currency exchange rates, and weather conditions influence the movement of cattle and hogs into the United States.

Canada and Mexico are important U.S. trading partners for live animals. The value of U.S. cattle and hog exports to Canada and Mexico was about $48 million in 2012 (**Table C-1**). The United States primarily exports breeding stock. In recent years, U.S. cattle and hogs have been shipped to more than 70 foreign markets. Prior to 2010, Canada and Mexico accounted for a majority of the value of breeding cattle exports, but since then, Russia and Turkey have been leading markets. Similarly, Canada and Mexico accounted for most of the value of breeding hog exports before 2008, but now China has become a leading market for U.S. breeding hog exports.

On the import side, the value of trade with Canada and Mexico is much greater. In 2012, the United States imported nearly $2.1 billion worth of cattle and hogs from Canada and Mexico (**Table C-1**). Almost all U.S. live cattle imports come from Canada and Mexico and almost all live hog imports come from Canada.

In volume terms, on average, cattle imports have accounted for about 6% of total U.S. commercial cattle slaughter since 2000. Over the same period, hog imports have accounted for nearly 7% of total hog commercial slaughter, but the hog share has dropped to 5% since 2009 as hog imports continue to decline.

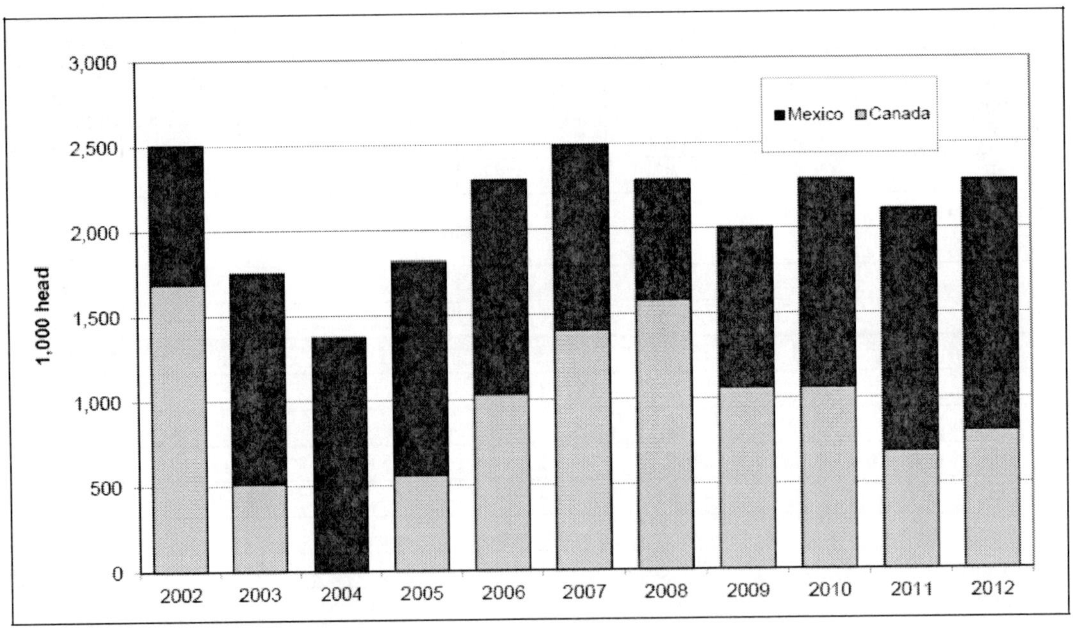

Source: USDA, FAS, GATS.

Figure C-1. U.S. Cattle Imports from Canada and Mexico.

U.S. Cattle Imports

U.S. cattle imports plunged in 2004 after the discovery of BSE in Canada in May 2003 and the subsequent U.S. ban on Canadian cattle imports. In 2004, all U.S. cattle imports came from Mexico. But once the border was reopened to Canadian cattle in 2005, imports steadily increased and reached near pre-BSE levels by 2007 due to the steady rebound in imports from Canada. In 2008, cattle imports dropped 8% to 2.3 million head, and fell 12% to 2 million head in 2009 (**Figure C-1**).

U.S. cattle imports during the first half of 2008 were almost 9% higher than the previous year, but import growth slowed during the second half of 2008, and by December cattle imports had fallen 8% below 2007. Imports from Canada continued to grow during 2008 and imports of Canadian feeder cattle were particularly strong in the first half of the year. Under COOL regulations, cattle that were in the United States before July 15, 2008, were considered U.S. origin cattle, which likely encouraged feeder imports from Canada during the first part of the year. Canadian feeder imports through June 2008 were 72% higher than the previous year, but ended the year only 16% higher. However, during 2008 cattle imports from Mexico were 35% lower than 2007, and the lowest imports since 1998. Good range and forage conditions in Mexico allowed producers to keep cattle on grass and resulted in reduced U.S. imports.

In 2009, U.S. cattle imports continued to decline, dropping 12%. But contrary to 2008, imports from Canada fell, while imports from Mexico increased. USDA's Economic Research Service (ERS) indicated that weaker U.S. cattle prices and weaker demand for beef in the United States, combined with a stronger Canadian dollar reduced Canadian returns and incentives to send cattle to the United States.[114] On the other hand, imports from Mexico started rising due to worsening drought conditions in Mexico during the latter part of 2009 that encouraged Mexican producers to ship cattle to the United States.

Some analyses attribute the import decline during the last part of 2008 and all of 2009 to COOL, but differ on the extent currency exchange rates may have contributed to this development. Cattle Fax, an industry-funded data and analysis service based in Colorado, observed that the 2008 decline in cattle imports was due to mandatory COOL regulations, and that imports would "face a big wild card in 2009" for the same reason.[115] Livestock sector analysts with the Chicago Mercantile Exchange (CME), examining cattle import trends through year-end 2008, commented that the COOL law "has been quite effective, if you measure effectiveness by the degree to which it has been able to stifle cattle trade in North America." They wrote that reductions in imports from both Mexico and Canada "came at a time when a significant devaluation in the value of the Peso and Canadian dollar normally would have been conducive of increased imports from these two countries. Under normal circumstances, one would expect cattle imports to actually increase rather than be cut by almost 40%."[116] However, USDA's ERS suggested that the currency exchange factor may be somewhat more involved and that Canada's available supplies of slaughter cattle were reduced by earlier strong shipments of feeder cattle.[117]

In 2010, U.S. cattle imports increased 14% from 2009 to 2.3 million head as shipments of feeder cattle from Mexico continued to expand, due to continued drought conditions and strong U.S. feeder cattle prices that further encouraged Mexican producers to send cattle north. Canadian cattle imports in 2010 remained flat. In 2011, total cattle imports into the United States turned down again, dropping 8% as increased imports from Mexico (+16%) were more than offset by a sharp drop in imports from Canada (-35%). Ample feed supplies in 2011 resulted in more cattle being fed in Canadian feedlots and, in addition, the relatively strong Canadian dollar dampened shipments to the United States.

In 2012, U.S. cattle imports increased 7% as shipments from both Canada and Mexico expanded. Strong U.S. feeder cattle prices coupled with continued drought in Mexico supported the movement of feeder cattle into the United States. Increased shipments of slaughter cows from Canada boosted U.S. imports for immediate slaughter in 2012.

Imports from Canada

A majority of Canadian cattle shipped to the United States are for immediate slaughter—79% in 2012 (**Figure C-2**). Most of the remaining imports are feeder cattle that are usually destined for U.S. feedlots to be fed out to slaughter-ready weights. Dairy cows and breeding stock account for a small share of imports from Canada. In 2011, the 15% feeder share of cattle imports was the smallest feeder share since 2000, as declining cattle inventories combined with the availability of relatively inexpensive barley supplies in Canada slowed shipments to the United States. In 2012, cattle imports from Canada increased 15% to more than 786,000 head as both feeder and slaughter cattle imports increased. Slaughter cattle imports in 2011 and 2012 remain well below the five-year average of imports from 2006 to 2010. A strong increase in slaughter cow imports in 2012 accounted for most of the 8% gain in total slaughter cattle imports. Feeder cattle imports increased 55% in 2012, but also remained well below earlier year levels.

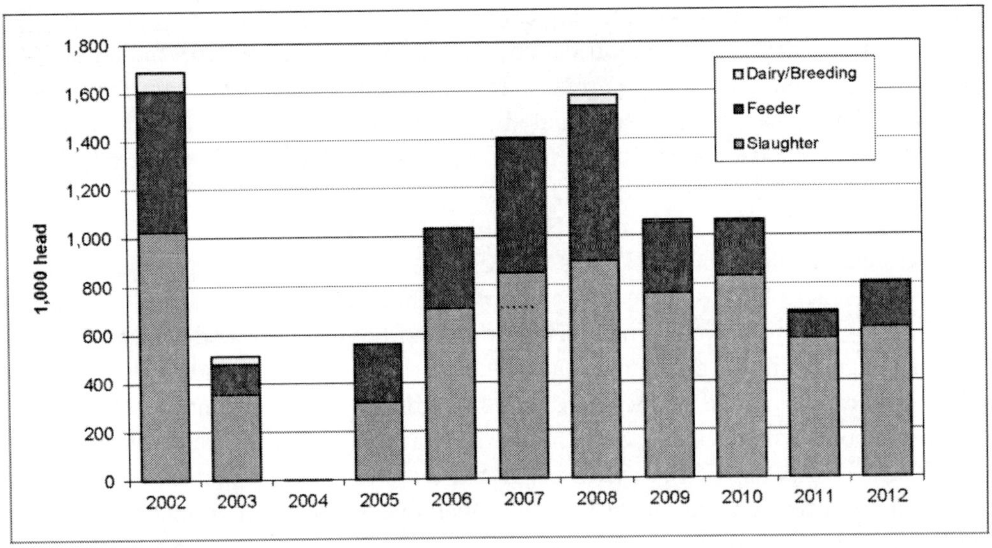

Source: USDA, FAS, GATS.

Figure C-2. U.S. Cattle Imports from Canada.

USDA estimates that Canadian cattle shipments to the United States will again increase in 2013. A feed cost advantage that Canada had for a couple of years has narrowed, and with a large expected U.S. grain crop, more feeder cattle could be sent to the United States for feeding. In addition, the closure of a beef cow slaughter plant in Quebec could boost the number of slaughter cows being shipped south in 2013.[118]

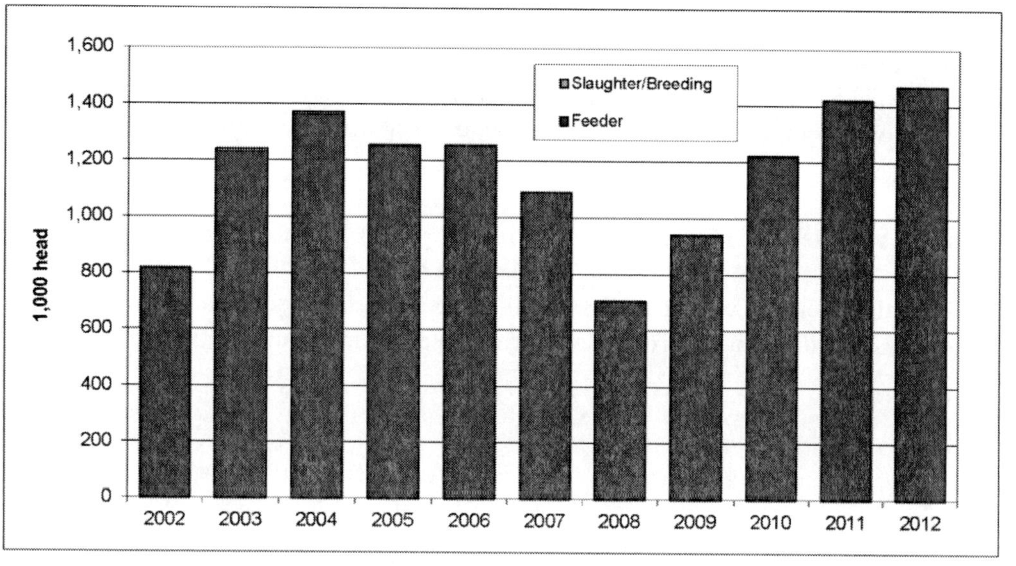

Source: USDA, FAS, GATS.

Figure C-3. U.S. Cattle Imports from Mexico.

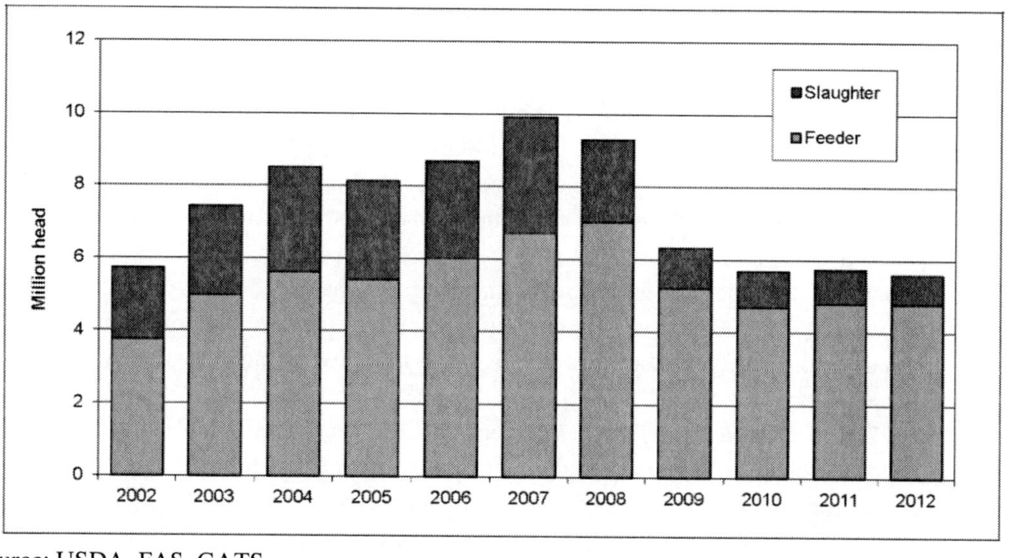

Source: USDA, FAS, GATS.

Figure C-4. U.S. Hog Imports from Canada.

Imports from Mexico

Almost 100% of Mexican cattle shipped to the United States are stocker or feeder cattle[119] that are usually raised in the northern states of Mexico, then shipped to the United States and placed on pasture or into feedlots **(Figure C-3)**.[120] Cattle imports from Mexico are often influenced by prevailing precipitation conditions in northern Mexico. Persistent drought since

2009 has led to an increasing number of cattle imports from Mexico. Cattle imports have steadily risen from the unusually low level of 2008, hitting double-digit growth from 2009 to 2011. In 2012, U.S. cattle imports from Mexico increased 3% to more than 1.47 million head. Continued drought conditions in the northern states of Mexico and strong U.S. feeder cattle prices encouraged Mexican producers to send cattle north.

This strong pace of imports from Mexico may not be sustainable in 2013 because of tight cattle supplies in Mexico. Mexico's large increase (+84%) in the shipment of heifers to the United States was a strong indication of herd liquidation in 2012. USDA estimates that Mexico's cattle inventory was about 18.5 million head on January 1, 2013, the lowest since the early 1960s. Cattle imports from Mexico are expected to decline in 2013 compared with 2012.[121]

U.S. Hog Imports

U.S. hog imports from Canada have grown sharply since the mid-1990s. U.S. hog imports were a record 10 million head in 2007, growing more than 13% per year on average during the previous 10 years. Furthermore, the composition of U.S. hog imports significantly shifted from hogs for immediate slaughter to feeder pigs.[122] At one time the U.S. hog industry was comprised of many small operations that raised hogs from birth to slaughter-ready weight (farrow-to-finish operations), but from the mid-1980s the hog industry moved toward vertical integration. With vertical integration there came increased demand for feeder pigs to meet the needs of finishing operations. Some Canadian producers focused their production on providing feeder pigs for shipment to the United States where access to abundant and cheaper supplies of grain made it more economical to feed pigs to slaughter weight.[123] The feeder pig share of hog imports increased steadily from the mid-1990s, peaking at 82% in 2009, and remained stable in 2010 and 2011.

U.S. imports of Canadian hogs dropped sharply from the 2007 peak. U.S. hog imports from Canada fell 7% in 2008 on a 30% drop in hogs for immediate slaughter. In 2009, hog imports dropped another 32% as both feeder pigs and hogs for immediate slaughter declined (**Figure C-4**).

An early 2009 USDA analysis suggested that COOL's implementation likely "made U.S. swine finishers reluctant to import Canadian finishing animals, in light of some major U.S. packers' stated unwillingness to process Canadian-origin animals."[124] Another report suggested that COOL was affecting the U.S. hog sector, particularly in Iowa, as packers moved to process only U.S.-born hogs. With many Iowa producers operating finishing operations that source feeder pigs from Canada, a USDA document on COOL implementation cited that some producers' barns are "empty because of a lack of an assured outlet for slaughter hogs of mixed country of origin" (i.e., Product of Canada and United States). USDA also reported that some lenders were not extending credit to operations that finish mixed-origin pigs, and that lower prices at times were "being paid for mixed origin slaughter hogs compared to hogs of exclusively U.S. origin."[125]

During 2010-2012 U.S. hog imports flattened. In 2012, hog imports declined 2% to 5.6 million head, the smallest amount since 2002. Imports for immediate slaughter averaged more than 2.3 million head from 2000 to 2009, but dropped sharply to just over 820,000 head in 2012. The number of feeder hog imports was unchanged in 2012, and have been around 4.7

million-4.8 million the last three years. Hog imports from Canada are expected to decline slightly in 2013.[126]

End Notes

[1] USDA, January 12, 2009, "USDA Issues Final Rule On Mandatory Country of Origin Labeling," available at http://www.usda.gov/wps/portal/usda/usdahome?printable=true& contentidonly=true&contentid= 2009/01/ 0006.xml; and 74 *Federal Register* 2658, January 15, 2009. This final rule replaced both the October 5, 2004, interim final rule for seafood (69 *Federal Register* 59708), and the August 1, 2008, interim final rule (73 *Federal Register* 45106) for all other covered commodities. An AMS fact sheet on the final rule, including a summary of changes from the interim final rules and estimates on COOL implementation costs, is available at http://www.ams.usda.gov/AMSv1.0/getfile? dDocName=STELPRDC5074847.

[2] USDA, "Vilsack Announces Implementation of Country of Origin Labeling Law," press release, February 20, 2009, http://www.usda.gov/wps/portal/usda/usdahome?contentid= 2009/02/0045.xml&navid= NEWS_ RELEASE&navtype= RT&parentnav=LATEST_ RELEASES&edeployment_action=retrievecontent.

[3] Wendy, J. Umberger, "Will Consumers Pay a Premium for Country-of-Origin Labeled Meat?," *Choices*, 4th quarter 2004, http://www.choicesmagazine.org/2004-4/cool/2004-4-04.htm.

[4] Gary, W. Brewster, et al., "Who Will Bear the Costs of Country-of-Origin Labeling?," available at http://www.choicesmagazine.org/2004-4/cool/2004-4-02.htm; Daniel D. Hanselka et al., "Demand Shifts in Beef Associated with Country-of-Origin Labeling to Minimize Losses in Social Welfare," *Choices*, 4th quarter 2004, http://www.choicesmagazine.org/2004-4/ cool/2004-4-03.htm; and Alejandro Plastina and Konstantinos Giannakis, "Market and Welfare Effects of Mandatory Country-of-Origin Labeling in the U.S. Specialty Crops Sector," American Agricultural Economics Association Annual Meeting, Portland, Oregon, 2007.

[5] USDA, AMS, "Mandatory Country of Origin Labeling of Beef, Pork, Lamb, Chicken, Goat Meat, Wild and Farmed-Raised Fish and Shellfish, Perishable Agricultural Commodities, Peanuts, Pecans, Ginseng, and Macadamia Nuts," 74 *Federal Register* 2682-2700, January 15, 2009.

[6] A slightly different COOL requirement applies to packaged honey if it bears any official USDA certificate, mark, or statement with respect to quality and grade. It was added by Section 10402 of the 2008 farm bill (P.L. 110-246) to the Agricultural Marketing Act, and took effect on October 6, 2009. For more information, see http://www.ams.usda.gov/ AMSv1.0/ams.fetchTemplateData.do? startIndex=1&startIndex=2&startIndex=1 &startIndex=2&template= TemplateN&navID=ProcessedFVUpdates&rightNav1=&topNav= &leftNav= &page=ProcessedFVUpdates& resultType=&acct=procsdgrdcert.

[7] The COOL statute uses by reference this definition of "retailer" laid out in the Perishable Agricultural Commodities Act to identify those retailers required to comply with COOL requirements.

[8] 7 U.S.C. 1638a.

[9] *Cattle Buyers Weekly*, August 4, 2008; and *Food Chemical News*, September 15, 2008.

[10] AMS, "Country of Origin Labeling (COOL) Frequently Asked Questions," September 26, 2008, http://www.ams.usda.gov/AMSv1.0/getfile?dDocName=STELPRDC5071922.

[11] USDA, AMS, January 12, 2009, fact sheet on the mandatory COOL final rule, p. 5, http://www.ams.usda.gov/ AMSv1.0/getfile?dDocName=STELPRDC5074847.

[12] "NFU Statement: USDA Issues Final Rule for COOL," January 12, 2009, http://nfu.org/news/news-archives/2009-news/86-agriculture-programs/198-nfu-statement-usda-issues-final-rule-for-cool.

[13] Letter to Secretary of Agriculture Tom Vilsack, February 3, 2009, http://web.archive.org/web/20090226012829/ http://dorgan.senate.gov/newsroom/extras/ 020309vilsack.pdf.

[14] USDA, "Vilsack Announces Implementation of Country of Origin Labeling Law," February 20, 2009, http://www.usda.gov/wps/portal/usda/usdahome?printable=true& contentidonly=true&contentid=2009/02/0045.xml. His letter is available at http://www.usda.gov/ documents/0220_IndustryLetterCOOL.pdf.

[15] Percentages calculated by CRS based on USDA estimates of retail-level COOL coverage in pounds, divided by total annual supply (USDA data on domestic production plus imports).

[16] AMS, "Frequently Asked Questions," January 12, 2009, available at http://www.ams.usda.gov/AMSv1.0/getfile? dDocName=STELPRDC5074846.

[17] For information on this related issue, see CRS Report R40832, *Animal Identification and Traceability: Overview and Issues*.

[18] AMS maintains an extensive website on COOL, with links to implementing regulations, cost-benefit analysis, and other materials at http://www.ams.usda.gov/cool/.

[19] USDA, Office of Budget and Program Analysis (OBPA), FY2014 USDA Budget Explanatory Notes for Committee on Appropriations for Agricultural Marketing Service, pp. 19-31 to 19-32, 19-86, http://www.obpa.usda.gov/exnotes/ FY2014/19ams2014notes.pdf.

[20] USDA, OIG, "Implementation of Country of Origin Labeling," August 2011, pp. 1 and 4, http://www.usda.gov/oig/ webdocs/01601-04-HY.pdf; USDA, OBPA, FY2014 Budget Explanatory Notes for Committee on Appropriations for AMS, pp. 19-32.

[21] USDA, AMS, COOL Compliance Data, "2012 Retail Review and Supplier Traceback Audit Compliance," http://www.ams.usda.gov/AMSv1.0/getfile?dDocName=STELPRDC5104265.

[22] U.S. Trade Representative, "Vilsack, Kirk Comment on Canadian Panel Request Regarding Country-of-Origin Labeling," October 7, 2009, http://www.ustr.gov/about-us/press-office/press-releases/2009/october/vilsack-kirk-comment-canadian-panel-request-regard.

[23] The Dispute Settlement Body has the sole authority to establish "panels" of experts to consider a trade dispute case filed by any WTO member country, and to accept or reject the panels' findings or the results of an appeal. It monitors the implementation of the rulings and recommendations, and has the power to authorize retaliation when a country does not comply with a ruling.

[24] Various trade publication reports, including *Cattle Buyers Weekly*, "MCOOL Has Cost Canadian Producers C$92M," December 8, 2008; *Agri-Pulse*, "COOL Regulations Create Heartburn for Canadians," December 3, 2008; and *Washington Trade Daily*, December 2, 2008, pp. 3-4.

[25] AMI, "American Meat Institute Tells U.S. Trade Representative That Mandatory Country-of-Origin Labeling Violates International Trade Obligations," January 8, 2010, http://www.meatami.com/ht/ display/ ReleaseDetails/i/ 56358.

[26] USCA, "USCA and Farmers Union Urge Vigorous COOL Defense," January 12, 2010, http://www.uscattlemen.org/ TheNewsRoom/2010_News/1-12COOLdefense.htm.

[27] R-CALF USA, "Canada, Mexico Have No Standing to Bring Complaint Against U.S. COOL Law," July 2, 2009, http://www.r-calfusa.com/news_releases/2009/090702-canada.htm.

[28] NCBA, "NCBA Statement on Canadian WTO Complaint against U.S. COOL Law," October 7, 2009.

[29] The TBT Agreement is summarized in CRS Report R41306, *Trade Law: An Introduction to Selected International Agreements and U.S. Laws*. The GATT 1994 commitment refers to the provision that requires laws and regulations to be administered "in a uniform, impartial and reasonable manner."

[30] WTO, *United States—Certain Country of Origin Labelling (COOL) Requirements*, Reports of the Panel, WT/DS384/R, WT/DS386/R, November 18, 2011, http://www.wto.org/english/tratop_e/dispu_e/384_386r_e.pdf. Background on the COOL dispute case is available on the WTO's website at http://wto.org/english/tratop_e/dispu_e/ cases_e/ds384_e.htm (Canada) and http://wto.org/english/tratop_e/dispu_e/cases_e/ds386_e.htm (Mexico).

[31] This "is a standing body of seven persons that hears appeals from reports issued by panels in disputes brought by WTO Members. ... Appellate Body Reports, once adopted by the Dispute Settlement Body (DSB), must be accepted by the parties to the dispute." See http://wto.org/english/tratop_e/dispu_e/appellate_body_e.htm.

[32] Reuters, "U.S. to appeal WTO ruling against meat labels," March 23, 2012 (hereinafter cited as Reuters); Agri-Pulse.com, "USTR will appeal WTO ruling on COOL," March 23, 2012. USTR's appeal submission to the WTO is available at http://www.ustr.gov/sites/default/files/US.AppellantSub.fin_.pdf.

[33] For details, see "Adoption of Panel Reports/Appellate Review (Articles 16, 17, 20)" in CRS Report RS20088, *Dispute Settlement in the World Trade Organization (WTO): An Overview*.

[34] The DSU is one of the multilateral agreements resulting from the Uruguay Round that provides the primary means for WTO members to settle disputes arising under WTO agreements.

[35] For details, see "Compliance Issues, Sequencing" in CRS Report RS20088, *Dispute Settlement in the World Trade Organization (WTO): An Overview*.

[36] Foreign Affairs, Trade and Development Canada, "Statement by Ministers Fast and Ritz on U.S. Country of Origin Labelling," press release, June 7, 2013, http://www.international.gc.ca/media_commerce/comm/news-communiques/ 2013/06/07a.aspx?lang=eng, and Embassy of Mexico in the United States, Ministry of Economy, "Mexico Will Continue Challenging the Country of Origin Labeling (COOL) Requirements Before the WTO," press release, June 10, 2013, http://embamex.sre.gob.mx/eua/index.php/en/comunicados2013/641-comunicado-de-la-secretaria-de-economia-mexico-continuara-impugnando-la-regla-de-etiquetado-de-pais-de-origen-en-la-omc.

[37] WTO, *WT/DS/384/25 Understanding Between the United States and Canada Regarding Procedures Under Articles 21 and 22 of the DSU*, June 13, 2013, and *WT/DS/384/24 Understanding Between the United States and Mexico Regarding Procedures Under Articles 21 and 22 of the DSU*, June 13, 2013.

[38] WTO, *WT/DS/384/26 Recourse to Article 21.5 of the DSU by Canada*, August 20, 2013, and *WT/DS/384/25 Recourse to Article 21.5 of the DSU by Mexico,* August 20, 2013.

[39] For details, see "Compliance Panels (Article 21.5)" and "Compensation and Suspension of Concessions (Article 22)" in CRS Report RS20088, *Dispute Settlement in the World Trade Organization (WTO): An Overview*.

[40] The panel made its determination on what is, and is not, a technical regulation with reference to TBT's Annex 1.1. It defines such to be a document that spells out "labeling requirements" among other features, including

administrative provisions, "with which compliance is mandatory." The panel concluded that the COOL statute and final rule are "legal instruments that are legally binding in US law," with wording clearly mandating compliance, while the Vilsack letter, rather than mandating additional labeling requirements, presents them as "suggestions for voluntary action."

[41] These involve applying mathematics and statistical methods to study relationships between economic variables.

[42] "Obama Administration Appeals Ruling On Country Labeling For Beef, Pork," *Inside US Trade*, March 30, 2012.

[43] WTO, United States—Certain Country of Origin Labelling (COOL) Requirements, 'Summary of key findings," available at http://www.wto.org/english/tratop_e/dispu_e/cases_e/ds384_e.htm.

[44] The panel rejected Canada's and Mexico's argument that COOL's objective is to protect the domestic U.S. livestock industry (p. 143 of WTO panel's report, footnote 30).

[45] WTO, United States—Certain Country of Origin Labelling (COOL) Requirements, 'Summary of key findings," available at http://www.wto.org/english/tratop_e/dispu_e/ cases_e/ds384_e.htm.

[46] USTR, "Statement in Response to WTO Panel Decision on Country of Origin Labeling," November 18, 2011, http://www.ustr.gov/about-us/press-office/press-releases/2011/november/statement-office-us-trade-representative-response.

[47] NCBA, "Statement ... [on] WTO Ruling on US Country of Origin Labeling," November 11, 2011, http://www.beefusa.org/newsreleases1.aspx?NewsID=1248; *Pork Magazine*, "NPPC: What's on Tap for 2012?," January 2012, http://www.porknetwork.com/pork-magazine/pork-exec/Whats-on-Tap-for-2012-136695033.html?view=all; AMI, "WTO Rules in Favor of Canada in Complaint Over U.S. Country-of-Origin Labeling Law," November 18, 2011, http://www.meatami.com/ht/display/ArticleDetails/i/73951.

[48] R-CALF, "U.S. Sovereignty Usurped by WTO's COOL Decision," November 18, 2011, http://www.r-calfusa.com/ news_releases/2011/111118-sovereignty.htm; USCA, "WTO Dispute Panel Issues Final COOL Report," November 21, 2011, http://www.uscattlemen.org/TheNewsRoom/2011_News/11-21WTO_DisputePanel.htm.

[49] FMI, "Food Retail Industry Applauds WTO Ruling on COOL," November 23, 2011, http://www.fmi.org/news-room/ news-archive/view/2011/11/23/food-retail-industry-applauds-wto-ruling-on-cool.

[50] NFU, "NFU Will Work With Administration to Ensure COOL Compliance With WTO Rules," November 18, 2011, http://nfu.org/news/65-international-policy/723-nfu-will-work-with-administration-to-ensure-cool-compliance-with-wto-rules; Public Citizen, "WTO Rules Against Country-of-Origin Meat Labeling Law: Third Ruling Against U.S. Consumer Safeguards in 2011," November 18, 2011, http://www. citizen.org/documents/release-wto-rules-against-coo-11-18-11.pdf; Food and Water Watch, "WTO Decision on COOL Attacks Consumers' Right to Know," November 18, 2011, http://www. foodandwaterwatch.org/pressreleases/wto-decision-on-cool-attacks-consumers%e2%80%99-right-to-know/.

[51] *High Plains/Midwest Ag Journal*, "TCFA Members Face Scary Issues from Washington," November 14, 2011, http://www.hpj.com/archives/2011/nov11/nov14/1109TexasCattleFeedersjmlsr.cfm.

[52] Office of Senator Tim Johnson, "Johnson, Enzi to Administration: Keep COOL Strong," December 15, 2011, press release with text of letter, http://johnson.senate.gov/public/index.cfm?p=PressReleases.

[53] Foreign Affairs and International Trade Canada, "Canada Wins World Trade Organization Case on U.S. Country-of-Origin Labelling," November 18, 2011, http://www.international.gc.ca/media_commerce/comm/news-communiques/ 2011/349.aspx?lang=eng&view=d; Farmscape, "Canada Hopes for Negotiated Resolution of M-COOL Dispute," November 22, 2011, http://www.farmscape.com/f2ShowScript.aspx?i=23812&q=Canada+Hopes+for+Negotiated+Resolution+of+M-COOL+Dispute.

[54] CPC, "Canadian Pork Producers Welcome the WTO Panel Decision on COOL," November 18, 2011, http://www.cpc-ccp.com/documents/news-releases/FINALWTOpaneldecisionpressrelease.pdf; CCA, "WTO Rules Strongly in Favor of Canada in COOL Case," November 18, 2011, http://www.cattle.ca/ media/file/original/ 1058_2011_11_18_CCA_News_Release_WTO_rules_strongly_in_favor_of_Canada_in_COOL_case.pdf.

[55] "R-CALF USA Applauds U.S. Appeal of WTO's Adverse COOL Ruling," March 23, 2012, http://www.tradereform.org/2012/03/r-calf-usa-applauds-u-s-appeal-of-wtos-adverse-cool-ruling/#comment-163002; "USCA Appreciates USTR Support for U.S. Cattle Producers," March 26, 2012, http://www.uscattlemen.org/ TheNewsRoom/2012_News/3-26USTRSupport.htm; "NFU Applauds USTR Decision to Appeal WTO Ruling on COOL," March 23, 2012, http://nfu.org/news/212-international-policy/947-nfu-applauds-ustr-decision-to-appeal-wto-ruling-on-cool-; Food & Water Watch, "President Obama Finally Stands Up for U.S. Farmers and Consumers: U.S. Appeals WTO Decision on COOL," March 23, 2012; "Public Citizen Applauds Obama Administration's Efforts to Defend Consumer Country of Origin Meat Labeling; Appeal of WTO Ruling Necessary First Step," March 23, 2012, http://citizen.typepad.com/eyesontrade/2012/03/public-citizen-applauds-obama-administrations-efforts-to-defend-consumer-country-of-origin-meat-labe.html.

[56] "NCBA Statement on USTR Appeal of WTO Ruling on Country of Origin Labeling," http://www.beefusa.org/ newsreleases1.aspx?newsid=2419; NPPC, "Capital Update, For the Week Ending March 23, 2012," http://www.nppc.org/2012/03/for-the-week-ending-march-23-2012/; Pork Network, "Pork, beef producers fear

retaliation from COOL appeal," March 26, 2012, http://www.porknetwork.com/pork-news/latest/Pork-beef-producers-fear-retaliation-from-COOL-appeal-144248155.html.

[57] Reuters; Secretaría de Economía, "México continuará la defensa legal en OMC del caso COOL," March 23, 2012, http://www.economia.gob.mx/eventos-noticias/sala-de-prensa/informacion-relevante/7646-boletin087-12.

[58] WTO, Communication from the United States to the Chairman of the Dispute Settlement Body, WT/DS384/19 and WT/DS386/18, August 23, 2012; John Maday, "COOL adversaries comment on ruling," Drovers CattleNetwork, July 2, 2012, http://www.cattlenetwork.com/e-newsletters/drovers-daily/COOL-adversaries-comment-on-ruling-161140725.html?view=all.

[59] 7 U.S.C. 1638a. See above "Defining and Labeling Origin for Meats."

[60] Rick Jordahl, "AMI urges U.S. to bring COOL law into compliance," *PorkNetwork*, July 2, 2012.

[61] Glynn T. Tonsor, Jayson L. Lusk, and Ted C. Schroeder, et al., Mandatory Country of Origin Labeling: Consumer Demand Impact, Kansas State University, Factsheet, November 2012, p. 2, http://www.agmanager.info/livestock/ policy/Tonsor_KSU_FactSheet_MCOOL_11-13-12.pdf.

[62] Steve Kay, "Clock Ticks On MCOOL Solution," *Cattle Buyers Weekly*, December 10, 2012.

[63] Ian Elliott, "Only small changes needed to comply with COOL ruling," *Feedstuffs*, December 24, 2012.

[64] WTO, *United States—Certain Country of Origin Labelling (COOL) Requirements*, WT/DS384/24 and WT/DS386/23, Arbitrator's Report, December 4, 2012, p. 14.

[65] Steve Meyer and Len Steiner, *Livestock Daily Report*, December 6, 2012.

[66] "USTR Abandons Regulatory COOL 'Fix' In Face Of Stakeholder Division," *World Trade Online*, February 2, 2012.

[67] Letter from Bill Bullard, CEO, August 22, 2012, http://www.r-calfusa.com/COOL/ 120822LetterToUSTRand USDAreCOOLStrategy.pdf.

[68] Steers and spayed heifers imported from Mexico must be marked M and M^x, respectively,and cattle from Canada must be marked with CAN [9 C.F.R. 93.427(c) and 93.436(b)(2)]. Cattle imported for immediate slaughter must be shipped in sealed conveyances from the port of entry to the slaughter facility [9 C.F.R. 93.420, 93.429, and 93.436(a)].

[69] This is the J-List exemption at 19 U.S.C. 1304(a)(3)(J). For background on the J-List, see **Appendix A**, Tariff Act. A list of products exempt from markings is found at 19 C.F.R. 134.33.

[70] NFU, "NFU Releases Analysis on COOL Compliance," press release, February 12, 2013, http://www.nfu.org /news/ current-news?start=18. Analysis available at http://cdn.e2ma.net/userdata/ 5030/assets/docs/ SS_COOL_Compliance_Memo_New_Final_Four_Groups.pdf.

[71] Letter from Senators Tester, Enzi, Johnson (SD) et al. to Secretary of Agriculture Vilsack and U.S. Trade Representative Kirk, January 31, 2013, http://www.tester.senate.gov/?p=press_release&id=2755.

[72] USDA, AMS, "Mandatory Country of Origin Labeling of Beef, Pork ... ," 78 *Federal Register* 15645, March 12, 2013.

[73] USDA, AMS, "Mandatory Country of Origin Labeling of Beef, Pork ... ," 78 *Federal Register* 31367, May 24, 2013. The rule amends 7 C.F.R. 60.124, 65.240, and 65.300.

[74] See footnote 72, pp. 15647-15652. USDA's cost estimate analysis is summarized in Table 1 on page 15650.

[75] See footnote 73, pp. 31377-31382. Adjustment costs are summarized in Table 4 on page 31381.

[76] Ibid., p. 31368.

[77] See footnote 5.

[78] NFU, "USDA Keeps COOL; Complies with WTO Ruling," press release, May 23, 2013, http://www.nfu.org/news/ 253-consumers-and-their-food/1766-usda-keeps-cool-complies-with-wto-ruling?tmpl=component&print=1&layout= default&page=.

[79] USCA, "USDA Finalizes COOL Rule," press release, May, 23, 2013, http://www.uscattlemen.org/Templates/ Press_Room/2013_Press_Room/5-23Final-COOL-Rule.html.

[80] R-CALF, "R-CALF USA Pleased With Final COOL Rule Released Today," press release, May 23, 2013, http://www.r-calfusa.com/news_releases/2013/130523COOL.htm.

[81] AMI, "Burdensome Country-of-Origin Labeling Rule Will Not Satisfy WTO or Trading Partners, But Will Harm U.S. Agriculture," press release, May 23, 2013, http://www.meatami.com/ht/display/ReleaseDetails/i/90194.

[82] NCBA, "NCBA Statement on USDA Issuing a Final Rule on Mandatory Country of Origin Labeling," press release, May 23, 2013, http://www.beefusa.org/newsreleases1.aspx?NewsID=2934.

[83] Brett Wessler, "COOL rules lead Tyson to close door on Canadian cattle," *Drovers CattleNetwork*, October 24, 2013, http://www.cattlenetwork.com/cattle-news/COOL-rules-lead-Tyson-to-close-door-on-Canadian-cattle-229151451.html.

[84] The plaintiffs are the American Meat Institute, the American Association of Meat Processors, the Canadian Cattlemen's Association, the Canadian Pork Council, the National Cattlemen's Beef Association, the National Pork Producers Council, the North American Meat Association, and the Southwest Meat Association. Subsequently, Mexico's National Confederation of Livestock Organizations joined the lawsuit. A copy of the lawsuit is available at http://www.meatami.com/ht/a/GetDocumentAction/i/92223.

[85] John Maday, "Eight organizations file legal challenge to new COOL rules," *PorkNetwork*, July 9, 2013, http://www.porknetwork.com/e-newsletters/pork-daily/Eight-organizations-file-legal-challenge-to-new-

COOL-rules-214758951.html, and Bryan Salvage, "'COOL' just got a lot hotter," Meat & Poultry, July 9, 2013, http://www.meatpoultry.com/articles/news_home/Regulatory/2013/07/COOL_just_got_a_lot_hotter.aspx?ID= {A8621462-A983-4A47-8580-408C09362D0C}&p=1.

[86] National Farmers Union, "COOL Lawsuit is Another Delaying Tactic," press release, July 10, 2013, http://www.nfu.org/news/current-news.

[87] R-CALF, "Group Circulates Petitions to Stop Federally-Funded NCBA from Suing to Eliminate COOL," press release, July 11, 2013, http://www.r-calfusa.com/news_releases/2013/130711-petition.htm.

[88] A copy of the injunction request is available at http://www.meatami.com/ht/a/GetDocumentAction/i/92882.

[89] In addition to USCA, the National Farmers Union, the American Sheep Industry Association, and the Consumer Federation of America joined the motion to intervene. On August 23, Food & Water Watch, R-Calf, the South Dakota Stockgrowers Association, and the Western Organization of Resource Councils also requested intervenor status.

[90] *American Meat Institute, v. USDA,* Civil Action No. 13-CV-1033 (KBJ) (U.S. District Court for the District of Columbia 2013).

[91] AMI, "AMI Disagrees With Denial of Request for Preliminary Injunction in Country-of-Origin Labeling Lawsuit; Will Appeal Ruling," press release, September 11, 2013, http://www.meatami.com/ht/display/ReleaseDetails/i/93815/ pid/287.

[92] NF, "COOL Appeal Another Attempt to Obstruct Consumers' Right to Know ," press release, September 12, 2013, http://www.nfu.org/news/current-news/244-livestock/1831 cool-appeal-another-attempt-to-obstruct-consumers-right-to-know?format=pdf.

[93] Canadian Cattlemen's Association, "U.S. continues to discriminate against cattle imports," press release, May 23, 2013, http://www.cattle.ca/news-read/363_us_continues_to_discriminate_against_cattle_imports.

[94] Canadian Pork Council, "US flouting of WTO Ruling on COOL shocking and appalling," press release, May 23, 2013, http://www.cpc-ccp.com/documents/news-releases/COOL_May_23_media_release_2_.pdf.

[95] Foreign Affairs and International Trade Canada, "Statement by Ministers Fast and Ritz on U.S. Country of Origin Labelling," press release, May 23, 2013, http://www.international.gc.ca/media_commerce/comm/news-communiques/ 2013/05/23a.aspx?lang=eng.

[96] Secretary of Foreign Affairs, Embassy of Mexico, "Mexico Opposes the New US Rule on Mandatory Country of Origin Labeling," press release, May 28, 2013, http://embamex.sre.gob.mx/eua/index.php/en/comunicados2013/631-comunicado-de-prensa-mexico-se-opone-a-la-nueva-regla-de-estados-unidos-sobre-etiquetado-de-pais-de-origen-cool.

[97] Foreign Affairs and International Trade Canada, "Statement by Ministers Fast and Ritz on U.S. Country of Origin Labelling," press release, June 7, 2013, http://www.international.gc.ca/media_commerce/comm/news-communiques/ 2013/06/07a.aspx. The retaliation list is included in the press release.

[98] Department of Finance, "Notice seeking comments on possible trade retaliation action against the United States in response to that country's failure to comply with the World Trade Organization ruling on certain country of origin labelling requirements," *Canada Gazette*, Vol. 147, No. 24, June 15, 2013, http://gazette.gc.ca/rp-pr/p1/2013/2013-06-15/html/notice-avis-eng.html#d115.

[99] Canadian Pork Council, "CPC Releases Report on COOL Damages to Canada's Pork Industry," press release, January 14, 2013, http://www.cpc-ccp.com/news.php?rev=e&ID=317&article=1&year=2013&da=0&incl=0. Report available at http://www.cpc-ccp.com/documents/news-releases/ 2013%20ESTIMATES%20OF%20MCOOL%20IMPACT%20ON%20CANADA%20final.pdf.

[100] Dan Sumner, *Canadian Losses from U.S. COOL Implementation*, prepared for the Canadian Cattlemen's Association, September 27, 2012.

[101] Letter from Ross Wilson, President and CEO, Texas Cattle Feeders Association, to USDA, April 11, 2013, http://www.regulations.gov/#!documentDetail;D=AMS-LS-13-0004-0806.

[102] See footnote 37.

[103] WTO, *WT/DS/384/25 Understanding Between the United States and Canada Regarding Procedures Under Articles 21 and 22 of the DSU*, June 13, 2013, https://docs.wto.org/dol2fe/Pages/FE_Search/FE_S_S009-DP.aspx?language= E&CatalogueIdList=117305,113648,104336,94619,61814,72904, 99959,28101,1026,87392& CurrentCatalogueIdIndex=0&FullTextSearch=. Document for the United States and Mexico agreement is WT/DS/386/24.

[104] Under WTO rules, the United States could not object to the second panel request.

[105] For example: Charles Abbott, "U.S. meat-labeling law, a WTO issue, now farm bill target," *Reuters*, October 30, 2013, and "Opponents Secure Lucas' Support In New Push To Change Law," *Inside Trade*, October 31, 2013.

[106] Letter from 69 groups opposing COOL to Leadership of the Farm Bill Conference, October 29, 2013, http://soygrowers.com/wp-content/uploads/2013/10/COOL-letter-10-29-13-FINAL.pdf.

[107] John Maday, "Groups encourage Congress to Preserve COOL rules," *Drovers CattleNetwork*, January 22, 2014. Letter from 96 groups supporting COOL to Farm Bill Conferees, January 22, 2014, available at http://www.r-calfusa.com/COOL/140122FarmBillConfereeCOOLletterWith98Groups.pdf.

[108] Jenny Hopkinson, "Tom Vilsack: More than agriculture at stake in farm bill," *Politico*, November 14, 2013, http://dyn.politico.com/printstory.cfm?uuid=9D01F578-806A-43EF-97FF-D125454D8BB2.

[109] Letter from Livestock and Poultry Industry groups to Conference leadership, *The Hagstrom Report*, January 27, 2014.

[110] U.S. Congress, House Committee on Appropriations, Explanatory Statement Submitted by Mr.Rogers of Kentucky, Chairman of the House Committee on Appropriations Regarding the House Amendment to the Senate Amendment on H.R. 3547, Consolidated Appropriations Act, 2014, 113th Cong., January 13, 2014, p. 12, http://docs.house.gov/ billsthisweek/20140113/113-HR3547-JSOM-FM-B.pdf.

[111] Letter from Representative DeLauro to Secretary Vilsack, January 23, 2014, http://delauro. house.gov/ images/pdf/ letter_to_usda_re_cool_fy14_approps.pdf.

[112] P.L. 107-171, Section 10816, approved May 13, 2002, 111 Stat. 533; and P.L. 110-246, Section 11002, approved June 18, 2008, 122 Stat. 2113. The COOL provisions in the AMA of 1946 are codified at 7 U.S.C. 1638 – 1638d.

[113] The J list is published in 19 C.F.R. 134.33, available at http://edocket.access.gpo.gov/cfr_2008/aprqtr/ 19cfr134.33.htm.

[114] USDA, Economic Research Service (ERS), *Livestock, Dairy, and Poultry Outlook*, December 17, 2009. p. 5.

[115] CattleFax, "CattleFax Long Term Outlook Special Edition," December 12, 2008, p. 3.

[116] *CME Daily Livestock Report*, January 7, 2009.

[117] USDA, ERS, *Livestock, Dairy, and Poultry Outlook*, December 18, 2008, p. 8. ERS analysts point out that prior to 2008, the United States was easing the BSE-related restrictions on Canadian cattle imports; in November 2007, cattle over 30 months of age were again permitted to enter from Canada.

[118] USDA, FAS, *Canada: Livestock and Products Semi-annual*, GAIN Report, March 1, 2013, p. 4.

[119] Stocker cattle are lightweight, usually 200 to 400 pounds, and are placed in grazing programs to grow the animals. Feeder cattle are heavier, mostly 400 to 700 pounds, and may be placed on grass or placed directly in feedlots.

[120] USDA, ERS, *Trade, the Expanding Mexican Beef Industry, and Feedlot and Stocker Cattle Production in Mexico*, by Darrell S. Peel, Kenneth H. Mathews, Jr., and Rachel J. Johnson, August 2011.

[121] USDA, FAS, *Mexico: Livestock and Products Semi-annual*, GAIN Report, March 4, 2013, p. 7.

[122] Feeder pigs are light-weight pigs—the majority weighing less than 15 pounds, others weighing between 15 and 100 pounds—that are shipped to the United States for feeding to slaughter-ready weight.

[123] USDA, ERS, *Market Integration of the North American Hog Industries*, November 2004, pp. 9-12.

[124] USDA, ERS, *Livestock, Dairy, and Poultry Outlook*, April 16, 2009, p. 4.

[125] Cattle Buyers Weekly, "MCOOL Hurts Iowa Hog Finishers," April 27, 2009.

[126] See footnote 118, p. 7.

INDEX

C

D

E

F

G

H

I

J

K

L

M

N

O

P

Q

R

S

X

Y